# "I" AND SELF

# "I" AND SELF

Re-visioning Psychosynthesis

## JOHN FIRMAN

*Psychosynthesis Palo Alto*

For information, contact:
Psychosynthesis Palo Alto
461 Hawthorne Avenue
Palo Alto, California 94301

Cover photograph: Roberto Assagioli and John Firman, Forence, Italy, 1973.

ISBN: 978-0-9987077-2-3 (pbk.)
ISBN: 978-0-9987077-3-0 (ebook)
Library of Congress Control Number: 2020915040
Psychosynthesis Palo Alto, Palo Alto, CA

*Pure intellectual light, fulfilled with love,*
*Love of the true Good, fulfilled with all delight ...*

—*Dante*


*For John*
*Forever, Annie*

# Contents

Foreword to the Newly Published Edition   *xiii*

Foreword to the Original Edition   *xvii*

Acknowledgments   *xix*

Introduction   *1*

CHAPTER ONE

Trouble in the Soul of Psychosynthesis   *15*

   *The "I Am Not" Formulation   15*

   *Dualism   17*

   *The Disidentification Exercise   20*

   *The War between Light and Dark   24*

CHAPTER TWO

Dualism and Psychosynthesis   *27*

   *World-wide Dualism   27*

   *Dualistic Denial   29*

   *Dualistic Denial and Psychosynthesis   31*

   *Psychoanalysis and Psychosynthesis   33*

   *Grief That Can't Be Spoken   37*

   *Holistic Gnosticism   41*

   *Monism   43*

   *A Possible Third Road: Transcendence-Immanence   46*

CHAPTER THREE

On "I"   47

*Assagioli's Original Insight into "I"   47*

*Assagioli's Approach to "I"   50*

*"I" as Distinct from Pure Awareness/Consciousness   52*

*"I" as Distinct from Self-Consciousness   53*

*Disidentification   55*

*Observing vs. Thinking   56*

*Disidentification vs. Dissociation   60*

*Will   61*

*The Strength to Be Helpless   63*

*The Consciousness-Will Split   66*

*More Conscious Than Thou   68*

CHAPTER FOUR

Transcendence-Immanence   71

*Transcendence   72*

*Transcendence and "No-thing-ness"   75*

*The Tasks of the "I" and "No-I" Approaches   80*

*Transcendence of Space   81*

*Transcendence as Infinity   83*

*Transcendence as Eternity   84*

*Transcendence as "One," Not "Wholeness"   87*

*Immanence   90*

*Immanence in Life Transitions   90*

*Immanence Means We "Are" Our Psyche-Soma   92*

*The* imago Dei   *93*

CHAPTER FIVE

The Idealization of "I" and Self   97

*Idealization of Disidentification   97*

*Identification with "Disidentification"   99*

*The Idealization of Self   103*

*The Broken Egg   106*

*Self of Abyss, Plain, and Peak   107*

*Idealization and Unity   111*

*Idealization and Timelessness   115*


CHAPTER SIX

Transcending the Levels of Consciousness   *119*

*Maslow's Experience   120*

*Staying Present to "I"   122*

*"I" as Distinct from Levels of Consciousness   124*

*Emanating the "Scale of Being"   127*

*The I-Self Relationship   129*

*The I-Self Unity   131*


CHAPTER SEVEN

Transcendence-Immanence and Therapy   *137*

*Transcendence-Immanence and Therapy   137*

*Self-Realization and Therapy   140*

*Dualistic Denial and Therapy   143*

*Peak Experiences—Healthy or Unhealthy?   147*

*Peak Experiences—What Do They Mean?   150*

*Larger Spiritual-Moral Contexts   155*

*"I" to "I"   156*

*Transference and Countertransference   162*

*Distinguishing Theory from Practice   166*

*In Sum   167*

APPENDIX ONE

"I" in Religious Traditions   *169*

    *The* Via Negativa   *170*

    *The* Via Positiva   *176*

    *All Roads Lead to Self   180*

APPENDIX TWO

"I" in Psychology   *183*

    *Freud and Ego Splitting   184*

    *Freud and the Narcissistic Mistake   187*

    *C. G. Jung and the Transcendent-Immanent Function   189*

    *Contemporary Psychology   191*

    *Gordon Globus   193*

    *Arthur Deikman   195*

    *In Conclusion   198*

APPENDIX THREE

Good, Evil, and the I-Self Relationship   *199*

    *Induction   200*

    *Induction and Abraxas   203*

    *Abraxas and Cosmic Consciousness   208*

    *The Shadow, Evil, and* Privatio Boni   *212*

APPENDIX FOUR

Individuality and Universality   *219*

    *Individual-Universal Consciousness   222*

    *Individual-Universal Self   225*

    *No Need for "Higher Self"   227*

    *One Self   229*

    *A Religious Postscript   231*

APPENDIX FIVE

Working with Roberto Assagioli   *235*

   *Spiritual Empathy   237*

   *Roberto Is Human   239*


Glossary   *241*

Notes   *247*

References   *257*

Index   *271*

About the Author   *279*

# Foreword to the Newly Published Edition

John Firman began to formulate the ideas presented in this book in the early 1980s, during the years in which he lived a solitary life in Washington, D.C., and later in both Atlanta and Macon, Georgia. Shortly afterward, in the mid-1980s, during a one-and-a-half-year period in which he drove an 18-wheeler back and forth across the nation, he continued to develop this material. He was probably the only trucker who carried in his cab a copy, among other books, of Jung's *Answer to Job*. In perusing this book recently, I discovered his bookmark-of-the-day: A pass for a "free, private shower" at a truck stop in Denver!

In 1987 when I reconnected with John after not having seen him for ten years, he had just begun to write the first draft of what was to become *"I" and Self*. He lived in Los Angeles at the time, and I lived in Palo Alto, California. For three years we spent many weekends either in his home or in mine, discussing the concepts that are presented in this remarkable book. Then, and now, I was taken with the breadth and depth of his knowledge. In preparing *"I"and Self* for publication, I reviewed the quotations and citations to ensure their accuracy. I found myself immersed in psychology, from psychoanalysis to object relations theory to transpersonal psychology; in theology, including the Christian mystics; in Eastern spiritual traditions; in mathematics; in infant research; in abuse and addiction literature; in Western philosophy; in poetry; and in physics and evolutionary science. John, in his thinking, was truly a Renaissance man.

The first publication of this book was in 1991, after John had moved north to Palo Alto. He showed an early copy of it to our friend the late Frank Haronian, a psychosynthesis psychologist in New Jersey, who eagerly wrote the foreword for the original publication of the book. We then printed *"I"and Self* at our local copy shop and distributed it in the psychosynthesis community.

John and I went on to publish three books together—*The Primal Wound: A Transpersonal View of Trauma, Addiction, and Growth* (1997); *Psychosynthesis: A Psychology of the Spirit* (2002); and *A Psychotherapy of Love: Psychosynthesis in Practice* (2010)—with SUNY Press in New York, but we never sought formal publication of *"I" and Self.* John died in 2008, and I now publish *"I" and Self* so that it will be available in future years for those who delve deeply into theory in their study of psychosynthesis.

The book, apart from the addition of appendix 5, remains the same as John wrote it, except for some small changes that I made: the correction of inaccurate references; the inclusion of citations to Firman and Gila's later writings; and the revision of a few points that I believe needed clarification. John had last looked at the original manuscript of this book in 2007, the year before he died, and had made some minor revisions at that time. I do not know whether, if he were to read it today, thirteen years later, he would make further changes. As it stands now, a few of the comments are dated—for example, the state of psychosynthesis writing. Many psychosynthesis practitioners have now written and published, adding to the body of psychosynthesis literature. John would be pleased; he frequently encouraged others to write their interpretation and development of psychosynthesis theory.

Appendix 5, the significant addition to this revised edition of the book, is John's recollection of the two-and-a-half months when he studied with Roberto Assagioli in Italy during the fall of 1973. Their meetings took place in both Florence and at Roberto's home in Capolona. Despite John's struggle with Assagioli's dualism, John loved Roberto, and Roberto remained an inner guiding presence for John for the rest of his life. I include here a portion of the letter John wrote to Roberto on leaving Florence in mid-December 1973:

*I would like to say to you that I am sorry and a little guilty that I did not help you more with writings of yours. I had said in Capolona that I would help you with your "aggression" paper, though I never did (I still think it's a valuable paper). It seems I got too involved in the raincloud to help you organize some of your "pools" of knowledge. Perhaps I can return some day to help you with some of your writings; my soul has made it pretty explicit that I am to do a lot of service by writing!*

*Well, I don't know what else to say, except that I love you and the light you have incarnated in your lifetime, more I am sure than I am aware of. I intend to follow the lead you have given for the rest of my life. I see clearly my "duty to joy" and service, and shall carry it out. My personality isn't adequate to express what I want to tell you, so I guess it doesn't have to; you'll hear it on a higher octave. Anyway, my personality really likes your personality too!*

*Namaskara,*

*Ann Gila*

# Foreword to the Original Edition

It must be at least a year since John Firman sent me a copy of an earlier version of his book dealing with the theoretical foundations of psychosynthesis. I was pleased and flattered that he asked me to read it and give him my comments. It took me a while to find the time but once I got into it I found it so fascinating that I had to finish it as soon as possible. In it, I found new and evocative ways of looking at standard psychosynthetic positions. If I had understood everything that he had written, the chore would have evoked a bored "Yeh, sure! So what's new?" But instead, I found myself challenged to learn, to think, and most excitingly, to grow!

It's a rare event when I choose to read a book a second time... or even to see a movie again. I have read John's book at least twice and plan to read the latest version in its entirety because every reading presents me with surprises! New ideas, new connections and a broader perspective on psychosynthesis stimulate my thinking.

When Sam Keen interviewed Roberto Assagioli for an article that was published in *Psychology Today*, he asked Roberto to tell him what was wrong with psychosynthesis. Keen gave Roberto an "A" for his reply to the effect that psychosynthesis was too "extensive," too "comprehensive." This over-inclusiveness has led to psychosynthesis remaining somewhat vague and undefined over the years. While it still offers a broad general vision of the whole person, it has developed relatively little precise articulation of the theory. John has taken a giant step toward correcting that deficiency. In doing so he has successfully avoided going to the other extreme of proposing a rigid and dogmatic system without room for expansion and correction.

I am grateful to John for opening my eyes to something that has been gestating in me for several years. Also, he has made me aware of some problems that I had not recognized. He has approached psychosynthesis as a lover who wants to help it to grow ever more adequate to its chosen task, not as a detractor who scorns its aspirations. John's study offers us an improved view of both the shortcomings and the potentialities of psychosynthesis.

*Frank Haronian*

# Acknowledgments

The seeds for this book began germinating in me during the winter of 1980 in Washington, D.C., and have only attained this final form in the past two years. Thus the influences on this material have spanned a decade, and have come from many far-flung and varied quarters. Allow me however to thank at least some of the people who have been important to my work along the way.

I would first of all like to thank Roberto Assagioli for conceiving psychosynthesis, and then Jim Vargiu for his further elaboration of psychosynthesis theory. While I take strong issue today with the dualistic philosophy of both these thinkers, I yet believe psychosynthesis potentially has a tremendous breadth, depth, and clarity as a psychospiritual approach to the human being.

I would also like to thank all those who worked, played, laughed, and cried with me over the years in the Psychosynthesis Institute, first in Palo Alto and then San Francisco. We learned a great deal the hard way.

Thanks as well to Fr. Vincent Serpa, O.P., who has been a faithful friend and wise advisor for many years. It was he who first introduced me to the idea that the human being might be thought of as a *union* of self and psyche-soma, rather than a self who *owned* a psyche-soma. And I give thanks to my friend and former co-worker Sr. Carla Kovack, O.P., who continues to teach me much about the daily struggles and joys involved in seeking a life of faith.

The writing of this book has for the most part been a lonely affair. But as I began to feel ready for the material to move towards readers, I turned to my friends and colleagues Tom Yeomans and Martha Crampton. I am deeply grateful for their useful comments on this work, and for their warm support of my efforts.

Other readers who deserve thanks for taking the time to go through earlier manuscripts are Dr. Nancy Howell, who brought her Christian feminism to bear on the book; and psychotherapist Robert Rosenbush, who commented from the perspectives of Buddhism and object relations theory.

I also turned to someone I had not known until fairly recently, Dr. Frank Haronian, the psychologist who had been the program director of the Psychosynthesis Research Foundation in New York City from 1967 to 1972. I, as many in psychosynthesis, had been influenced by his classic article, "The Repression of the Sublime," which argued that spirituality could be repressed just as any other aspect of the person. As I was working on this book, I was pleased to discover Frank's other excellent psychosynthesis articles in *The Journal of Humanistic Psychology* and *Pastoral Psychology* (see References).

When I decided to contact Frank about the piece I was writing, he responded very kindly, and gave me thoughtful and useful feedback on my work both via tape recordings and personal meetings. So I am indebted to him for taking the time to read and respond to this book, and for the wonderful personal support and encouragement he has given me.

I would also like to say that I feel extremely grateful and blessed that my father, Joseph H. Firman, and my mother, Catharine K. Firman, bequeathed to me the financial means which enabled me to work unhampered during the final stages of the writing and publishing of this book.

Last, and yes, by no means least, I would like to thank my colleague and wife, Ann Russell [Ann Gila]. She more than any other has lived the birth pains of this book with me. Through countless long discussions, heated arguments, doubts and uncertainties, and readings and re-readings of various manuscripts, Ann has "been there" for this book and for me.

Many of the ideas herein are a direct result of extended theoretical struggles between Ann and myself, as we developed and presented workshops and classes over the past several years. Indeed, while in no way shirking my full responsibility for this book, I must say that without Ann's assistance I could neither have developed nor written most of the material as it now stands.

# Introduction

*What we hope to see developed over a period of years,*
*and certainly do not claim has yet been achieved,*
*is a science of the Self...*
—Roberto Assagioli

## The State of Psychosynthesis Theory

The Italian psychiatrist Roberto Assagioli began developing psychosynthesis in 1910, as an approach which would address both the psychology and the spirituality of the human being.

He sought a developing open-ended system which would understand not only the healing of childhood trauma and the integration of the personality, but in addition, the *spiritual* or what has been termed the *transpersonal* dimension of human experience. This latter includes what Abraham Maslow (1971) called *peak experiences*, those moments of profound insight and joy encountered during such activities as intense creative endeavor, aesthetic appreciation, or religious practice.

Thus, psychosynthesis was one of the forerunners of the fields of both humanistic psychology and transpersonal psychology, the two movements spawned by the work of Maslow and his successors. Indeed, many of Assagioli's core concepts have subsequently emerged in the parlance of transpersonal psychology: *disidentification*; *"I"* or *observing self*; *subpersonalities*; the *superconscious*; and the *Transpersonal Self*.

However, psychosynthesis itself has undergone very little theoretical growth, especially as compared to psychological theories of a similar age such as the Freudian and Jungian approaches (remember for example, that the birth of psychosynthesis pre-dates Jung's break with Freud by several years). In stark contrast to his prolific contemporaries Freud and Jung, Assagioli wrote only two books about psychosynthesis in his lifetime (a third book, a collection of miscellaneous writings, was posthumously published thirteen years after his death). Thus the psychosynthesis theorist has been left with a very slight foundation on which to build.

But even Assagioli's small seminal theoretical base has not received much serious attention in the intervening years within psychosynthesis literature (here as throughout, I refer to published, English-language literature only). Professionals outside the field will be shocked and perplexed to learn that after nearly 80 years, there are almost no critical evaluations of specific psychosynthesis concepts in print.

For example, there has been little or no published critique and extension of fundamental concepts such as *personal self*, *will*, *Self*, the *superconscious*, or the *lower unconscious*. These tremendously central concepts seem to be nowhere dealt with directly, in a manner which would clarify and expand our understanding of them. (An exception to this trend in the literature was the now-defunct journal *Synthesis*, which in the 1970s set out to elaborate rigorously and systematically the specific concepts put forth by Assagioli.)

From what I can ascertain to date, most psychosynthesis theoretical literature is largely limited to one of the following categories:

(a) Discussions of clinical work and technique, which refer only very generally to pre-existing theory (sometimes inadvertently giving one the mistaken impression that the applied theory is elaborated elsewhere).

(b) Attempts to relate theories of other approaches to psychosynthesis (often a premature and confusing effort, given the underdeveloped state of psychosynthesis theory itself).

(c) Presentations of Assagioli's work which seek to make it more accessible to those outside the field (although at this stage, such work simply perpetuates and disseminates the weaknesses in Assagioli's work, and too, as we shall see below, may quietly add new difficulties).

(d) Efforts to put forth newly-developed concepts without making it clear how these correct and/or extend pre-existing psychosynthesis thought (thus new concepts remain disconnected from the theoretical base, add little to the growth of that base, and in the extreme, may seem unrelated to psychosynthesis at all).

However important any such types of work may be, they currently far outdistance any ongoing published development of the body of psychosynthesis theory per se. For example, while there are indeed those applying psychosynthesis to the field of addiction, there is no developed theoretical model of addiction and treatment founded on central psychosynthesis concepts (such as, the I-Self relationship and the levels of the psyche; or disidentification and the core personality). Additionally, psychosynthesis has found itself unable to develop a comprehensive clinical theory; or a lifespan developmental theory; or even a personality theory much beyond Assagioli's first general outline.

The upshot of this lack of development is of course that as a psychological theory, psychosynthesis can today be applied only very generally and imprecisely to contemporary issues of psychological dysfunction and health. Recent important work in areas such as narcissistic and borderline disorders; codependency, abuse, and addiction; and developmental psychology; all remain unaddressed by published theory in a complete way. This is regrettable, because I believe developed psychosynthesis theory has the potential to illuminate many deep dynamics of these areas, as well as to suggest new research and treatment approaches.

Furthermore, without a strong developing theoretical base, there may be eventually no "psychosynthesis" at all to attract the serious theorist and clinician. If there is not a shared body of work carefully built by criticizing, correcting, and elaborating Assagioli's original thinking, it may come to pass that psychosynthesis becomes a theoretical non-entity.

That is, with no organic developmental direction to the ideas, there is nothing for practitioners to come to terms with as an initial baseline, no need to explain how new data and insights correct or improve accepted theory. Thus, with no developing "stem" growing up from Assagioli's original "seed," psychosynthesis becomes a mere catch-all term for an eclectic collection of unrelated opinions, ideas, and techniques. This of course in turn discourages creative thinkers from considering serious work in the field, which in turn leaves psychosynthesis bereft, which in turn discourages serious work, and so on—and a vicious cycle is set in place.

We shall in the present work, therefore, attempt to assist the development of this undernourished stem of psychosynthesis thought. We will examine principles outlined by Assagioli, then carefully critique these, and only then, suggest formulations to correct or refine the earlier work. The specific concepts we shall consider in this way are *personal self* or "*I*," and the notion of *Higher Self*, also called, *Transpersonal Self* or more simply, *Self*.

## Re-visioning Psychosynthesis

However, in our exploration of "I" and Self we will find that there is "trouble in the soul of psychosynthesis." That is, we will discover fundamental difficulties with these central concepts as understood by Assagioli, and thus with the basic view of the human being which underpins the entire system of psychosynthesis.

As we offer changes to this basic view then, we will find that psychosynthesis as a whole is thrown into a new light. Psychosynthesis is here perhaps a bit like a person undergoing a shift in identity—the person remains the same unique individual as before, but at the same time one's experience of self and world are fundamentally altered. Changes at such a basic contextual level of any system affect the entire system, although the various areas of the system may remain quite intact.

Our current study thus comprises not only an assessment and development of specific aspects of psychosynthesis thought, but as well, a re-visioning of psychosynthesis as a whole. For example, we suggest a new understanding of the word "psychosynthesis" itself (see "Idealization and Unity," in chapter 5).

While this re-visioning touches the very core of psychosynthesis, with implications for both theory and practice, I believe it nevertheless maintains continuity with the original thrust of Assagioli's work. In fact, I believe Assagioli himself would approve of most, if not all, found in these pages.

Also, to the extent that transpersonal psychology makes use of material similar to that of psychosynthesis, this book can be taken as a commentary on transpersonal psychology as well. Transpersonal psychology is a much more general field than psychosynthesis, representing the "fourth force" in psychology, following the earlier movements of psychoanalytic theory, behaviorism, and humanistic/existential psychology. The student of transpersonal psychology who wishes to explore concepts such as the observing self, cosmic consciousness, Transpersonal Self, or the spectrum of consciousness, just may find these pages thought-provoking.

Let us turn now to a brief outline of the three major concepts addressed in this current work: *"I," Self,* and *transcendence-immanence.* We offer this outline not only in order to introduce these concepts to those new to psychosynthesis, but also to indicate the approach we will take to each of them. They form the foundation and pillars for the other ideas in the book, and will be dealt with more fully in the remaining chapters.

## On "I"

The concept of personal self or "I" as the seat of personal identity is central to psychosynthesis. This core concept directly or indirectly conditions all spheres of theory and practice within the field. According to Assagioli:

> The Self (with a capital S) is often somewhat misleadingly considered to be the central concept in psychosynthesis ... [but] the idea which is of capital importance, and around which the entire personal psychosynthesis revolves, is that of a personal self ... (Assagioli 1965, 87)

But again, as with most psychosynthesis concepts, there has been to date no major examination of personal self within psychosynthesis theory. Most of the theoretical literature in psychosynthesis simply refers to aspects of Assagioli's original formulation, without undertaking any close examination or further development of this concept.

The one exception to this dearth of material is Betsie Carter-Haar's excellent article, "Identity and Personal Freedom" (1975). This article outlines many dynamics surrounding "I" vis-à-vis personality integration, and seems to be the best elaboration of these dynamics available to date. But as we shall see, Carter-Haar's article, as useful as it is, yet suffers from the many difficulties intrinsic to the notion of "I" in current psychosynthesis thought.

The biggest of these difficulties with the classic notion of "I" can be seen in Assagioli's fundamental formulation:

> I *am not* my body....
> I *am not* my emotions....
> I *am not* my intellect.
> (Assagioli 1965, 118)

We will below maintain that this "I *am not*" formulation posits a fundamental split between personal identity and the psyche-soma, and is an instance of what has been called *dualism*.

Assagioli's dualism is a variety that views the human person as a "soul with a body." Here, rather than considering the person a holistic soul-body unity, the human being is seen as an entity to whom the body, feelings, and mind, are merely "vehicles."

The soul or self here thus becomes a pure spiritual essence, an invisible homunculus living somewhere within the psyche-soma. We shall see that this "I *am not*" formulation is an ideological belief held by Assagioli, and that this belief is not proven by phenomenological observation as he claims.

After our dispelling the dualistic "I *am not*" formulation, we then find ourselves free to follow Assagioli's brilliant and more empirical observations into the nature of "I." Here we explore "I" as the core identity of the human being, a center of consciousness and will. "I" will be here understood as distinct *but not separate* from the changing processes of psyche and soma.

We shall see that indeed, "I" can observe the various psychosomatic processes such as sensations, feelings, and thoughts, and that therefore "I" is not identical to these changing processes. However, we need not infer from this fact that "I" is an incorporeal visitor from some purely spiritual realm who has incarnated in matter. *Psyche and soma, together with the people and events of our world as a whole, are completely integral to our lives and cannot be thought to be in any way extraneous to our deepest identity.*

In pursuing Assagioli's more accurate (non-dualistic) view of "I," we shall see also how his insight is starkly contrasted to a view of personal identity which equates human being with consciousness alone. This latter view, current in some psychosynthesis and transpersonal psychology circles, is formulated in the statement, "I am pure consciousness." This formulation of course leaves out a fundamental aspect of Assagioli's view of human identity—will. For Assagioli, will and consciousness are both essential to the person.

We will see how the notion of "I" as solely consciousness implies a pure passivity at the core of human being, and thus creates a dualistic split between one's essence and one's engagement with the world. At various points too, we shall examine how this formulation can confuse the attainment of higher levels of consciousness with Self-realization, that is, with the daily choices of a life lived in ongoing relationship with Self.

## On Self

In spite of Assagioli's hope that psychosynthesis develop into a "science of the Self" (Assagioli 1965, 194), his concept of Self has received even less attention in psychosynthesis literature than has the concept of "I." But since "I" is considered a "reflection" of Self (20), we will here use our study of "I" to move towards a beginning exploration into the nature of Self as well.

For example, since "I" is distinct but not separate from psychosomatic processes, Self too can be thought to be distinct but not separate from these processes. But since Self represents a more profound depth of being than "I," Self can also be considered distinct but not separate from the content and processes of the unconscious as well, whether of the superconscious/higher unconscious or of the individual and collective unconscious.

That is, Self is revealed as quite different from the notion of Self as a collective archetype of wholeness, a primitive undifferentiated totality out of which differentiates the ego. Rather, Self is distinct from all content, whether this content is individual or collective, spiritual or mundane, whole or fragmented.

Too, Self is the direct reflecting source of "I," of a someone, a person, an individual, a center of consciousness and will. It follows therefore that Self also must be a deeper someone, deeper person, deeper individuality, a deeper center of consciousness and will. Self is therefore not cosmic energy, universal wholeness, or a collective image, but is instead Deeper Personal Being—a greater "I am that I am." As a reflection of Self, "I" may be thought to be an image of Self, what has been called the "image of God," or the "*imago Dei*."

As we apply our study of "I" to Self, we shall see further that contrary to dualistic psychosynthesis thought, Self is not an ideal blissful entity existing in a transcendent, timeless, or superconscious/higher unconscious realm. Rather, we shall find Self to be even *more* engaged in spacetime than is "I," and thus possessing the ability to be fully present to us not only in the heights of our spiritual experiences, but in the depths of our isolation and pain, and indeed, in every moment of our lives.

Self is quite distinct, therefore, from experiences of wholeness, unity, and light, and Self-realization does not necessarily involve peak experiences. While communion with Self may include peaks, it may just as often include experiences of disintegration and pain, experiences which Victor Frankl (1988, 83) called *abyss experiences*. But looking beyond both peak and abyss, we shall find that Self-realization is much more a matter of developing a personal ongoing relationship with Self throughout the ordinary daily round of human existence.

The reader familiar with psychosynthesis will note too that we do not use Assagioli's terms, *Higher Self, Transpersonal Self*, and *Universal Self*, but instead elect to use the simple term, *Self*. As we shall see, our use of Self does not equate exactly with any of these other terms used by Assagioli. The differences and similarities will become apparent as we proceed, and are an integral part of the "re-visioning" of psychosynthesis. (Appendix 4 is devoted to a full discussion of this issue of various greater "Selves" in psychosynthesis theory.)

## Transcendence-Immanence

Our approach to "I" and Self will attempt to avoid two common approaches to this subject—*dualism* and *monism*. We shall instead attempt to find the middle way between these two extremes.

As we have stated, dualism maintains that deepest human essence is completely separate from the psyche-soma. Here we may be led to think of "I" as a mysterious invisible entity existing somewhere within the psyche-soma, what philosopher Gilbert Ryle in *The Concept of Mind* rightly criticized as, "the dogma of the Ghost in the Machine" (Ryle 1949, 15–16). At the best, dualism encourages otherworldly philosophies that consider the human being to be a soul who laudably chooses to take on a physical body. At the worse, these philosophies consider the soul to be trapped in the illusion or evil of physical reality from which it must seek escape to the "spiritual."

Throughout this continuum can be found the psychospiritual dynamic we shall call a *transpersonal identification* (Firman and Gila 2002, 100–102; Firman and Gila 2006). Such an identification refers to an intense involvement with spiritual or higher unconscious realities that limits one's ability to engage other dimensions of the human condition, such as existential aloneness, anxiety, evil, and mortality.

The second traditional psychological approach to human identity—monism—confuses self with the processes of the psyche-soma. A most prevalent form of this monism considers human selfhood as derivative of, if not identical to, physiological and social processes. There is here no conception that deeper personal identity transcends these processes and thus no recognition that human beings may participate in a supraordinate unity that includes self, other, and world.

This type of monism can lead eventually to a sense of isolation and meaninglessness in life which has been called the *existential vacuum* (Frankl 1985, 128–30), the *existential crisis* (Firman and Vargiu 1980, 99–103), or the *existential neurosis* (Maddi):

> The personal identity out of which this [existential] neurosis originates involves a definition of self as simply an embodiment of biological needs and a player of social roles ... The resulting symptom pattern is characterized by chronic alienation, aimlessness, and meaninglessness. (Maddi 1976, 256)

Throughout this work, we shall develop an alternative to both the dualistic and monistic poles of thinking. Here deepest human identity shall not be considered to be a transcendent soul with a body. But neither shall that identity be considered as essentially a product of psychosomatic and social forces.

Rather, we shall conceive deepest human identity to be *transcendent-immanent*. That is, human being is on one hand distinct from—transcendent of—processes such as feelings and thoughts, or attitudes and actions. But on the other hand, human being can in no way be considered separate from such processes, that is, it is at the same time completely immanent, completely one with them.

Furthermore, we will show how these two seemingly opposed concepts of transcendence and immanence are actually two facets of one reality—transcendence implies immanence and vice versa. These are not two "pieces" to be united in a whole, nor two pieces which can be split apart. By transcendence and immanence we do *not* mean:

1. A transcendent, timeless, spiritual realm up there in the soul/higher unconscious, versus,

2. An immanent, material spacetime realm down here in the personality.

The two terms transcendence and immanence are instead thought to represent one unbroken reality seen from two different points of view, and this single reality—the foundation of deepest human being—can be thought to be distinct but not separate from the content and processes of psyche-soma and the world at large.

## Some Limitations of This Book

The discussion of "I" and Self in these pages is a preliminary exploration, and should in no way be considered an exhaustive treatment of these highly elusive and complex topics. Indeed, by the very nature of the subject, we believe it is quite impossible to finally pin down or define the mystery of human being. It is hoped however, that some of this work might spark further thinking, discussion, and development of these important concepts in psychosynthesis theory.

The reader will note too that this book is focused upon the conceptual and experiential rather than upon the clinical and applied. This has been necessary because the task here is to critique, and to offer improvements to, the basic conceptual underpinnings of psychosynthesis. Thus the areas covered, as well as the scope of the discussion, do not lend themselves easily to short clinical illustration, and the inclusion of extended case material would simply be too cumbersome. See Firman and Gila (1997; 2002; 2010) for the application of the concepts to in-depth case material.

Another missing piece in this book is that it does not deal fully with the development of personal identity as it proceeds, or fails to proceed, within the social matrix of the human lifespan. Although much contemporary family systems theory, object relations theory, self psychology, and infant research (see especially Daniel Stern, 1985) goes quite far in this direction, development of psychosynthesis theory along these lines is exciting to contemplate. Such development could indeed make good use of the concepts of "I" and Self elaborated in these pages. Again, see Firman and Gila (1997; 2002; 2010) for this elaboration.

The present work does, however, offer a foundation for a psychosynthesis understanding of the social matrix of human development, and we do throughout imply the indispensable human need for this matrix. While "I" is an immediate reflection of Self, this action of reflection is not solely an intrapsychic event, but even more so, comes to us through the mirroring by, and relationship to, the significant others in our lives.

Self acts in and through other people and not simply within the bounds of our private interior worlds. Indeed, we would say that I-amness is only fully realized insofar as Self can act through authentic empathic relationships, *authentic unifying centers* (see Firman and Gila 1997; 2002; 2010), beginning—it is hoped—with our parents and families of origin. Only in this way can we be reflected or mirrored, and thus realize our true identity. Some of these dynamics are examined in chapter 7.

Our intention in this book is to provide an understanding of human being that can help facilitate just such authentic relationships, both in and out of therapy. We are maintaining that empathic "I-Thou" relationships are not served by treating human beings as selves inhabiting bodies, nor on the other hand, as entities whose selves are simply derivative of psychosomatic processes. Rather, we find that optimum human relationships are imbued with the perception that while there is indeed a transcendent aspect of human identity, this transcendence does not imply a separation or difference from the world, but exactly the reverse—a radical immanence, a fundamental union with the world.

In any case, we must remember that in discussing views of human being, we are not ultimately talking about consciously-held philosophical or psychological notions. We are talking rather about an essential sense of who we are in the world, an a priori sense which itself conditions our experience and beliefs. And it is this deep sense of our own humanity by which we contact the humanity of others, be they our family, friends, or clients. One might even say that our experience of self at this level is *the* fundamental operating principle in our lives. Our hope here is but to point towards this deepest sense of self.

## Three Last Comments

In order to close this introductory section, we would like to make three comments about the terminology used in this work. First, we use the terms *higher unconscious* and *superconscious* interchangeably, following a similar practice by Assagioli in his writings.

Second, note that herein we shall use the term "I" rather than Assagioli's other term for this concept: *personal self*. We do however consider "I" and personal self to be equivalent terms, following the psychosynthesis convention of reserving them to denote identity or I-amness, rather than states of consciousness, identifications, or even consciousness itself.

In other words, the terms "I" and personal self are applied traditionally to the enduring experiencer, and are not limited to indicating changing experience of any sort. In psychosynthesis, any sort of "self" is not merely a type or state of consciousness, but a living, willing, being. However, we find it less confusing simply to select one of these terms—"I"—for our use. Our subject is elusive enough as it is, and we do not need a plethora of terms muddying the waters. Thus we have for the most part retired the term personal self, while continuing to consider it identical to "I."

As for Assagioli's other synonym for "I"—the *ego*—this term runs the very real risk of confusing the concept of "I" with the ego as described in many other psychological theories. We therefore do not consider ego as equivalent to "I." Ego is thereby freed to be used in the traditional psychoanalytic sense (see the section on Freud in appendix 2).

Our third and last comment is that the terms *"I"* and *Self* (and often, *will*) are here not objectified by prefacing them with the articles "a," "an," or "the." This is avoided because usages such as, "the 'I'" or "a Self," tend to give the impression that these are objects or contents of awareness rather than the subject who is aware.

This experimental convention does however lead to some awkward phraseology. For example the phrase, "When the 'I' becomes identified," is changed to read, "When 'I' becomes identified." However, this awkwardness may serve to remind us that the phrase does not refer to an object to be discovered "out here," but to the one who is "back there" reading the phrase. I am indebted to psychotherapist Ann Russell for this insight and convention.

# CHAPTER ONE

# Trouble in the Soul of Psychosynthesis

*And is not purification really ... to separate*
*as far as possible the soul from the body,*
*and to collect itself together out of the body ...*
*to dwell alone by itself as far as it can,*
*being freed from the body as if from a prison?*
—Plato

## The "I Am Not" Formulation

Assagioli's concept of "I" is founded on the insight that "I" can be distinguished experientially not only from the outer world of the physical body, observable behavior, and social roles; but in addition, can be distinguished from the inner world of sensations, images, feelings, and thoughts.

In other words, "I" can experience being distinct from both the world of "soma" and the world of "psyche." This insight led Assagioli to his familiar formulation:

I *have* a body, but I *am not* my body....
I *have* emotions, but I *am not* my emotions....
I *have* a mind, but I *am not* my mind....
*I am a center of pure self-consciousness and of will.*

(Assagioli 1973, 214–15)

Assagioli's initial recognition of a distinction between "I" and psyche-soma is a profound and accurate insight into the lived subjective experience of "I." We shall closely examine Assagioli's original insight in chapter 3. However, his "I *am not*" formulation of this subjective experience presents problems, and this is the subject of this current chapter.

It is interesting to note that this "I *am not*" formulation, so central in both of Assagioli's books, has been dropped from use by some practitioners of psychosynthesis today. For example, of the few writings by psychosynthesis theorists which have found major publishers, one book includes this formulation only as a footnote (Ferrucci, 1982), while the other leaves it out altogether (Whitmore, 1986). Too, this formulation has been added to, altered, or eliminated by various psychosynthesis training programs in the United States and Europe with which I am acquainted.

For all of the apparent dissatisfaction with Assagioli's "I *am not*," the underlying problem does not seem to have been articulated by anyone in the field, with the exception of the psychosynthesis therapist and teacher Miceal O'Regan. In his article, "Reflections on the Art of Disidentification," O'Regan claims that this formulation is actually dangerous and can lead to the erroneous idea that "I" is fundamentally *separate* from the body, from the feelings, and from the mind. He has this to say about the "I *am not*" formulation:

> ... this kind of thinking and effort is illusionary and the basis of ego inflation. At best it becomes a practice in positive thinking, at worst it becomes a practice in denial and repression. (O'Regan 1984, 44)

It seems clear that Assagioli's radical "I *am not*" is more than a simple comment about the distinction between the I-experience versus the psyche-soma experience. This is more than a mere discrimination among different aspects of the human person, such as distinguishing lungs from heart, or feelings from thoughts.

That is, the statement, "I *am not* my body," has far greater psychological and philosophical implications than, for example, the statement, "A sensation is *not* a thought." This "I *am not*" formulation, unlike the latter statement, suggests an actual dissociation or splitting of human identity and other spheres of experience.

Here we can envision "I" as somehow above and beyond the vicissitudes of daily human existence, as somehow essentially uninvolved in personal responsibility, human relationships, and existential suffering. Of course, this view might well maintain that the honorable thing to do is to fully engage human existence, to integrate the personality, and to help the evolution of humanity. But this engagement is not seen as *essential* to human being. (This is the view which we shall later call *holistic gnosticism.*)

I believe this implied dissociation of "I" and the psyche-soma is the reason the "I *am not*" formulation has been altered by some in the field. This alteration seems to imply a rejection of the dualistic splitting of these two spheres of experience, a de facto rejection of the Neoplatonic-Gnostic-Theosophical dualism which claims the human person *is* a self who merely *owns* a psyche-soma.

> *Salvation belongs only to the soul;*
> *the body is by nature corruptible.*
> —Gnostic Text

## Dualism

It has long been known by many psychosynthesis practitioners that Assagioli was influenced by the Theosophical movement, and particularly by Alice Bailey. When I worked with Assagioli in 1973, one could not miss the picture of the renowned Theosophist Madame Blavatsky in his hallway, nor the full-volume set of Bailey's works on his shelf. During my meetings with him we discussed, among other things, theosophical concepts and principles such as "the seven rays" typology (which is mentioned in his work; see the "septenary classification," in Assagioli 1973, 250–51).

Many who knew of Assagioli's work in both Theosophy and psychology spoke of maintaining a "wall of silence" between these two areas of his work, and thus this connection has not generally been acknowledged. (Although one wonders why this was so, when for example C. G. Jung's obvious love of Alchemy and Gnosticism allowed these to become explicit parts of his body of work. Much the same might be said of Freud too, whose respect for classical mythology gave us concepts such as the Oedipal complex and narcissism.)

Furthermore, as Jean Hardy has outlined so thoroughly and convincingly, Assagioli was profoundly influenced not only by Theosophy, but through this, by Neoplatonic and Gnostic thought as well:

> But the direct descent of Theosophy from gnostic traditions is significant in the whole of his [Assagioli's] thinking and affects the basic assumptions upon which psychosynthesis was founded. (Hardy 1987, 124)

Hardy states that, as has been said of Jungian psychology, psychosynthesis could be considered "gnosticism in twentieth century dress" (ibid.).

For our purposes, the important thing to note here is that all of these systems which so influenced Assagioli have one important thing in common—they all consider the human person as a "self with a body," rather than as a holistic "self-body unity."

It is therefore quite understandable that this dualistic view has crossed the "wall of silence" and affected psychosynthesis. Hardy states plainly that psychosynthesis, "assumes a person is a soul and has a personality" (196). That is, the person *is* a self and *has* a body-feelings-mind, a psyche-soma. (She states that this is also the view of transpersonal psychology in general.)

This is indeed a gnostic view of the person. According to Bentley Layton in his introduction to *The Gnostic Scriptures*, Gnostics considered that "the true person is the soul, and the body is merely a 'garment' that we must 'put on' and 'wear'" (Layton 1987, 18). Compare this to Assagioli:

> In other words, one becomes a self who uses the body, the feeling-apparatus and the mental abilities as tools, as instruments, in the same way as a car is the extension of a driver ... (Assagioli 1965, 122)

Assagioli's statement clearly implies a gnostic separation of soul and body, of self and psyche-soma. Here the person becomes someone who owns a psyche-soma and who can therefore presumably relate to it much as one does to any other "apparatus" or "tool" included in one's personal property. The body becomes a mere vehicle or trapping of the human being, with no fundamental ontological unity between body and self. Thus self becomes Ryle's "ghost in the machine," an entity animating the personality like some mysterious homunculus living somewhere inside the body.

This tendency to separate or dissociate any two aspects of reality—especially soul and body, spirit and matter, or self and personality—is generally called *dualism*. This dualism is what we are calling *trouble in the soul of psychosynthesis*.

> *Woe unto you who put your hope*
> *in the flesh and in*
> *the prison that will perish.*
> —Gnostic Text

The core of Assagioli's dualism resides in his Exercise in Dis-identification (Assagioli 1973, 214–15). Here one is invited to make a series of dissociative affirmations:

I *have* a body, but I *am not* my body....
I *have* emotions, but I *am not* my emotions....
I *have* a mind, but I *am not* my mind.

The above statements of (supposed) disidentification then culminate in the self-identification:

*I am a center of pure self-consciousness and of will.*

The experience gained through practicing this exercise of disidentification/self-identification is at the very center of psychosynthesis:

The conscious and purposeful use of self-identification—or dis-identification—is basic in psychosynthesis. (Assagioli 1965, 111)

This can only mean then, that the dissociative idea contained in this disidentification exercise is also basic to psychosynthesis as understood by Assagioli. Let us therefore carefully examine the influence of this dualism in the disidentification exercise.

## The Disidentification Exercise

In analyzing Assagioli's dissociative "I *am not*," it is important to see that he begins with a true experiential approach to "I," but is then led astray by gnostic-theosophical concepts.

Assagioli begins his approach to a discussion of "I" in a beautifully empirical way, introducing the Exercise in Dis-identification with a section entitled "*Procedure*" (Assagioli 1965, 114–16). In this preliminary section he outlines the procedure for what I consider true (non-dualistic) disidentification:

> The procedure for achieving self-identity in the sense of the pure self-consciousness at the personal level ... can be summarized in one word ... *introspection*. It means, as its terminology clearly indicates, directing the mind's eye, or the observing function, upon the world of psychological facts, of psychological events, of which we can be aware. (114)

Assagioli quite rightly says that such simple observation of inner processes will open one to the empirical fact that one is not identical to such inner processes, that one can experience disidentification from these. This disidentification amounts to the clear and simple realization that "I" exists throughout all these changing processes:

> This objective observation produces naturally, spontaneously and inevitably a sense of dis-identification from any and all of those psychological contents and activities. By contrast, the stability, the permanency of the observer is realized. (116)

This "observer" is "I." "I" describes the empirical ability of the human subject to endure through, and therefore engage all, changes in the inner environment. (The pure subjectness of this experience can perhaps also be formulated alternatively as a *noself* experience; see "Transcendence and No-thing-ness," chapter 4.)

As far as Assagioli in this "Procedure" section is focusing on the actual lived experience of "I" in the here and now, he is on safe phenomenological/empirical ground. He is here describing the stance of objective inner observation which is fundamental to Western contemplative prayer, as well as to Eastern insight meditation such as vipassana or zazen.

However, Assagioli almost immediately wanders away from this useful empirical approach. Immediately after this "Procedure" section, he launches into the formal Exercise in Dis-identification (116–25)—a technique which he claims will facilitate the aforementioned objective inner observation.

But this objectivity is completely lost in the very first sentence of the exercise, which reads,

> The first step is to **affirm with conviction** and to become *aware* of the fact: "I *have* a body, but *I am not* my body." (116, emphasis in bold added)

He goes on to repeat this affirmation vis-à-vis feelings and mind as well.

Note well that the phrase, "affirm with conviction," is a sharp break from objective inner observation. This is not the simple observation of here-and-now inner events he has just finished describing as central to the disidentification experience. In moving from the objective "Procedure" section into the Exercise in Dis-identification, Assagioli makes two very large leaps:

1. He shifts from the act of observation to the act of affirmation, which is basically a shift from empirical witnessing to a profession of belief. And as Assagioli himself points out elsewhere, affirmation is a method used by advertising agencies to sell their products, as well as a technique used in brain-washing (Assagioli 1973, 174–75). Thus, as O'Regan pointed out, we are here in the realm of positive thinking, and have lost completely the objective introspection just previously described.

The effect of this shift is that the experiential authenticity of the actual introspective experience—the simple observation of inner events—is quietly transferred to the more abstract philosophical belief. One is therefore led unwittingly into accepting a particular (gnostic) belief about one's experience.

2. The second leap has to do with the nature of this affirmed belief. Again with no accompanied explanation, Assagioli eliminates the word "sensations" he used earlier (Assagioli 1965, 114), and substitutes the word "body" (116). However, this exercise involves observing sensations come and go in awareness; that is, one here witnesses for example the changing experiences of physical tension and relaxation, heat and cold, or muscular twitches and digestive sounds. We are *not* in fact observing the whole physical body come and go in awareness.

Assagioli has here moved away from the objective observation of sensations, to a statement of belief about the entire soma. The inner distinction between self and sensations thus becomes a philosophical statement describing a separation between self and the entire physical world.

Assagioli performs this same shift later in the exercise, quietly replacing the earlier "*mental activity*" (emphasis in the original) and "mental contents" (115), with the much larger concepts of "intellect" and "mind" (117)—but again, one is observing mental contents or thoughts pass through one's awareness, not the whole of cognitive functioning implied by mind or intellect.

The effect of this leap is to distort one's notion of "I." One is in effect affirming that "I" is in essence so radically different from psyche-soma that "I" can observe—is transcendent of—large-scale changes undergone by the body and mind in toto. Here is an image of "I" which has "I" standing back some distance from the entire psyche-soma; indeed, here is Ryle's "ghost in the machine."

But even if such a perspective were possible, it is irrelevant to disidentification. The Exercise in Dis-identification does not purport to produce such extreme dissociation in the practitioner; it is ostensibly inviting us merely to recognize a distinction between ourselves as observers, and the inner flow of changing sensations, feelings, and thoughts that we observe.

Together, the two leaps above can therefore create an unconscious acceptance of an inflated or idealized notion of "I." Here one unwittingly affirms the belief that "I" is essentially spiritual and separated from physical and mental existence, that one is a transcendent spark of spirit belonging most fundamentally to some non-physical realm. Furthermore, this dualistic view of "I" may then—still unnoticed by the practitioner—grow into a dualistic notion of Self (see "The Idealization of Self" in chapter 5).

The fact that Assagioli makes both of these shifts with no explanation whatsoever, strongly indicates the influence of an unconscious a priori belief system. And the influence of this unconscious dualism is not limited to the Exercise in Dis-identification, but influences other expositions of theory as well:

> The observation, the calm dispassionate, objective observation of the flow of these sensations makes us realize how fleeting or impermanent many of them are and how easily they alternate (and sometimes one is substituted by its contrary). This gives us the certainty—let us say *scientifically demonstrates*—that the self is not the body ... (114–15, emphasis added)

No, this dispassionate observation does not at all demonstrate that "the self is not the body." Such observation merely allows the realization that one is distinct, but not separate, from sensations. Anything more than this is not scientifically demonstrated, but quite the contrary, is a statement of dualistic belief. Here we see again Assagioli's dualism unconsciously superimposed over objective experience.

In short, in Assagioli's Exercise in Dis-identification we are not invited to uncover the objective disidentified experience of "I." Rather, we are being asked to make an affirmation of dissociative dualistic belief. Here Assagioli, apparently caught in dualistic thinking himself, is asking us to utter a credo concerning a gnostic-theosophical belief about the nature of the human being. And this dualism is not limited to the Exercise in Dis-identification, but is an unconscious assumption in other psychosynthesis theory as well.

## The War between Light and Dark

In traditional Gnosticism of course, dualism involves an actual antagonism between self and body—"The body is a 'bond,' 'bond-age,' 'fetter,' or 'prison' of the soul" (Layton 1987, 18). Further, the "true home" of the gnostic soul is "the spiritual universe ... the light" (ibid.), while the material universe is the "'prison' ... the 'dark place'" (Rudolph 1987, 109).[1]

This antagonism is an aspect of the larger view in which the cosmos is seen as a struggle between two fundamental forces, light/spirit and dark/matter. Here spirit is trapped in matter, and salvation involves gaining freedom from the limitations of the body and the world. According to Mircea Eliade:

> For the Gnostics and the Manichaeans, redemption is tantamount to collecting, salvaging, and carrying to heaven the sparks of the divine light which are buried in living matter, first and foremost in man's body. (Eliade 1976, 113)

In Gnosticism therefore, salvation is a process of what Eliade calls *separation*, an escaping from the prison of the body and a return to a God who is absolutely transcendent of (that is, separate from) the world.

One can easily recognize in Assagioli this gnostic notion of a transcendent divine spark—"I"—which is separate from, but imprisoned within, matter: "Every time we identify ourselves with a physical sensation we *enslave* ourselves to the body" (Assagioli 1965, 117, emphasis added); and, "It [self] is not being the *prisoner* of the body ... " (160, emphasis added).

Clearly for Assagioli, as for the Gnostic, self can be enslaved by matter, the psyche-soma. Self is in a pitched battle with fractious psychosomatic forces, a battle in which imprisonment or freedom hang in the balance. The gnostic notion of separation and the "I *am not*" formulation seem to be quite similar, and both seem to underlie these telling words of Assagioli:

But even when these forces within ourselves are temporarily stronger, when the conscious personality is at first overwhelmed by their violence, the vigilant self is never really conquered. It can retire to an inner fortress and there prepare for and await the favorable moment in which to counter-attack. It may lose some of the battles, but if it does not give up its arms and surrender, the ultimate issue is not compromised, and it will achieve victory in the end. ... We should create a "psychological distance" between ourselves and them, keeping these images or complexes at arm's length, so to speak, and then quietly consider their origin, their nature and—their stupidity! (23)

I have often heard such "Assagiolian" language explained away as a function of his turn-of-the-century mentality, as unfortunate anachronisms which somehow do not affect the theory and practice of psychosynthesis. But if such attitudes infuse his very language, how are they not to condition his system? No, this language is not merely the use of outdated metaphor—it is a dualistic strain of thought we can recognize in many aspects of psychosynthesis theory even today.

Assagioli did in fact build a system with a strong dualistic bias. We can recognize in psychosynthesis the gnostic forces of spirit and light—Self and higher unconscious—ranged against the forces of matter and darkness—the complexes and obsessions of the lower unconscious.

At worst, Assagioli portrays an antagonism between self and the "stupidity" of unconscious forces. At best, he envisions a fundamentally spiritual self who cares for, and expresses through, the psyche-soma. But either way, self is seen as fundamentally different from the psychosomatic "vehicle."

And if psychosynthesis is to remain true to the holistic viewpoint implied by its very name, this dualism must not be overlooked. Assagioli's thought must not simply be re-conditioned by more contemporary metaphors, with no critical examination of the ideas themselves. Simply dropping or changing older formulations—like the "I *am not*"—does not allow theorists to recognize this dualism, and thus prevents correcting this dissociative tendency throughout the system as a whole.

# CHAPTER TWO

# Dualism and Psychosynthesis

*Be wakeful and pray with entreaties*
*that you might not dwell in the flesh*
*but might leave the bondage of bitterness*
*belonging to this life.*
—Gnostic Text

## World-wide Dualism

Psychosynthesis is of course not alone in its immersion in dualism, for one could fairly say that our world is awash in this dissociating tendency. A short list of current dualisms might include:

1. The alienation between the human and natural worlds, as seen in the world-wide ecological crisis, is an obvious instance of a dualism of humanity and nature. Here we consider ourselves as so transcendent of nature that we are completely free to use it as we see fit, with little or no concern for its integrity or our fundamental unity with it.

*The cosmos is the fullness of evil.*
—Gnostic Text

2. The patriarchal exaltation of *masculine spirit* in a hierarchy over *feminine matter* is clearly dualistic. Here is the adherence to an exclusively masculine image of Spirit, accompanied by

the devaluation of the feminine, matter, and the natural world. As noted feminist theologian Rosemary Ruether points out, the idea of matter as inferior and feminine was a gnostic trait, although Gnostics did believe, "that woman too can rise above her carnal femaleness" (Ruether 1983, 101). Feminists of many religious traditions, women and men alike, are currently attempting to correct this one-sidedness.[2]

> *For every female (element) that makes itself male*
> *will enter the kingdom of heavens.*
> —Gnostic Text

3. According to Hans Jonas (1963), existentialism, nihilism, and the "death of God" movement can also be seen as instances of dualism. He points out that the distant, exclusively transcendent God of the Gnostics is operationally equivalent to a dead God—in both cases we have a world with no God.

Too, if we are merely wearing our bodies like clothing, human death is wrapped in a comfortable simile of "changing our clothes," thus defending us from a confrontation with the true depth of human suffering. Here the tragedies of suicide, murder, war, and abortion can become dangerously minimized and nihilism encouraged. Ironically, both positivistic materialism and spiritual dualism seem to make the body into a mere object.

4. Similarly, dualism supports the continued repression of traumatic childhood experiences of abandonment, pain, isolation, and shame. Such hard facts of life may be minimized or ignored by a dualism which considers these less real than the transcendent and spiritual. The growing recognition of endemic abuse in childhood—sexual, physical, emotional, mental, and religious—points to the fact that much of what we call normal functioning is actually a dissociation from these early experiences. Here the person develops what D. W. Winnicott termed a *false self* (1987, 133–34) which is dissociated from the helplessness and terror of these all-too-common early experiences.

While this false self may be a valuable and important compensatory structure early in life, it does eventually stand in the way of healing in adulthood (see the work of D. W. Winnicott, Alice Miller, John Bradshaw, and Charles Whitfield).

## Dualistic Denial

This last item above (#4) is of special concern to psychosynthesis psychotherapy. The reason for this is that the dissociation implied by the "I *am not*" formulation can support a sense of a spiritual or centered self which becomes split off or dissociated from the rest of the personality. When a dualistic spirituality is used to separate from other—often more painful—aspects of life, we can call this generally *dualistic denial*. Dualistic denial is a central dynamic found in the clinical presentation of metaphysical dualism.[3]

There are many forms of dualistic denial, but a common form occurs when we attempt to avoid our grief by affirming that a dead loved one is "in a better place now," or "has merely dropped the physical vehicle." But whether or not such beliefs are valid, we are yet left with a deep human grief to work through. And such grief does not indicate a lack of faith or less enlightenment, as Plato implied. Being with our grief is an acceptance of our human-ity, and dualistic denial can be an attempt to avoid this. (As with all defensive or compensatory structures, dualistic denial can be used as a needed respite from stressful powerful experiencing, and thus properly managed can serve the healing process rather than retard it.)

Dualistic denial can also be seen in the person who, raised in a dysfunctional family, developed heightened spiritual sensitivi-ties as a refuge from the early traumatizing environment. In this case we might find that a spiritual or religious false self has devel-oped, creating problems in later adult life. Such a personality type may be fueled by *actual* spiritual or mystical experiences of love, joy, and beauty, while at the same time disowning, if not totally repressing, feelings of anxiety, abandonment, and rage.

Dualistic denial seems also linked to what psychotherapist and psychosynthesis teacher Ann Russell (1990) has called the "Heaven-Is-Just-Around-The-Corner Syndrome." Here there is the hope and quest for some magical situation—the right house, lifestyle, therapy, relationship, religious practice, etc.—which will trigger an idealized spiritual state. The often-unconscious assumption is that the treasure at the end of the quest will erase the wounds of life, and eliminate the need for creating a realistic lifestyle which accepts these wounds. And of course, limited acceptance of woundedness translates into limitations of the healing process.

However, dualistic denial need not present as a search for an idealized state, but may simply take the form of an unconscious belief that such states are somehow more real than other experiences in life. Thus, engagement with the reality of human existence will ever involve painful disillusionment, as again and again, one is surprised by the reality of intrinsic human suffering and brokenness. Here a redemptive coming to terms with the human condition is blocked by the belief that higher spiritual experiences are truly the way life ought to be. (It is interesting that a depressive mode can here result—derived, paradoxically, from not accepting the inherent suffering of life.)

Often the healing of dualistic denial, the coming to terms with one's human brokenness, may be couched in phrases such as, "I need to choose to incarnate," or "I am a soul learning to embody in matter." But the framing of the issue in these terms remains dualistic. Underlying such phrases is still the assumption that we are discarnate spirits learning to incarnate.

We might instead consider that the human person is, from the very beginning of life, an essential unity of "I," psyche, and soma. This holistic view would maintain that the consciousness of this fundamental unity has been blocked or broken by developmental difficulties and trauma, and that facilitating the healing of this wounded consciousness is a matter for psychotherapy and/ or spiritual direction. In such healing then, we are not learning to incarnate at all, but are instead resolving the dualistic denial caused by an early dysfunctional environment.

Again, the idealized notion of "I" as centered, whole, and separate from the psyche-soma, eminently supports all such types of dualistic denial. It is no surprise then that psychosynthesis often has a blind spot in this area, and can be ineffective in recognizing and dealing with dualistic denial.

*Psychosynthesis seemed to offer me a direct way to heaven,*
*when I didn't even know I was in hell.*
—Former psychosynthesis teacher

## Dualistic Denial and Psychosynthesis

Dualistic denial in psychosynthesis theory can be seen in a certain spiritual or superconscious dissociation from the past and the lower unconscious (see "The Broken Egg," chapter 5). For example, Will Friedman, co-founder of the Psychosynthesis Institute of New York, has pointed to this dissociation in his criticism that psychosynthesis "has lost touch with its psychoanalytic roots" (Friedman 1984, 31).

And Frank Haronian, psychologist and former vice-president of the Psychosynthesis Research Foundation, states:

> … if you forget that you have human weaknesses and limitations, there is something wrong. And that's what psychosynthesis tends to encourage. Those who are careless may become infatuated with the sublime, and become victims of spiritual ambition. (Haronian 1983, 31, 27)

Too, psychologist Sheldon Kramer has implied in the literature that psychosynthesis can encourage "pseudo-individuation" rather than authentic personal growth. He states that the reason for this is that many psychosynthesis practices focus on developing spirituality and do not include interpersonal and family-systems theory and technique (Kramer 1988, 98).

Lastly, psychosynthesis therapist Victoria Tackett has felt the need to warn psychosynthesis practitioners not to minimize the wounding from childhood abuse by treating this as "merely an unruly victim subpersonality to be integrated" (Tackett 1988, 29). Tackett's point is that this is a completely inappropriate and superficial approach to such core trauma, because a *subpersonality* (Assagioli 1965, 74–75; Vargiu 1974) is just that—a semi-autonomous subsystem within the psyche-soma, much like the *ego states* of Eric Berne's Transactional Analysis (1961). However, most workers in the field of abuse know well that such wounding is inflicted to the entire person, and cannot be limited to one subsystem within the personality.

I have noticed this same type of superficiality in talk about alcoholics having an "alcoholic subpersonality." Here again, this terribly underestimates the profundity of both the disease and the path of recovery. Major addictions, as well as wounding in childhood, affect the whole person—physical, emotional, mental, spiritual—and to couch these in simple terms of subpersonalities shows a naiveté about the depths of these waters.

It is however understandable that a psychosynthesis practitioner might attempt to understand complex psychological dysfunction in terms of subpersonalities, because most extant psychosynthesis theory concerning the integration of the personality is limited to subpersonality theory. Subpersonality theory (and to a minor extent, body-feelings-mind theory) seems to be virtually all psychosynthesis has to offer in the way of understanding personality development, that is, of conceptualizing *personal psychosynthesis*. Thus, when one reaches the limit of the theory, the practitioner is left either to proceed towards the spiritual dimension (*spiritual psychosynthesis*), or to look to other systems for more sophisticated understandings of personal integration and dysfunction.[4]

Again, since psychosynthesis theory does not offer depth models of psychological development and disturbance, practitioners can be led into misguided attempts to apply known psychosynthesis theory in clinical situations far beyond its scope. Too often, such attempts to understand depth issues within known psychosynthesis theory are irrelevant at best, and at worst, may serve to work against the client's recovery.

Given the above cautions and criticisms from psychosynthesis practitioners—from both old hands and relative newcomers alike—there seems to be an inherent tendency within the approach to ignore the depths of the psyche in favor of the heights. Here is a dualism which, among other things, prevents the system from developing a rigorous understanding of childhood trauma and abuse; of the conditioning family system; and of the development of object relations.

## Psychoanalysis and Psychosynthesis

Criticisms such as those mentioned above can be heard especially from psychosynthesis-trained therapists and guides who find psychosynthesis inadequate in working with more severely disturbed clients. Here the therapist may encounter the borderline or narcissistic personality for example, and realize that there is nothing in psychosynthesis theory which addresses the challenges these present.

But in realizing this inadequacy, one may be led to another type of splitting in which one begins to consider psychoanalysis (for example) as the preferred theory and treatment for childhood issues of the lower unconscious, while psychosynthesis is somehow reserved for the higher levels of human functioning represented by the spiritual dimension or higher unconscious. Thus psychosynthesis apparently would be limited to what is known as *spiritual direction* or *spiritual guidance*. But if this occurs, the vital question becomes: "What type of spirituality is being espoused? Christian? Buddhist? Theosophical?" One does not undertake spiritual guidance without being very clear about the spirituality involved.

The elaboration of a spirituality, however, will take one beyond psychosynthesis, having more to do with theology and religious practice than it does with psychology. And as Assagioli maintained, psychosynthesis is not a spirituality nor a religion:

> Psychosynthesis does not aim nor attempt to give a metaphysical nor theological explanation of the great Mystery—it leads to the door, but stops there. (Assagioli 1965, 6–7)

And too, turning psychosynthesis away from the lower unconscious and towards the superconscious can serve to support dualistic denial. The reason for this is that even the supposedly "normal neurotic" and "self-actualizer," thought at one time to have completed their healing of childhood, can be far more deeply wounded than was once suspected.

More and more we are realizing that dysfunction, narcissism, childhood trauma, and compulsivity are not the sole property of severely disturbed personalities, but underlie even the healthiest functioning specimens among us. Thus, childhood work is not something we complete in order to move to more existential or spiritual issues, as if the former is a lower rung on some ladder of enlightenment. Thinking like this minimizes the deep influence of early conditioning and ignores the life-long need to be open to that dimension of experience.

As awareness of the dysfunction in "normal" families grows in the culture, we are discovering that the "Happy Childhood" often is a romantic fantasy. Even the "normal" parent may at some important level be negligent and/or abusive, and the most "normal" child may at some essential level be traumatized.

> *A lot of what we consider to be*
> *normal parenting is actually abusive.*
> —John Bradshaw

Thus, even the healthiest self-actualization is beginning to show its dysfunctional shadow. For many then, existential and spiritual issues increasingly cannot be separated from an exploration of early unresolved issues, nor from a struggle with current compulsions and addictions.

Note too that we are here speaking to a level of human brokenness which has not been fully addressed by classical psychoanalysis either. Indeed, it appears that while Freud recognized the prevalence of child abuse from the reports of his patients, he chose to interpret such material as a product of fantasy only (see Jeffrey Masson's *The Assault on Truth*). Thus traditional psychoanalysis itself has missed the centrality of childhood abuse, and can find itself at times searching for the roots of psychological dysfunction where the answer is not.

In the contemporary "Recovery Revolution" however, vast numbers of people are awakening to the painful fact of their own traumatized childhoods, and the compulsions and attachments connected to these. For example, we see self-help groups for codependency; the inner child; sex, romance, and relationship addiction; women who love too much; and adult children of alcoholics.

All of these are components of a far-reaching raising of consciousness apparent in society at large, a collective movement which will eventually touch all our lives in some way. This revolution in consciousness is a cultural phenomenon in which increased awareness of psychological wounding is giving birth to an increased awareness of what psychological health and human fulfillment can be. In psychosynthesis terms, this revolution is opening the way for a much clearer insight into the nature of "I" and Self than ever before possible.

But the endemic nature of dysfunction does not of course mean that there exist no gradations of psychopathology. The recognized forms of mental illness are obviously severe, and often present a striking contrast to the functioning "normal neurotic" adult. We are not disclaiming such distinctions.

Rather, we are saying that the functioning adult has much deeper dysfunctional roots than has heretofore been suspected in the history of Western psychology. It has taken the current collective awakening to the prevalence of childhood neglect and abuse, and of adult addictive behavior, to show us that there are very few among us who are not grappling with a dysfunctional childhood in one way or another.

And again the point for psychosynthesis is this: If we attempt to focus simply on the superconscious, and only superficially on the lower unconscious, we will create a situation in which spiritual experiencing will have less and less foundation in serious psychological understanding. This can lead in turn to dualistic denial, to repression and dissociation, and to the distortion of true superconscious experiencing by unconscious dynamics from childhood.

Even with all his dualism, Assagioli himself had an appreciation for lower unconscious work which is unmatched by many of his successors. For example, in the chapter from *Psychosynthesis* (1965) entitled, "General Assessment and Exploration of the Unconscious," he states, "The preliminary step in psychosynthesis ... is a thorough knowledge of the conscious and unconscious aspects of one's personality" (68). He then devotes this chapter to describing the importance of gaining an understanding of, among other things: family influences such as those from the father and his family; the mother and her family; siblings; ethnic and cultural influences; and ancestors in general.

It is also refreshing to remember that Assagioli moves on from this 30-page general assessment chapter into a full 90 pages on *personal psychosynthesis* (the integration of the personality, self-actualization). This is followed by a mere 32 pages on *spiritual psychosynthesis* (work involving the integration of superconscious energies). Thus we have almost a full three-to-one weighting of personal over transpersonal work—a weighting lost by most subsequent psychosynthesis theory.

However, in these chapters Assagioli still implies a progression away from the lower unconscious and towards the higher unconscious. One seemingly moves from the assessment, through personal psychosynthesis, and finally to spiritual or transpersonal psychosynthesis. This tends to suggest the gnostic progression up the *ladder of enlightenment* or *scale of being*. There is little sense here that lower unconscious dynamics are an integral, pervasive, and ongoing aspect of all human growth, no matter how spiritual one's life becomes.

Psychosynthesis needs to remember that we never fully leave behind our childhood legacy, and that in the search for healing and self knowledge, we must remain aware of this legacy as an ongoing influence in our daily life experience. Lower unconscious work, via psychoanalysis or other approaches, cannot in any way be outgrown, because our past is ever a part of our present. The lower unconscious and higher unconscious form a whole, a whole pervaded by Self. Self is distinct from both, and present throughout both.

Assagioli himself, however, had perhaps good cause for not fully integrating the psychoanalytic thought of his time. Early psychoanalytic theory was fraught with nineteenth-century positivism and a reductionism vis-à-vis spiritual experience. But current psychosynthesis theory has less and less excuse for not looking seriously to psychoanalytic theory and its contemporary developments and extensions.

Indeed, psychoanalytic thought since Assagioli's time has *far surpassed psychosynthesis in uncovering the mystery of human I-amness*. This movement can be seen beginning with Anna Freud and Heinz Hartmann (see Yankelovich, 1970), and moving into the approaches of ego psychology, object relations theory, and self psychology. The work of people such as Klein, Fairbairn, Winnicott, and the Balints, as well as Meissner, Kernberg, and Kohut, to name a few, represents an increasingly clear focusing upon the elusive "I."

Thus analytic theory has been in effect building an ascending stairway from the lower unconscious, up through instincts and id, towards the living, willing person. The challenge for psychosynthesis is to perform an analogous task—to build a *descending* stairway from the higher unconscious, down through the dynamics of superconscious experience, towards the living, willing person. But more than this, I believe that as the stairways begin to meet, we must seek a comprehensive understanding of the higher unconscious and lower unconscious as a unity, while retaining unique human personhood at the center. It is only from such a perspective that we may begin to develop a general theory of *Self-realization.*

If psychosynthesis can play a part in this task, it may yet live up to its promise to elaborate in precise terms how the spiritual and psychological dimensions relate in the human person. To the extent it does not shoulder this task, it is, I fear, doomed to becoming a pop pseudo-psychology or New Age religion.

## Grief That Can't Be Spoken

It should be carefully noted too that dualistic denial *does not prevent one's significant engagement with childhood issues.* Indeed, one may work in quite dramatic and cathartic ways on the pain, rage, and shame of childhood—*while yet maintaining the denial.* The issue is not so much an affinity for the superconscious as it is a basic belief that one is not what one is experiencing.

Dualistic denial allows one to base all such childhood work on the assumption that early trauma did not in reality happen to me ("I am not my pain"), but to my body, feelings, and mind. Since it is not really "I" who suffers, this must be only a temporary condition, a transitory problem to be dealt with in order to be able to then move beyond it.

Indeed, suffering may be seen as only a function of my identi-fications and attachments—as if we should tell the abused child or the socially oppressed that their pain is caused by their attachment and ignorance! One may even here blame the victim, as people are seen as the cause of their own suffering, as choosing their plight in some way. Pain is seen here as merely a necessary hurdle on the way to a "more real" centered and whole Self-realization.

What dualistic denial will not admit is that there is brokenness in human life which is never *healed* so much as *lived through*. And this pain or brokenness is not a neurotic attachment to a victim role; nor a holding on to suffering for secondary gain; nor an ignorant attachment to desire. Rather, this is a suffering which is intrinsic to human existence, and a suffering which remains ulti-mately a mystery, in spite of thousands of years of thought and theories.

Such wounds are carried by us all, though they are perhaps carried in more virulent forms by those severely traumatized as children. Psychological wounds like these are analogous to physi-cal deformity—while the condition itself is incurable, one can still live a meaningful and productive life in and through this debility.

For example, certain abandonment anxieties, compulsions and addictions, and childlike emotional reactions to particular situations may not immediately disappear from one's life via psychotherapy, like dew in the morning sun. One may find instead the need to change one's life in order to manage such issues, rather than attempting to force oneself violently into an idealized self-actualized life.

But more than this, missed opportunities for growth in our lives are lost forever. While we may indeed perhaps gain back some of the potential we lost to earlier wounds, we shall never be *that* actual person again, inhabiting *that* actual time and place. We will have lost forever the potential we had for healthy develop-ment at that actual time in our lives. There are deep wells of grief here, and engagement with these depths can be a crucial part of the healing process.

And this holds for other human losses as well. When do we fully "get over" the death of a loved one? True, the initial focus on the loss and the grieving yields to other interests, new relation-

*[Handwritten margin notes, left: "He misses the point completely. These are not missed opportunities, they are opportunity for alchemy"]*

*[Handwritten margin notes, right: "Good! And this I cannot be. I do not have a body which I have a place, but must transcend"]*

*[Handwritten note in text: "No must be. This is alchemy."]*

ships, and life goes on. However, there is forever something lost. That particular person—even if we think she or he is in a "better place"—has left our life with a unique void in it, that is, a void not ever to be truly filled by another. Yes, there will be others, and life can indeed flow on into deeper meaning than ever before. Yet there is a real existential hole left in our lives, an absence which perfectly matches the former presence of the other.

However, dualistic denial recoils from true and complete acceptance of these abiding depths of human suffering and grief. Within dualistic denial, the feelings may be felt and expressed in good solid therapeutic work, but when all is said and done, the wounding is not to *me* but to my psyche-soma. As long as I am not my psyche-soma, there is <u>no way in the world to accept</u> a core wounding of myself, *a brokenness through which I will live my entire life.*

This denial is founded on an idealized image of an enlightenment or Self-realization which precludes incurable wounds, and thus refuses to accept such existential human limitations. Here dualism may even cause one to suffer guilt and shame for not having worked through all one's "unspiritual" grief and "childish" responses to life.

By the way, this rejection of existential human limitations obviously makes dualistic denial incompatible with overt dependence on another—as, for example, in the therapeutic transference. Such a dependency is too great an admission of human frailty, a supposed indication that Self-realization is not occurring. Indeed, the ideal at times implied by psychosynthesis is independence from all outside figures, or at the outside, an interdependence among equals. One is to achieve a personality integration which is finally dependent on no one but "one's higher Self." Any dependency on what Assagioli called an *external unifying center* (Assagioli 1965, 26), while possibly acceptable for a time, is not, in his words, "the most direct way or the highest achievement" (25).

This attitude of course has not helped psychosynthesis deal with wounding to the core personality, as in narcissistic, borderline, and self disorders, and in survivors of childhood abuse. Treatment of all such wounding demands an informed and accepting attitude towards transference and countertransference dynamics, as well as the skill to work with these. But people suffering from these afflictions are, if we follow the idealization, not yet capable of Self-realization—this seems to be reserved for the elite, to the supposedly highly-evolved people that Gnostics historically have called *pneumatics*, those defined as escaping the doom of the material world. We shall take up transference and countertransference more fully in chapter 7.

Again, an idealized and dualistic notion of "I" is a central aspect of all such dualistic denial, for example, "Who I really am is this spiritual centered self; I have transcended (or worked through) the trauma of my past." This denial also can be couched as, "My ego is an illusion, I do not exist; therefore the trauma of my past is also an illusion and a trap" (see "Transcendence and 'No-thing-ness,'" chapter 4). By their very nature, such beliefs work to prevent an acceptance of fundamental human brokenness, limitation, and mortality.

But as we proceed, we hope to show that "I" is at home not only in experiencing centeredness and wholeness, but quite as much in experiencing pain and brokenness. "I" is not to be confused with feeling centered, just as Self is not to be confused with feeling blissful. Such notions only feed dualistic denial; they link deepest human identity with joy and pleasure and separate it from pain and suffering.

> *Our Real Self feels both joy* and *pain.*
> —Charles Whitfield

The larger process of Self-realization is not even a matter of deep work on the past, object relations, and the family system in order to then feel centered and blissful. Self-realization involves a deep and complete acceptance of all we are, and thus cannot be separated from—though it cannot be reduced to—an *ongoing* openness to deeper and deeper levels of our childhood, and to the joys and sorrows of life as a whole.

In other words, Self does not exist solely in superconscious peak experiences, even though much of psychosynthesis theory implies this. Self is present throughout both the lower unconscious as well as the higher unconscious, and operates in all our interpersonal relationships as well. Thus an ongoing communion with Self may involve experiencing anything at any time. Self-realization is distinct from any single realm of life experience, is limited to none, and can include all.

Therefore in Self-realization we are invited to a range of experience which includes the depths as well as the heights of human existence, not to mention the mundane plodding of normal daily life. In fact, one may at times begin to feel distinctly **un**centered and **un**blissful as Self-realization proceeds!

Enlightenment is not a matter of ascent into the spiritual heights, but rather a radical openness to a relationship with the entire psyche-soma, to other people, and to the world at large. We shall discuss all of these issues in greater detail as we proceed.

## Holistic Gnosticism

Of course dualism of any sort ignores the fact that no matter how distinct and individual we feel ourselves to be, we do not discover ourselves as in any way separate from the world. Even our breathtaking transcendent experiences of Supreme Reality are only to be had in the world. We ever find ourselves inescapably in relationship, affecting and being affected by the world around us. Experientially, we are self-body wholes inseparable from a greater network of life.

Thus, it would seem that we are not the gnostic sparks of spirit lost in matter, needing to escape and go home; we are not souls who wear our bodies like suits of clothes; we are not monads separate from each other and the world. In other words, the distinctness implied by transcendence, whether human or divine, is never found in isolation from immanence, from a fundamental intimate engagement in the world.

The confusing thing about Assagioli's dualism (and a reason perhaps it is not often fully recognized) is that it co-exists with exactly the unitive perspective we have just described. For all his affirmations of "I am not," I believe he would be in agreement with much of the two preceding paragraphs.

Indeed, his very use of the concept *synthesis* implies just such a deep recognition of the unbroken relatedness of all life. Assagioli's sense of a Universal Principle is most definitely *not* the distant dissociated God of classical Gnosticism:

From a still wider and more comprehensive point of view, universal life itself appears to us as a struggle between multiplicity and unity—a labor and an aspiration towards union. We seem to sense that—whether we conceive it as a divine Being or as cosmic energy—the Spirit working upon and within all creation is shaping it into order, harmony, and beauty, uniting all beings (some willing but the majority as yet blind and rebellious) with each other through links of love, achieving—slowly and silently, but powerfully and irresistibly—*the Supreme Synthesis.* (Assagioli 1965, 31)

This is obviously not the statement of the Gnostic who is seeking escape from an evil illusory world to the far-off pure pleroma of separate spirit. These are the words of one who sees a growing realization of the intimate unity of spirit and matter, through the power of love.

Thus, Assagioli's gnosticism might be called *holistic gnosticism*. This gnosticism still views spirit as separate from matter, but believes that the role of spirit is to enter into, and transform, matter. Here the human being is still fundamentally a dualistic self-with-psyche/soma, but the work of this self is to incarnate in matter, to serve the plan of evolution towards a harmonious larger whole. So here we feel good about our physical "vehicles" and the world, and commit to the task of helping matter evolve towards this final Cosmic Unity of spirit and matter.

However, the final Cosmic Union of holistic gnosticism is still flawed by dualism. To couch it in crude terms, the statement of the final Synthesis would be something like, "I have the universe, but I am not the universe; I am a pure Universal Center of consciousness and will." Here is the image of a Universal Spirit clothed in the universe, much as the human being is supposedly clothed in the psyche-soma. But there is still a fundamental split between spirit and matter, even though they now form a whole.

If this dualism did not exist at the universal level in the system of holistic gnosticism, there would be no ontological source for the dualism of the human "I *am not.*" The latter would simply float in the universe, self-sufficient and isolated, with no ontological roots, no reflective source. That is, with no universal dualistic

"I *am not*" as the source of the human dualistic "I *am not*," the system would not make sense, because then, in Assagioli's words, "the microcosm would be superior to the macrocosm—indeed a ridiculous conceit!" (Assagioli 1973, 130).

Speaking psychologically, we may say that holistic gnosticism, like classical Gnosticism, still supports dualism at the level of the person—I am still *not* my psyche-soma. Even if I work to form a harmonious union with my body, feelings, and mind, these remain ontologically separate from, and cannot help but take a secondary position to, my true self.

So for all this holism, Assagioli nevertheless remains dualistic in speaking of the deepest core of human identity. Here Assagioli finds himself faced with an ineffable transcendence, and lapses into dualism when attempting to describe this transcendence. Transcendence here becomes a splitting of human identity and psyche-soma. And his attempt at a transcendent formulation—"I *am not* my body, feelings, or mind"—is but only very weakly countered by the more immanent, "I *have* my body, feelings, and mind." This latter is an ineffective attempt to bridge the gaping chasm created by the radical, "I *am not*."

In spite of Assagioli's vision of unity, his "I *am not*" sounds a strong dualistic note which echoes throughout psychosynthesis. From here issue forth idealizations of "I," of disidentification, and of Self; a split between "I"/Self and psyche-soma; and a separation between the higher unconscious and the lower unconscious.

## Monism

We may think of dualism as a conception of transcendence which has no immanence. That is, here there is a fundamental separation between for example, self and personality, spirit and matter, or God and nature. At a psychological level, when all is said and done, "I *am not* my psyche-soma."

However, when correcting for this dissociation we must attempt to avoid the opposite extreme which is called *monism*. We may think of monism as the idea of immanence with no transcendence. Thus, monistic systems might consider self and personality, spirit and matter, or God and nature, as fundamentally one and the same.

Psychologically, monism might lead to the statement, "I *am* my body, feelings, and mind." Such monism is implied too by statements such as, "I *am* my body, but I am *more* than my body."

Psychological monism might also lead to a formulation which claims there is actually no "I" at all, but only the ongoing processes of the psyche-soma (although such a formulation properly understood may be simply heuristic; see "Transcendence and 'No-thing-ness,'" chapter 4).

We can think of monism in psychological theory then, as any concept which seeks to reduce the multiple aspects of the human being into a unity in which important distinctions among the aspects are lost. Monism is represented for example by the behaviorists who consider only observable behavior as valid for scientific study, and who thus reduce self and psyche to soma alone.

We can see monism as well in certain mind-over-matter orientations which consider all physical disease as an expression of one's psychological process; here, soma is reduced to psyche. And lastly, monism is evident in those personality theories which consider self to be the totality of the psyche. This reduces self to psyche.

Whereas dualism splits apart aspects of a whole, monism merges them together, losing distinctions among them. As with all opposites, it is quite easy to flee from one extreme and run into the arms of the other. Here is Hans Jonas, at the close of *The Gnostic Religion*, warning us about falling into monism in an effort to correct such dualism (we note that he uses "man" in the generic sense):

> The disruption between man and total reality is at the bottom of nihilism. The illogicality of the rupture, that is, of a dualism without metaphysics, makes its fact no less real, nor its seeming alternative any more acceptable: the stare at isolated selfhood, to which it condemns man, may wish to exchange itself for a monistic naturalism which, along with the rupture, would abolish also the idea of man as man. Between that Scylla and this her twin Charybdis, the modern

mind hovers. Whether a third road is open to it—one by which the dualistic rift can be avoided and yet enough of the dualistic insight saved to uphold the humanity of man—philosophy must find out. (Jonas 1963, 340)

That is, it is important to save "enough of the dualistic insight"—enough transcendence—because this is a recognition of the individual uniqueness and multiplicity within a holistic view that all things in the universe are connected. In monism one loses (among other things) the distinct unique personhood of "man as man," as this is merged into a universal whole in which individuality is lost. But Assagioli is extremely clear that the human self is *not* lost in communion with universality:

The chief quality [in the experience of Self]...is the realization of individuality and universality...[Self] feels itself at the same time individual and universal. (Assagioli 1965, 87)

For Assagioli, the deepest experience of Being is not a monistic merging into unity, not an immanence without transcendence, in which unique human selfhood is annihilated. He takes pains here and throughout his writing to mark himself unequivocally as a non-monist, and as we have seen, he leans much more towards the dualist end of the spectrum when addressing the question of personal identity.

In sum then, the problematic dualism in psychosynthesis may be thought of as a transcendence without immanence. This view considers "I"/Self as radically other than, separate from, psyche-soma.

However, this dualism will not be corrected by a monistic immanence without transcendence, reducing "I"/Self to other aspects of psyche-soma. It seems clear that Assagioli himself attempted to avoid both of these extremes, but was thwarted by gnostic-theosophical theology. What is needed is a formulation which holds *both* transcendence *and* immanence.

# A Possible Third Road: Transcendence-Immanence

In any attempt to correct for the dualism within psychosynthesis, therefore, it would be important to be sensitive to the monism which awaits at the other end of the spectrum. With this in mind, we shall throughout the following chapters develop a possible approach to "I" which attempts to navigate Jonas' "third road" between dualism and monism.

This navigational instrument is the notion of *transcendence-immanence*, developed as a psychological/experiential concept rather than as a religious one. Here the continuity and distinctness of "I" throughout the changing contents of experience can be termed *transcendence*, while "I"s fundamental unity with changing experience in the world can be called *immanence*.

Thus "I" is not seen as a transcendent self who owns a body, not a soul fundamentally untouched by time and change. But neither is "I" simply immanent; it is not merely identical to the flow of changing life processes, and therefore an artificial and illusory construct imposed on our experience. Rather, the notion of transcendence-immanence understands "I" as a paradoxical synthesis of two seemingly contradictory experiences of personal identity: *permanence and change.*

Transcendence-immanence is a theme which forms the developing backbone of our current exposition. It will immediately appear again in the next chapter as we begin looking directly at "I," but it will also eventually lead us into an examination of Self, as well as some of the practicalities of the clinical situation.

> *In the one soul we may distinguish two aspects.*
> *The one is the soul as suchness,*
> *the other is the soul as birth-and-death.*
> *Each in itself constitutes all things,*
> *and both are so closely interrelated*
> *that one cannot be separated from the other.*
> —Asvaghosha's "Doctrine of Suchness"

# CHAPTER THREE

# On "I"

*As long as there is a dualistic way of*
*looking at things there is no emancipation.*
*Light stands against darkness;*
*passions stand against enlightenment.*
—Hui Neng

As we have seen, Assagioli initially saw "I" as a center of identity realized through objective inner observation of psychic events. Through such observation one realizes that "I" is distinct but not separate from the flow of inner contents.

This original insight was unfortunately formulated into his Exercise in Dis-identification, which affirmed a series of beliefs about "I." These beliefs—"I am not my body, feelings, or mind"— tended towards an inflated notion of "I" and encouraged a sense of dissociation from the body, feelings, and mind.

However, if we ignore Assagioli's dissociative "I *am not*" formulation for the moment, and focus simply on his original insight, we can see that this latter represents a profound understanding of the nature of "I." In this chapter we will therefore elaborate this original insight, and not comment on the "I *am not*" belief system.

## Assagioli's Original Insight into "I"

For Assagioli the concept of the term, "I," denotes something which is distinct from the world of soma, that is, from the objective world of the physical body and outward behavior:

> My body may find itself in different conditions of
> health or sickness; it may be rested or tired, but that
> has nothing to do with my self, my real "I." My body
> is my precious instrument of experience and of action
> in the outer world, but it is *only* an instrument. I treat
> it well; I seek to keep it in good health, but it is *not*
> myself. I *have* a body, but *I am not* my body. (Assa-
> gioli 1965, 118)

This means for example, that "I" cannot be reduced to any
aspect of the physical organism, nor to any patterns of observable
behavior—"I" is distinct from soma.

Assagioli not only considers "I" as distinct from soma, but
from psyche as well. Just as "I" is not to be confused with contents
in the outer objective world, so it is not to be confused with
contents of the inner subjective world. Therefore, such private
inner events as feelings and desires, or images and thoughts, are
distinct from "I" as well:

> What remains after having disidentified myself from
> my body, my sensations, my feelings, my desires, my
> mind, my actions? It is the essence of myself—*a center
> of pure self-consciousness*. (Assagioli 1973, 216)

This *"center of pure self-consciousness"* refers to "I." Note
that the term *self-consciousness*, as used in psychosynthesis,
is a technical term pertaining to a sense of existing as a unique
individual human being. The term is not used in its more popular meaning, to wit, feeling embarrassed, painfully visible, and
vulnerable to ridicule by others.

As a center of pure self-consciousness then, "I" can experience disidentification from both psyche and soma. Thus, "I" is
different from the Freudian ego when defined as for example, "a
coherent organization of mental processes" (Freud 1960, 7)—"I"
is distinct from any organization or mental process. Neither is
"I" to be confused with the ideas or images we have of ourselves,
whether we call these self-images or self-representations—"I" is
distinct from ideas and images.

Assagioli's notion of "I" is also different from W. Ronald D. Fairbairn's *central ego* or "I," which is seen as comprising elements split off from the *original ego* (1990, 104–105); from D. W. Winnicott's concept of *True Self,* which is defined as "the summation of sensori-motor aliveness" (1987, 149); and as well, from Heinz Kohut's idea of *nuclear self,* which is thought of as a "structure" made up of "constituents" (1977, 177–79). "I" is to be thought of as distinct from any summation of parts, from any sort of structure fashioned from psychosomatic contents.

Assagioli considers "I" to denote a subject who is to be distinguished from any and all contents and processes of both soma and psyche. "I" is the responsible experiencer of somatic and psychic events, potentially able to observe these, and therefore distinct from these. Assagioli seems quite in agreement with this passage from philosopher Hywel D. Lewis:

> ... in addition to states of mind [psyche] distinct in nature from physical states [soma] but constantly interacting with them, there is also a subject, or a self or soul, which remains constant and is uniquely involved in all the flow of our mental states or experiences. This notion has a long ancestry. It appears for example, in celebrated ways in the work of Plato, Augustine, Descartes, and Kant. (Lewis 1982, 40)

And these words of the philosopher Thomas Reid could have been written by Assagioli himself:

> I am not thought, I am not action, I am not feeling; I am something that thinks, and acts, and suffers. My thoughts, and actions, and feelings, change every moment; they have no continued, but a successive, existence; but that *self,* or *I,* to which they belong, is permanent, and has the same relation to all the succeeding thoughts, actions, and feelings which I call mine. (Reid 1973, 195–96)

Turning to the East, we can see that Assagioli's approach seems quite akin to these words of Ramana Maharshi, illustrating his "Who am I?" approach to Self-realization:

> D. [Devotee]: Who am I? How is the answer to be found?
> B. [Ramana Maharshi]: Ask yourself the question. The body (*annamayakosa*) and its functions are not 'I.' Going deeper, the mind (*manomayakosa*) and its functions are not 'I.' ... the individuality is operative as the cognizer of the existence of thoughts and their sequence. This individuality is the ego, or, as people say, 'I.' *Vijnanamayakosa* (intellect) is only the sheath of the 'I' and not the 'I' itself. (Ramana Maharshi 1978, 116)

> B: The 'I' is always there, whether in deep sleep, in dream or in the waking state. The one who sleeps is the same as the one who is now speaking. There is always the feeling of 'I.' If it were not so you would have to deny your existence. (117)

## Assagioli's Approach to "I"

Given the above, of course, the term "I" becomes highly elusive and difficult to conceptualize. We are here attempting to map something which thwarts our normal ways of thinking about objects of study, something which demands we go beyond our usual methods of representing phenomena. For all of this however, Assagioli states that the term "I" does apply to a real and verifiable human experience, however elusive this may be:

> In my opinion, the direct experience of the self ["I"], of pure *self-awareness* ... is a true, "phenomenological" experience, an inner reality which can be empirically verified and deliberately produced through appropriate techniques. (Assagioli 1965, 5)

Consistent with this phenomenological or experiential orientation, Assagioli's initial approach to "I" is not via an a priori theory, but is rather an a posteriori approach, proceeding from actual phenomenological experience. He attempts to plumb the depths of the lived experience of "I," and then to develop concepts which clarify this experience.

As we saw in the previous chapter, Assagioli's procedure for discovering the I-experience begins with an emphasis on simple inner observation, or introspection. One simply notices carefully and at some length the inner sensations, feelings, and thoughts passing continually into and out of one's awareness.

Assagioli says that it is through such introspection that "... we acquire a more focused and clear awareness of what William James called the mind-stream, ceaselessly flowing within ourselves" (114).

In carefully practicing such inner observation, a sense of identity is realized which is experienced as distinct from the ever-changing parade of inner events: "By contrast the stability, the permanency of the observer is realized" (116). It is as if "I" finds itself able to be aware of the passing "mind-stream" without being swept along by it. We might diagram this:

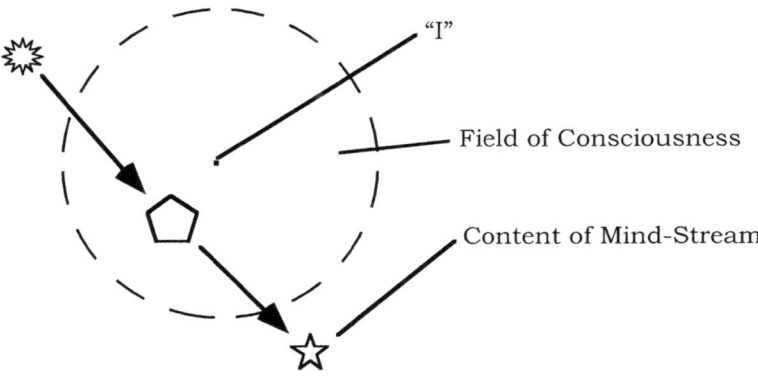

*Figure 3.1*

## "I" as Distinct from Pure Awareness/Consciousness

Note that in figure 3.1, "I" is illustrated as distinct not only from the contents of consciousness, but from consciousness itself. "I" is not identical to the field of consciousness/the field of awareness. (We, with Assagioli, consider *awareness* and *consciousness* as equivalent terms.) "I" is not a center of awareness in the sense of being something made up of awareness, but in the sense of being a dimensionless point, "in but not of" the field of awareness/consciousness.

Another term for our notion of a dimensionless point might be "a point without extension"—the words used by the psychiatrist Gordon Globus to describe "I" (1980, 419; see also appendix 2). "I" is thus distinct from awareness, because awareness has extension, and is able for example, to contract and expand.

Assagioli does however confuse us at times about this distinction between "I" and awareness—he sometimes describes "I" as "pure consciousness" (for example, Assagioli 1965, 117).

But if "I" is thought of as "pure consciousness," the implication is that "I" is identical with the field of awareness/consciousness, albeit, a "pure" field of awareness/consciousness. If this were the case, we would then alter figure 3.1, first by eliminating the point at the center, and then by changing the term *field of consciousness* to "I." Thus we would have something like this:

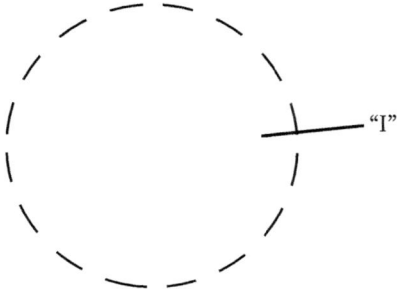

*Figure 3.2*

However, Assagioli's use of "pure consciousness" in relation to "I" seems to be simply a short-hand form of the more precise formulation he uses in both of his books: "I" is a center of *"pure self-consciousness"* (Assagioli 1965, 119; Assagioli 1973, 216), or "pure self-awareness," Assagioli 1973, 216).

That is, "I" is not simply consciousness, pure or otherwise, but is self-conscious: "Human beings go beyond mere animal awareness and *know that they are aware"* (Assagioli 1973, 11, emphasis in original). This implies a center distinct from mere awareness—a center which can somehow be conscious of consciousness, which can know that it knows. If this is the case, then figure 3.1 seems a more accurate representation than figure 3.2, because figure 3.1 represents "I" as distinct from simple awareness. But it would be even more accurate to then add self-consciousness to our map, as we shall do forthwith.

## "I" as Distinct from Self-Consciousness

But even as we accept Assagioli's statement that "I" is a center of pure self-consciousness, "I" must be understood as distinct from this self-consciousness itself—that is, it is a *center* of self-consciousness. We might add self-consciousness to our diagram in order to distinguish it from both "I" and simple consciousness, as shown in figure 3.3:

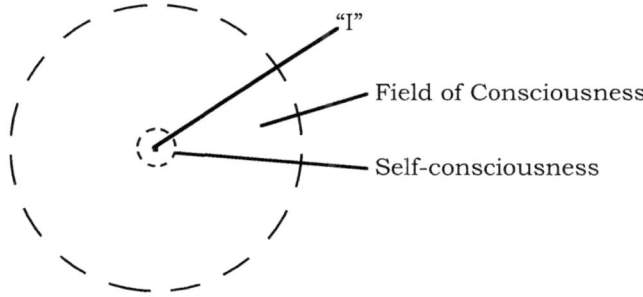

*Figure 3.3*

Self-consciousness can then be thought of as that portion of the field of consciousness/awareness which is most intimately touched by "I." It is as if self-consciousness is the first ripple made by "I" in the pool of consciousness. It is at this point of contact between "I" and the field of consciousness, that the field is transformed from mere *knowing*, an ability shared with animals, to a *knowing one knows*. Somehow, at that very point of contact, awareness can turn back on itself and know awareness:

> From our experimental point of view, reflection is, as the word indicates, the power acquired by a consciousness to turn in upon itself, to take possession of itself as of an object endowed with its own particular consistence and value: no longer merely to know, but to know oneself; no longer merely to know, but to know that one knows. (Teilhard de Chardin 1975, 165)

This "consciousness of consciousness," or self-consciousness, implies the operation of something which is distinct from consciousness itself. To make it possible for awareness to reflect on awareness, there must logically be something which is at least partially non-identical with awareness; there must be some place to stand, so to speak, from which knowing can know knowing. This something must be transcendent of consciousness, in order to make it possible for consciousness to, in Teilhard's words, "take possession of itself as of an object." This something is actually a some*one*—the one who knows, the one we call "I."

*Whereas awareness reflects on objects of awareness, "I" makes it possible to reflect on awareness itself, thereby creating the experience of self-consciousness.*

This distinction between the human self and self-consciousness is born out by modern infant research. The work of Daniel Stern indicates that there is a sense of *emergent self* in the very first few months of life which pre-dates the appearance of self-consciousness (Stern 1985, 38).

In conclusion it appears reasonable to consider "I" as distinct from any sort of consciousness or awareness at all, even from pure consciousness or self-consciousness. I am "I" whether conscious or not: "I have my consciousness, but I am distinct from consciousness." Thus "I" may be thought of as a center which continues in existence not only amongst the changing contents of awareness, but within the fluctuations of awareness/consciousness itself.

Similarly, by the way, "I" is also distinct from its other intimate function, *will*. "I" is not only able to will, but can *know* "I" is able to will. Thus too, then: "I am I whether I can will or not." (We shall discuss will later in this chapter.)

## Disidentification

Practicing inner observation over time, then, can lead to a deeper sense of "I," an experience of identity which cannot be reduced to the passing contents of awareness and/or the fluctuations of awareness itself.

Although various inner events such as strong feelings or intense thinking may momentarily obscure the sense of "I," with increasing introspection these events are felt more and more to be various experiences through which I pass. This can be described as one type of the experience called *detachment* or *disidentification* in relation to intrapsychic currents. One here becomes conscious that any and all inner events can be allowed to come and go, with no need to control them in any way.

> There are no elements of the personality which are of
> a quality incompatible with the "I." For the "I" is not
> *of* the personality, rather it *transcends* the personality.
> (Carter-Haar 1975, 81)

Again, this attitude of disidentification could only be possible if in fact "I" were distinct from awareness and objects of awareness. The experience here is that some aspect of personal identity endures through time, even though sensations, thoughts, feelings, images, and even consciousness and will, change over time.

And of course, so emphatic was Assagioli about this distinction between "I" and all else in the personality, that his Exercise in Dis-identification uses the extreme wording:

I *have* a body, but I *am not* my body. ...
I *have* emotions, but I *am not* my emotions. ...
I *have* a mind, but I *am not* my mind.

(Assagioli 1973, 214–15)

We have seen that this dualistic wording is highly problematic, but this formulation does show beyond doubt that Assagioli saw "I" as of a different order from that of the changing contents and processes of the psyche.

## Observing vs. Thinking

Disidentification must not of course be confused with any sort of mental analysis of the inner world. Such an inner stance is not a disidentification at all, but quite the opposite—it is an identification with the process of mental analysis. This type of identification might be diagrammed:

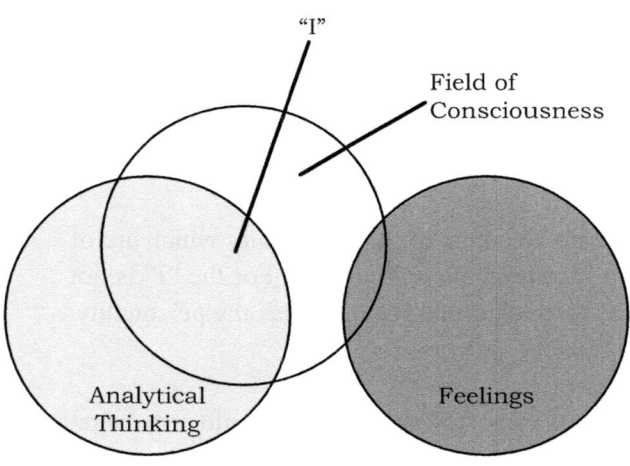

*Figure 3.4*

This figure represents not an experience of observation, but rather an experience of thinking analytically about that which is observed, in this case, feelings. Here I experience that I *am* mental analysis. This identification then conditions my total awareness as if analysis were the lens through which I experience everything. (And too, I would here relate not only to my inner world via analysis, but to my outer world of relationships and events as well.)

Although such a mental identification is often referred to as "objectivity," it is clearly biased towards the thinking function, and operationally cuts off "I" from the immediate experience of other dimensions of the psyche-soma, such as sensations, feelings, images, or intuition.

For example, if feelings are not totally filtered out by this identification, they will at best be experienced only through the lens of rational thought, will not be experienced in their own right, and will be considered "other" by the person—"Feelings are not me." (In psychoanalytic parlance, feelings here become *ego-dystonic* versus *ego-syntonic*.)

To use Betsie Carter-Haar's description of this phenomenon, one here has disowned one's feelings. Carter-Haar describes *disowning* as seen in identifications with subsystems or subpersonalities within the personality:

> When we are strongly identified with something, such as a major subpersonality, most of our energy flows through it. And our energy is filtered by it as well. In other words, only energy of a quality compatible with the basic quality of that subpersonality will be allowed to flow. (Carter-Haar 1975, 69)

If I became angry, for example, I might say, "I *think* I am feeling anger." Inwardly I may be aware only of a vague mild discomfort, although blood-pressure and galvanic skin response are fluctuating wildly. Or if I do happen somehow to feel and recognize the anger, I will consider it "not me."

If however, I am not identified with thinking, I am more apt to be in direct contact with the feeling, to own my feelings. In this case I may say, "I am angry," while vividly experiencing rapid breathing and a pounding heart. Here the energy of my feelings is not filtered, and that energy can be experienced and utilized directly. Only then, paradoxically, can I truly take responsibility for my feelings—otherwise they remain, "These alien things which happen to me."

So identification with mental analysis is very different from disidentification, from simple introspection in which a distinction is realized between "I" and the contents of awareness. Identified with analytic thought, one is at least partially dissociated from non-rational experience. Here one is only aware of thinking, and so is relatively unaware of feeling; thought serves to mask the feeling, rendering the feeling experientially distant.

But "I" has the potential to disidentify from the thinking process. Such disidentification would initially entail simply observing the analytical thoughts, without becoming involved in their activity. The experience would then shift naturally from the experience that, "I am thinking," to the more receptive experience, "I am aware of thoughts passing through my awareness." Thoughts gradually join other inner events as objects of awareness, distinct from "I" who is aware. This might be illustrated:

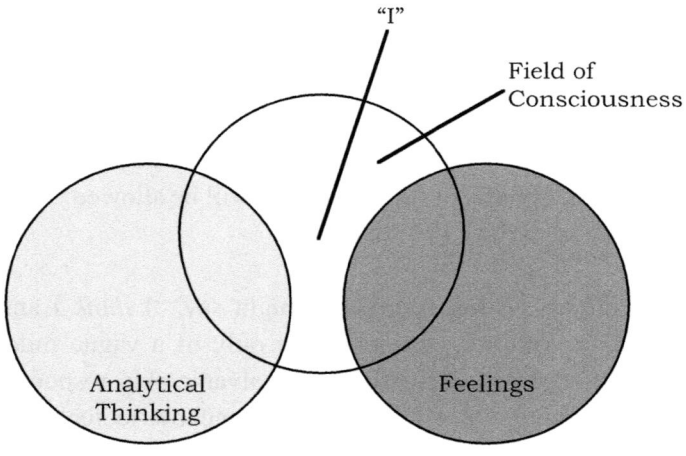

*Figure 3.5*

Figure 3.5 represents a person who experiences disidentification from thoughts, and thereby has become directly aware of not only thoughts, but now feelings as well. There is an intensification of "I" such that "I" now knows itself as distinct from (transcendent of) both feelings and thoughts, and can thus include both (be immanent in both). Here the one-sided involvement in rational processes has yielded to a broader awareness of inner resources.

Note that in this experience of disidentification from analytical thinking, there is not any sort of distancing or dissociation from thoughts. Quite the contrary, there is an ability to be *more* aware of thoughts than when identified with them. Our simple diagram of disidentification (figure 3.5) unfortunately suggests a movement of "I" away from thoughts. However, disidentification from thoughts would not be any sort of distancing at all, but rather, *an increased awareness of both thought and feeling.* Transcendence immediately implies immanence.[5]

Such disidentification might happen quickly in the moment, as for example when I break my concentration on a difficult problem in mathematics, and suddenly become aware that I am feeling frustrated with the task. In this instance, I have experienced disidentification from the single perspective of thinking, and expanded my consciousness to include feelings as well.

But a shift in identification like this may also be seen in long-term transformations of the personality as a whole. For example, the analytical identification (figure 3.4) may represent not just a momentary involvement in thought, but rather the "aloof intellectual" type who exhibits no empathy or warmth, approaching life only logically. Similarly, a feeling identification might represent an "impulsive romantic" type devoted to a life of dramatic action and intense feeling, distrusting any rationality as cold and lifeless.

In such all-encompassing identifications, figure 3.5 might then represent the results of a long-term process of personality change in which the person's entire experience of self and world is transformed. Perhaps facilitated by psychotherapy, here the "thinker" might have become more empathic and sensitive, or the "feeler" might have become less impulsive and more thoughtful. For an excellent case study of this type of long-term process, see Betsie Carter-Haar (1975).

Whatever the scale of change involved in the disidentification experience, it can help over the long term to develop a richer and more flexible experience of oneself. The transcendent aspect of

"I" allows for a potential immanent inclusion of an ever-widening range of human experience.

## Disidentification vs. Dissociation

An identification with any mode of experience will render all other modes relatively inaccessible—one becomes dissociated from other modes. If I identify with analytic thought, I not only distance myself from feelings, but from other more synthetic and creative modes of mental functioning as well. Here I can do nothing but analyze, and I disown other cognitive modalities. (This type of dissociation can be quite useful, however, in such activities as focusing on an important task; it usually only becomes problematic when it is unconscious and chronic.)

Similarly, if I identify with a particular feeling, I will not only distance myself from thought, but from other feelings. For example, I may become chronically identified with my rage, thus obscuring not only rationality, but the potential for feeling any happier emotions as well. In the extreme, I may become a "rage-aholic" whose very way of being in the world is as an angry person.

On the other hand, the practice of disidentification works not to reduce and dissociate awareness, but to increase and expand awareness. By such practice, the thinking-identification may yield to an awareness of feelings and to new modes of thinking; and the feeling-identification may evolve towards an awareness of thought processes and to a discovery of other feelings.

The increased potential for personal freedom in disidentification is obvious, as one hereby may become aware of a much wider range of responses from which to act in life:

> It gives us the freedom to choose at any moment to become
> fully identified with any part of ourselves—an emotion
> or habit pattern or subpersonality—to be involved in it
> and experience it deeply. (Carter-Haar 1975, 78)

Although Carter-Haar's words apply only to one particular type of disidentification experience (we will take up others below), we can see here a central paradox of "I"—the more fully one knows one is distinct from any particular content of experience, the more one can be open to, and enter into, all the many types of human experience. In other words, *the more transcendent I know myself to be, the more I am capable of immanence.*

Note then that it is identification rather than disidentification which is the dynamic underlying dissociation. It is an identification with one particular mode of experience—sensing, feeling, thinking, intuiting, life roles, and so forth—which renders other modes remote. Identification, not disidentification, is dissociative. Thus we can perhaps avoid the common confusion in which one thinks of disidentification as dissociation, as separation from experience. (Again, this is not to say dissociation and identification are not useful and important human abilities.)

## Will

The realization that "I" is distinct from psychosomatic contents and process is often accompanied by an increased experience of freedom—if I experience myself as distinct from sensations, feelings, thoughts, images, etc., I am not only more aware of each, but I am potentially less controlled by them as well. Assagioli writes,

> *We are dominated by everything with which our self is identified. We can dominate and control everything from which we dis-identify ourselves.* (Assagioli 1965, 111, emphasis in original)

His use of the word "dominate" here is unfortunate, in that it mistakenly may be read to mean a forceful repressive type of inner control—not what he means at all. Rather, Assagioli is apparently attempting to indicate the freedom which emerges when we are not identified with the limited perspective of a single part of ourselves.

For example, disidentification from the single mode of feeling or thought allows one the freedom to draw on either feeling or thinking in response to life's changing circumstances. I am more able to experience and express the richness of my multiplicity, rather than being limited to one aspect of my personality alone. In the words of the psychiatrist Arthur Deikman:

> By dis-identifying with automatic sequences we lessen their impact and provide free space in which to choose an appropriate response. Thus, we achieve autonomy where previously we were overwhelmed and helpless. (Deikman 1982, 108)

Again, this disidentification is not a dissociation, nor a standing back and deciding what to do (although one may be free to do even this as well!). Rather, this is moving naturally and easily from that alive sense of "I," from that *who* who is not limited to a single part of our personality and who can thus potentially engage them all.

Here we know we are not identical to any one part, or even all parts together, and so are able to "dance" with the whole.

> *At the still point, there the dance is.*
> —T. S. Eliot

This ability to "dance" derives paradoxically from the "still point" of "I." This inner freedom, the freedom to express more and more of our inner resources in the world, Assagioli called *will*. Assagioli's concept of will is that of a graceful inner freedom and empowerment derived from an openness to all that we are.

Thus, Assagioli's idea of will should in no way be confused with the harsh repression of aspects of ourselves represented by the Puritanical or Victorian notion of *will power*. This latter is not emanating from a disidentified sense of I-amness; it is a dictatorial power wielded by a single aspect of the personality.

> The Victorian conception of the will ... [is] a conception of something stern and forbidding, which condemns and represses most of the other aspects of human nature. But such a misconception might be called a caricature of the will. The true function of the will is not to act against the personality drives

to *force* the accomplishment of one's purposes. The will...balances and constructively utilizes all the other activities and energies of the human being without repressing any of them. (Assagioli 1973, 10)

With the words, "without repressing any of them," Assagioli indicates the operation of a someone who is distinct but not separate from all contents, and thus able to include all contents. Again, in the words of Carter-Haar (1975), there are no elements of the personality which are of a quality incompatible with "I," because "I" transcends all such elements. Following Assagioli (Assagioli 1973, 49), we might add will to our diagram:

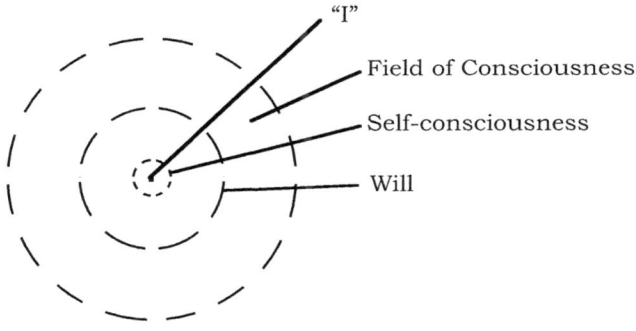

*Figure 3.6*

In figure 3.6, the field of will appears smaller than the field of consciousness, because most often one is aware of far more content than one can directly affect. Of course the relative sizes of all the fields would constantly fluctuate throughout daily living; in an act of intense concentration, for example, the fields of consciousness and will would nearly match. The point is that with disidentification often comes not only increased awareness, but increased potential to act on that awareness.

## The Strength to Be Helpless

Having said all this about the freedom of will, we must point out too that this increased potential for freedom can mean at times an increased experience of weakness and helplessness—we are free to accept such abyss experiences as well.

There are times in life—some would say all times in some way—which call us to accept our very real human limitations, to come to grips with the fact that we are far less in control of ourselves than we would like to think we are.

For example, some of the deeper layers of our psyche may contain wounds from traumatic experiences of helplessness and victimization. Thus, when these memories begin to re-emerge and disrupt our lives, it is often necessary to enter into a full experiencing of the powerlessness characteristic of the original painful events. Only in this way can we accept them and then begin to heal. Plumbing these depths shows true disidentification, because here one may actually choose to give up for a time any sense of independence and freedom, in order to embrace and redeem wounded aspects of ourselves.

If during these times we attempt to maintain a centered, choosing, self-actualizing persona, we are in effect dissociating from the depth of our own humanness. And this is dissociation, not disidentification; it is an identification with a false persona. Obviously, this identification can be supported by a dualistic, inflated, and idealized notion of "I."

> *Outwardly Homo sapiens may pretend*
> *to be satisfied and strong;*
> *inwardly he is poor, needy, vulnerable ...*
> —Abraham Heschel

If on the other hand, we accept such existential helplessness, we can then disidentify from the false-centered persona and move towards a deeper experience of true "I"—we "lose self to gain self."

This truth is indicated by the very first step in the Twelve Steps of Alcoholics Anonymous. The Twelve Steps have freed millions from most known addictions, from gambling and drugs, to sex and relationships, to debt and overeating. Here is that well-known first step, which is sometimes considered one of the most difficult of the twelve:

> *We admitted we were powerless over alcohol—that*
> *our lives had become unmanageable.* (*Twelve Steps*
> *and Twelve Traditions* 1953, 21, emphasis in original)

This admission stands at the very beginning of the recovery process. Without such a defeat of human hubris there can be no freedom, because the truth of the *lack* of freedom is denied. If one cannot admit one is in prison, there is no hope of escape.

Acceptance of our real weakness leads to finding our true strength. This acceptance allows us to break denial, move through the abyss of powerlessness, and eventually proceed towards a more authentic experience of freedom than ever before.

There is a profound universal principle in this acceptance of our human weakness and limitation. We may infer from Assagioli that helplessness and dependence are not simply manifestations of early childhood experience, but are actually at the very core of our being—because our very existence is totally dependent on a deeper Self:

> The reflection ["I"] appears to be self-existent but has,
> in reality, no autonomous substantiality. It is, in other
> words, not a new and different light but a projection of
> its luminous source [Self]. (Assagioli 1965, 20)

The process of Self-realization may involve the discovery and acceptance of this ontological dependence and helplessness. There may be times on this path when we are invited to experience the fact that we are severely limited creatures, indeed, that we have "no autonomous substantiality." If Assagioli is correct in the above statement, there will indeed be times when we are called to meet Self in experiences of helplessness, disintegration, and loss of identity. We shall return to this subject later when we discuss the nature of the I-Self unity.

Paradoxically, at this level of experiencing, the true will of "I" is so very free that it can engage the experience of absolute helplessness and dependence. The transcendence-immanence of "I" is such that it allows a "dance" with freedom *or* helplessness, strength *or* weakness.

## The Consciousness-Will Split

Having discussed will, we are in a position to examine a more crucial reason for not confusing "I" with consciousness. This reason is that considering "I" as pure consciousness implies that consciousness is more fundamental to "I" than is will. This notion creates a conceptual split between "I" and will, and thus encourages an experiential dissociation between them as well.

This conceptual dissociation of consciousness and will can be seen in psychosynthesis writings and practices in which an exercise in self-identification culminates in the statement, "I am a center of pure consciousness." This is a major truncation of Assagioli's formulation of self-identification, which is: "I am a center of awareness **and of power**" (Assagioli 1965, 119, emphasis in bold added) or "*I am a center of pure self-consciousness **and of will***" (Assagioli 1973, 215, italics in original, emphasis in bold added). For Assagioli, "I" is not solely a center of consciousness, but *equally* a center of will.

But if "I" and consciousness are separated from will, we have the concept of "I" as merely conscious, merely aware; the core of human identity is represented as only receptive. This would mean that human growth and/or spiritual development can be explained essentially as changes in consciousness, with no necessary references to choice, responsibility, or active engagement in the world.

This is a concept of human being which places "being" at one pole in a being-doing polarity. The statement of this position would be, "Who I really am is receptive being, while my doing, my will, is something I merely own." However, being is not to be set over against doing in this way. Human being—"I"—is distinct, but not separate, from activity *and* receptivity. Human being is transcendent of any such polarity, able to be immanent in either or both of these opposites. "I am I, whether receptive or active."

This aspect of I-amness seems quite like the Taoist principle of *Ying ning*, described as:

> ...a tranquillity in the action of non-action, in other words, a tranquillity which transcends the division between activity and contemplation...(Merton 1965, 26)

The notion that consciousness is more basic to human identity than is will can be seen as an aspect of dualism, the gnostic notion of human being devoid of any fundamental active engagement in the world. One's consciousness becomes more valued than one's responsible action in the world.

And this is a particular dissociation which Assagioli himself emphatically rejected—the thrust of his entire second book, *The Act of Will*, is precisely that there is something central to human identity which involves choice, responsibility, and personal power. According to Assagioli we might even consider ourselves to *be* will:

> The third phase of the discovery [of will], which renders it complete and effective, is that of *being a will* (this is different from "having" a will). (Assagioli 1973, 7, emphasis in original)

"Being a will" does not imply a distant relationship to will, with consciousness playing a more central role. It seems quite clear that will for Assagioli was every bit as fundamental to "I" as consciousness, whether "self-consciousness" or "pure consciousness." Here Assagioli states the principle in no uncertain terms:

> At the heart of the self there is both an active and a passive element, an agent and a spectator. Self-consciousness involves our being a witness—a pure, objective, loving witness—to what is happening within and without. In this sense the self is not a dynamic in itself but is a point of witness, a spectator, an observer who watches the flow. But there is another part of the inner self—the will-er or the directing agent—that actively intervenes to orchestrate the various functions and energies of the personality, to make commitments and to instigate action in the external world. So, at the center of the self, there is a unity of masculine and feminine, will and love, action and observation. (Keen, 1974)

It is not that I *am* self-consciousness and I *have* will. Rather, "I" is a *center* of self-consciousness and will, distinct but not separate from both. In other words, I am "I" whether or not I am self-conscious (aware of self) or willing (able to act).

## More Conscious Than Thou

If we equate consciousness with I-amness, with personhood, we may begin to fall into bigotry and elitism. We may begin to feel ourselves superior to those who are deemed less human because they seem less conscious than ourselves. This is a dynamic involved in the disregard and mistreatment of children; the ill; the mentally disabled; the elderly; and the supposedly "primitive" cultures—anyone seen to be less-than-conscious is seen as less-than-human.

This bigotry can extend to the spiritual or religious sphere as well, as those dubbed less conscious are seen as less evolved and somehow inferior to those who have enjoyed exalted expansions of consciousness.

> *They postulate three species of human beings:*
> *spirituals; animates; those consisting of dust.*
> —Gnostic Text

But human being may be considered distinct from consciousness, and indeed there are many "less conscious" individuals who seem to live more authentic lives than many of the "more conscious." The sincere elderly woman putting flowers at the foot of the Virgin Mary statue each day may be living a more holy and Self-realized life than the sophisticated explorer of higher states of consciousness.

Also, many who have formerly been considered less conscious, and so less human, are turning out to be quite active and aware. Today even the human fetus, that seemingly not-yet-an-"I," is gradually being recognized as a living, feeling, human being. The following passage is by Dr. Thomas Verny, from his report on research into the life of the unborn child (he states that he uses the pronoun "he" to avoid confusion):

> The unborn child is a *feeling, remembering, aware*
> being, and because he is, what happens to him—what
> happens to all of us—in the nine months between
> conception and birth molds and shapes personality,
> drives and ambitions in very important ways. (Verny
> 1981, 15, emphasis in original)

Current infant research too, is leading to the conclusion that
the human infant experiences some sense of self even in the first
months of life. It appears that the infant does not, as formerly
thought, exist in a state of unconscious self–other oneness prior
to "separation-individuation" (Mahler 1975). The work of Daniel
Stern indicates that early infancy is not characterized by a primal
unconscious unity, but by an ongoing and active relationship
between self and other:

> Infants begin to experience a sense of an emergent self
> from birth. They are predesigned to be aware of self-
> organizing processes. They never experience a period
> of total self/other undifferentiation. There is no confu-
> sion between self and other in the beginning or at any
> point during infancy. They are also predesigned to be
> selectively responsive to external social events and
> never experience an autistic-like phase. (Stern 1985, 10)

The surprising early existence of "I" can be seen too in the
following childhood memory, showing an obvious and wonderful
blossoming of self-consciousness and will:

> I had this strong sense when I was a baby in arms. Natu-
> rally I don't know how old I was—perhaps 1 to 2. I was
> screaming and being carried downstairs ... I suddenly
> had this feeling of what I should now call emerging
> into self-consciousness. It was a sense that I need not
> scream, that I could choose not to. It was in my power
> to do this. It was a wonderful feeling, like what I'd
> now say was a religious sense. (Robinson 1983, 118)

It seems obvious that one must be extremely careful in creating a concept of human development resembling a ladder of consciousness leading from Unconsciousness up to Cosmic Consciousness. On such a chain of being, one may begin to think that the apparently more conscious individuals are closer to Reality, while the masses struggle down below. This misuse of such a model is pure gnostic elitism (see "'I' as Distinct from Levels of Consciousness," in chapter 6).

One can also create an elitism based not upon consciousness, but upon will—here, we are what we do, what we achieve. In this case, the most human are the most active and productive, and therefore activity is most valued while inactivity is denigrated.

This is seen in the Puritan work ethic, and is most pronounced in the syndrome of *workaholism*. Here we find it very difficult to relax, to enter into the quiet of leisure time or the solitude of prayer, and may consider ourselves superior to those who seem less productive (that is, they can only be "unmotivated" or "lazy").

Neither consciousness nor will seem more fundamental to human identity, and neither fully describes human being. Deepest human identity is distinct but not separate from these two functions.

In sum, then, if awareness is the receptive aspect of "I," will is the dynamic aspect. Both awareness and will describe fundamental functions of the distinct (transcendent) "I," and together allow human beings to be intimately involved (immanent) both in the private inner world and in the outer social world.

"I" is distinct but not separate from, in but not of, the psyche-soma, as well as awareness-will.

> *The life of a healthy individual is characterized by fears,*
> *conflicting feelings, doubts, frustrations,*
> *as much as by the positive features.*
> *The main thing is that the man or woman feels he or she*
> *is living his or her own life, taking responsibility for*
> *action or inaction, and able to take credit for success*
> *and blame for failure.*
> —D. W. Winnicott

# CHAPTER FOUR

# Transcendence-Immanence

*If one does not know the Constant,*
*One runs blindly into disasters.*
*If one knows the Constant,*
*One can understand and embrace all.*
*If one understands and embraces all,*
*One is capable of doing justice.*
—Lao Tzu

In the preceding pages we have been alluding to the idea that the concepts of transcendence and immanence seem to be quite useful in pointing to the nature of human spirit, of "I." Not only do these terms avoid both dualism and monism, but they appear to be promising phenomenological constructs which can perhaps help lead us towards the lived insight into the nature of "I" in oneself and others.

Transcendence refers to a radical distinction between "I" and all content—whether mass, energy, space, or time—and processes, whether biological, psychic, or spiritual. The psychiatrist Gordon Globus, writing in the *American Journal of Psychiatry,* calls "I" a "singularity" (1980, 418–19), an extensionless point at which the fundamental rules of the universe break down (see appendix 2).

Immanence on the other hand means that "I" cannot be thought of as in any way separate from mass, energy, space, or time. In Globus' terms, "I" is "coupled to an address" (419), that is, "I" exists at a specific unique point in spacetime. Thus, even as one ponders the breathtaking transcendence of "I," one must avoid the temptation to think of "I" in isolation from psyche-soma. (As Globus points out, dualism is avoided by his "singularity" conception, because only one domain is required—there is no need to posit another, far-off, transcendent domain.)

Transcendence and immanence together hold a central paradox of "I." They are not polarities, but descriptions of the same singular phenomenon from two different vantage points. Perhaps this paradox is analogous to the incongruous nature of light, which from one point of view acts like undulating waves, and from another, as bundles of corpuscles. Each view seems to contradict the other, yet neither can be eliminated.

But let us turn now to a closer inspection of the concepts of transcendence and immanence. As we shall discover, a clear understanding of these terms can assist us in seeing through the wonders of peak experiences, through the despair of life's dark times, and even through the normal unfolding of daily existence, to the unique, living, willing being who lives all of these experiences.

## Transcendence

To begin our discussion of transcendence, we must point out that we are not using the term transcendence according to these definitions from *Webster's New World Dictionary* (Second College Edition, 1979):

> 2. *Philos.* a) beyond the limits of possible experience ...
> 3. *Theol.* existing apart from the material universe:
>    said of God

Contrary to definition number two, our usage does not conceive of transcendence as so radically "other" that it is completely beyond, outside, and distant from human experience. Such an approach will tend to disallow direct experiential knowing of the Divine, that knowing sought in contemplation and mysticism.

Quite the contrary, our notion of transcendence is that it is not only deeply within us each, but that it describes an aspect of essential human being itself. While the experience of transcendence is definitely unlike all other modes of human knowing (and can even be called *unknowing* or *non-experience*), it nevertheless constitutes a lived inner reality.

As well, contrary to definition number three above, we do not consider transcendence to imply even the smallest hint of the meaning, "apart from," applied either to human being or Divine Being. We are using transcendence to mean: distinct from content—whether mass, energy, time, or space—and processes, whether biological, psychological, or spiritual. We in no way mean to imply any sort of separation from content and such processes, nor any notion of a far-off transcendent domain.

In the field of psychology, the term transcendence is used by many respected figures. C. G. Jung (1972, 110) spoke of what he called the *transcendent function*, by which he meant the shifting of the center of the personality so that new material from the unconscious may be integrated (see appendix 2).

Abraham Maslow too, in the chapter "Various Meanings of Transcendence," outlines no less than 35 different meanings of the word, from the experience of the loss of self-consciousness to the ability to see beyond one's personal value system (1971, 269–79).

And Rollo May uses the word to describe the human capacity "to abstract, to use symbols, to orient one's self beyond the immediate limits of the given time and space" (1958, 73).

For all of this psychological use of the word "transcendence," however, May finds it necessary to warn us that the term has a certain "inciting-to-riot quality" among those who consider it "vague and ethereal" (72). We do however commiserate with some of this "riot," because the term is indeed used vaguely and imprecisely in much psychological and even spiritual writing (usually it is used merely as a synonym for "going beyond").

We shall therefore attempt to describe carefully our use of the word in the present context. Our use of "transcendence" regarding "I" is meant to carry this meaning:

> "I" is not to be identified with any object of awareness; nor with any biological, psychological, or spiritual experience; nor with mass, energy, space, or time; nor with the functions of awareness and will.

In short, "I" as transcendent is to be conceptualized as no *thing* at all.

So "I" is to be conceptualized (or non-conceptualized) as distinct, but not separate, from the experience of: my feelings; my ecstasy; my despair; my family; my job; my country; my universe; and my consciousness and will. If there were not in fact such a distinction, disidentification would seem to be impossible, as would be "knowing I know" and "knowing I will" (see chapter 3).

A corollary to this meaning of transcendence is that no concept will ever adequately describe "I." That is, since concepts themselves can be objects of awareness, "I" is distinct from them, and thus "I" is ultimately beyond their grasp. Indeed, since "I" is the very one who is seeking to grasp "I," I will never be able to grasp "I." As Schumacher states:

> How is it possible to study that which does the study-ing? How, indeed, can I study the "I" that employs the very consciousness needed for the study? (Schumacher 1977, 23)

And again, this a-conceptual nature of "I" must not be confused with the experience of blotting out cognitive function-ing, because one may experience this distinctness from thought *even while thinking.*

Assagioli himself uses the term transcendence in a variety of different ways, but he approaches our use of the word when he says:

> ...transcendent Reality...can be indicated or hinted at only through negations: not-this, not-that, no-thing, the "Void." This aspect of Reality has been empha-sized by some schools of Northern Buddhism and in the West by Meister Eckhart. (Assagioli 1973, 129n)

From this description of transcendence, it may be inferred that Assagioli himself thought of "I" as transcendent, because we find this same type of wording occurs in his disidentification exercise: "I *am not* my body, feelings, or mind." Thus he brings into play the notion of transcendence at the exact point at which he attempts to describe the experience of "I." (But as we have seen, he neglects the equal importance of immanence in so doing.)

It is important to note then that by transcendence we do not mean to indicate some transcendent substance mysteriously existing in the recesses of the cerebral cortex, the "ghost in the machine." Transcendence does not tell us what "I" is, but only what "I" is *not*; it is a heuristic device, not a description of a thing per se.

Of course, in speaking about "I," one cannot avoid referring to it as an object—as we just did. But remember that when we say "I," what we mean is *the unique subject which cannot be named, and which you are.*

## Transcendence and "No-thing-ness"

As the psychotherapist Ann Russell (1989) often maintains in psychosynthesis circles, it can be useful to say simply that there is no "I" at all. This is quite a valid approach—perhaps it is better not to say anything at all, rather than attempt to use transcendence to say we cannot say anything at all!

Assagioli too might agree with this strategy. If "I" is but a reflection of Self, then "I" only "appears to be self-existent but has, in reality, no autonomous substantiality" (Assagioli 1965, 20). In this sense, "I" is indeed an illusion.

> *He sent out Science to seek his pearl, and got nothing.*
> *He sent Analysis to look for his pearl, and got nothing.*
> *He sent out Logic to seek his pearl, and got nothing.*
> *Then he asked Nothingness, and Nothingness had it!*
> —Chuang Tzu

Russell further points out that this notion of the illusion or non-existence of "I" seems consistent with the Buddhist concept/ experience of "noself" (*anatman* or *anatta*). This notion also seems consonant with the contemporary Western rejection of the notion of "substantial self," a rejection seen in the thought of Alfred N. Whitehead (1985) as well as in Christian Process Theology.[6]

This concept of noself is also referred to by transpersonal researchers, such as Roger Walsh (1978) and Jack Engler (1986) in their writings about Buddhist vipassana meditation. In speaking of the non-existence of "I," Walsh says,

> This concept seems analogous to the Buddhist doctrine of *anatta* or "not self," which states that both awareness and objects of awareness exist as automatic processes devoid of any "I."[7] (Walsh 1978, 10)

Thus, contact with Reality would mean a loss of one's normal, illusory, sense of separate identity.

In the Jewish tradition, one thinks of the idea that to see the face of God means death (see Exodus 33:20). Or, in the Christian tradition, we are reminded of God's words to St. Catherine of Siena: "You are she who is not, and I am who is." (Raymond of Capua 1980, 85)

This insight is still quite current in modern Christian spirituality, as seen in the work of Thomas Merton or in these words of Father Timko from the Slavonic Orthodox tradition:

> And, as Saint John Chrysostom said, "He alone truly knows himself, who knows himself as nothing." Let us just be what we actually are—*nothing!* (see Dorje 1987, 158)

However, this "I do not exist" formulation does not satisfy completely as a "non-concept" concept either. For example, examine Walsh's vivid account of a personal experience of noself:

> Immediately there followed a powerful awareness accompanied by intense emotion that "I" did not exist, and all that existed were "I" thoughts following rapidly one after another. Almost simultaneously the thought, "My God, there's no one there!" arose, and my consciousness reverted back to its accustomed state. (Walsh 1978, 7)

We are still left, however, with: "Who had this experience?" For all of this reported non-existence, we can still here sense a somebody/nobody who experienced "a powerful awareness." There is still some thread here running through even the "'I' did not exist" experience. *Someone* experienced this and thus was able later to describe it—*even though* this was an objectless, content-less "'I' did not exist" experience.

The question remains, "Who is it that *does* exist; who is able to experience this non-existence?" Arthur Deikman pointedly asks this very same question:

> Once again, the voice in the night declares that there is no voice in the night. "He knows 'I am' to be a miscon-ception." Who knows that? (Deikman 1982, 141)

If one were truly non-existent in such moments, there would be no one present to engage the experience, no one there to experience anything at all. Therefore, it would be in fact impossible to ever have such an experience, and we would never hear about it from others—in no case would there ever be anyone there to have the experience or report it.

A true moment of personal non-existence would seem to constitute a non-experience, permanently inaccessible to any sort of knowing at all. If a tree falls in the forest, and you hear the sound, aren't you there somehow?

So in Walsh's description above, there yet seems to be a some-body/nobody who experiences disidentification from I-thoughts, and this may perhaps be called an experience of emptiness; the void; no-thing-ness; the insubstantiality of self; *shunyata*; or loss of self in God. But if we elect to say therefore that "I" does not exist, how are we to refer to the one who *does* live and move in these experiences—the source of Deikman's "voice in the night"?

An alternative is to say simply that this noself experience is a seeing through our normal everyday experience of ourselves as objects, to experience that true "I" is not what we *have* but who we *are*. Here there is a dispelling of the mistaken idea that I am a content of awareness which I can possess like a feeling or a thought (this is called the "narcissistic mistake" in appendix 2).

*"No-Self"*
*Is "True-Self."*
—Chuang Tzu

The Christian monk Thomas Merton talks about this realization of pure subjectivity as dispelling the illusion of the false or "empirical self," to experience the no-thing-ness of our "true self":

> As long as there is an "I" that is the definite subject of a contemplative experience, an "I" that is aware of itself and of its contemplation ... then we have not yet passed over the Red Sea, we have not yet "gone out of Egypt. ... " The true inner self, the true indestructible and immortal person, the true "I" ... does not "have" anything, even "contemplation." This "I" is not the kind of subject that can amass experiences ... for this "I" is not the superficial and empirical self that we know in our everyday life. (Merton 1961, 279)

> Our reality, our true self, is hidden in what appears to us to be nothingness and void. What we are not seems to be real, what we are seems to be unreal. ... And that is why the way to reality is the way of humility which brings us to reject the illusory self and accept the "empty" self that is "nothing" ... (281)

And here is Ramana Maharshi with a quite similar notion of an illusory false self which hides an enduring true self:

> L. [Devotee]: If "I" am always—here and now—why do I not feel so?
> B. [Ramana Maharshi]: Who says that you do not? Does the real "I" or the false "I"? The false "I" is the obstruction which has to be removed in order that the true "I" may cease to be hidden.
> (Ramana Maharshi 1978, 118)

This true self or true "I" is the source of Deikman's "voice in the night"—the one who discovers "I am" does not exist. It is an impoverished, empty, no-thing, noself. So the no-thing-ness experienced in the disidentified emptiness of meditative insights does not imply any loss in the experience of existing as a responsible agent actively engaging the world. Such selflessness does not involve a psychotic loss of ego boundaries nor any diminishment of personal responsibility.

Our use of the term transcendence is an attempt to say that this *one* who exists is not at all our habitual experience of identity as an object, nor is it simply an experience of pure consciousness or will. Transcendence is here a paradoxical term denying any thingness at all, and thus is a no-thing concept.

Transcendence holds the idea that "I" is distinct from all things and therefore is not completely limited or defined by things. Thus, "I" can experience any thing, or no thing. "I" can experience the changing contents of the inner world and changes in awareness and will. "I" can even experience non-existence and live to tell about it. ("You shall see the face of God and live.")

So transcendence is simply a tool pointing to "I" as unknowable in the usual subject-object manner, and in that, it seems to have some affinity with the noself idea.

Transcendence does not imply the existence of a transcendent no-thing, nor does it imply the non-existence of any thing. "I" who can be named is not the constant "I" (and even "noself" is a name, and thus can befuddle our understanding).

Here is psychosynthesis thinker Jim Vargiu quoting some words which sum up the whole issue very nicely:

> This paradoxical nature of the Self is perhaps best stated by the Buddhist formula: "Neither being, nor not-being, nor both being and not-being, nor neither being nor not-being"! (Vargiu 1973, 8)

And of course, in the Judeo-Christian West, Pseudo-Dionysius is no slouch with transcendent-immanent wordings, either. He too seems to recognize a human self/non-self as one approaches the Divine:

Here, renouncing all that the mind may conceive, wrapped entirely in the intangible and the invisible, he belongs completely to him who is beyond everything. Here, being neither oneself nor someone else, one is supremely united by a completely unknowing inactivity of all knowledge, and knows beyond the mind by knowing nothing. (Pseudo-Dionysius 1987, 137)

Clearly, language gets tied in tortuous knots as it attempts to twist itself around this central mystery. Any conceptualizing here is doomed to paradox and counter-paradox, never touching the reality it is trying to denote. The essence of human identity, and its communion with the Divine, cannot be encapsulated in any concept, for that identity is the "who" who experiences these very concepts.

Whether we say self is transcendent of all things, or that it is no-thing, all we can hope to do is to develop imperfect notions which point towards "I." As is said, "The finger which points at the moon is not the moon."

*Subjectivity as such escapes by definition from*
*that which we know about ourselves by means of notions.*
—Jacques Maritain

## The Tasks of the "I" and "No-I" Approaches

Before leaving this discussion of the "I-approach" and the "no-I approach," let us just say that there are different tasks or mandates incumbent on each of these orientations.

On one hand, the "I"-approach demands much ongoing clarification that "I" is definitely not our chronic experience of self as object. This objectification of "I" must be avoided at all costs. Here one must be sure not to portray "I" as in any way something we own, as something we develop, as something we must protect, or as some sort of static material standing behind all changing process—otherwise we are left with the "ghost in the machine." It is on this rock that people applying I-approaches are apt to founder (see note 6).

On the other hand, the no-I-approach has the responsibility for ongoing clarification that this notion does not constitute a psychotic loss of unique individual personhood, nor a diminished capacity to be deeply engaged in the world—otherwise noself can become passivity, irresponsibility, and a repression of full humanness. It is on this rock that people applying noself approaches may founder (and have done; see Engler 1986).

Given these different strategies and obstacles, perhaps both schools might help the other in their respective tasks. And perhaps too, such mutual assistance may form an important dynamic in the ecumenical dialogue between Eastern and Western religions.

The West has traditionally castigated the East for its supposed monistic "annihilation of individuality" feared in noself terminology; while the East has been critical of the apparently dualistic "substantial self" in Western thought, seen as the isolated, individualized ego. See Dorje (1987) for one promising approach to such East-West dialogue.

But let us refine this tool of transcendence still further, so it may help to fulfill the obligations of an I-approach. It is hoped that this concept, with immanence, can point us more accurately to both the self and noself nature of "I."

## Transcendence of Space

It is quite common to use transcendence in a way which confuses it with distance, with the experience of space. For example, if in a particular situation we are able to overcome a strong feeling of anger, and then become tranquil, we might say, "I transcended my anger." However, this experience is simply a shift from one state of consciousness to another, a change from the psychological space of anger, to the space of tranquility. It would be more accurate to say simply, "I became unaware of anger and then I became aware of tranquility."

For "I," such a supposedly transcendent movement is operationally no different from shifting our awareness from the roar of traffic in the street outside, to the quiet ticking of a clock inside the room. In this latter case we first have become unaware of the traffic noise, and then become aware of the ticking—just as formerly we had become unaware of our anger and then aware of tranquility. Both experiences are simply a change in awareness, a movement from one psychological space to another.

But do we transcend the noise in the street by becoming aware of the clock ticking? No. The street noise and the ticking are both of the same order, just as are anger and tranquility, or agony and ecstasy—all are changing aspects of experience.

We would not apply transcendence to these types of changes in space. Rather, we are using the word transcendence here to mean, "distinct from the experience of space." Transcendence means *no-thing*, while space is a *thing*. (According to Einstein, gravity can be thought of as a curvature of spacetime, that is, space changes.)

Therefore, since "I" can engage many different psychological spaces, and can undergo changes in these spaces, "I" can be thought of as distinct but not separate from space. Whether feeling a crushing lack of space, or an exciting expansion of space in our lives, we ever remain transcendent of spatial experience.

So transcendence does not mean, "Way over there, far away from everything." This conception of transcendence leads to dissociation rather than disidentification. Making this mistake, we may attempt to transcend our pain by going far away from it, that is, by repressing it. Or, if we are told about a transcendent God, this God might be thought to exist far away in another place, dualistically dissociated from the world (when actually, as St. Augustine said, the transcendent God is closer to us than we are to ourselves).

Again, transcendence does not apply to space at all, but to the one who can experience space—"I." Transcendence is a description of the very nature of "I," no matter where "I" is. And because "I" is distinct from space, "I" can engage any and all spaces— transcendence is entirely immanent, in but not of any possible space. "I" is therefore always completely present, because it is not identical with any particular space at all. As has been said,

"NO MATTER WHERE I GO, THERE I AM."

## Transcendence as Infinity

Of course, a term for this transcendence of space is the word *infinity*. But we must not then think of infinity here as an endless series, as a progression to which something more can always be added. This latter is not infinity in the transcendent sense, but the snake continuously eating its own ever-growing tail, the mythological uroboros. Here is how *An Illustrated Encyclopaedia of Traditional Symbols* defines uroboros, or "ouroboros":

> "My end is my beginning." It symbolizes the undifferentiated; the Totality; primordial unity; self-sufficiency. It begets, weds, impregnates, and slays itself. It is the cycle of disintegration and reintegration, power that eternally consumes and renews itself; the eternal cycle; cyclic time; spatial infinity; truth and cognition in one; the united primordial parents; the Androgyne ... (Cooper 1978, 123)

Here is a notion of a totality of space, of spatial infinity. True, the word "in-finite" means, "no-finish," and in this sense, such a uroboric progression is infinite—it has no finish because one more step (one more bite) can always be taken.

But we are using infinite to mean "no finish" in the sense that it does not partake of the very processes of start, continuation, or finish at all. Here, infinity is distinct from all process, no matter how unending this process might be, whether infinite regress or infinite progress.

Infinity is simply to be thought of as distinct from all space. Thus beginning and ending, or starting and finishing, or endless change, have nothing to do with our transcendent concept of infinity here.[8]

And thus we are not here implying the existence of some sort of infinite substance which exists in a far-off realm beyond space, but are merely applying the idea of transcendence to space—*every concept and experience of space is distinct from "I."* "I" can therefore be thought of as infinite, distinct from space. And as we next shall see, "I" can also be thought of as eternal, transcendent of time.

## Transcendence as Eternity

Since "I" can observe changing contents of awareness, as well as experience changes in awareness and will, "I" can be thought of as distinct from the experience of change. "I" means continuity through time, a continuity not based on a continuity of any object of awareness, nor on any continuity in awareness or will.

> *The real self allows a person to recognize*
> *within herself that special "someone" who*
> *persists through space and time ...*
> —James Masterson

Whether I feel my sensations change from pleasure to pain; or feel my emotions change from despair to joy; or find my beliefs changing from agnostic to theist; or awaken from a period of un-self-consciousness; or find myself possessed by, and then free of, an obsession; it is still "I" who experiences these changes—I am here in my despair, I am here in my joy, I am here in my realization of unconsciousness, I am here in bondage or freedom. And these are not different "I"s, not a series of infinite multiple personalities, but the same "I" moving through different experiences.

This use of the word transcendence thus points to continuity in time. Transcendence means "I" is distinct from the experience of time, that is, it is eternal. By eternal is meant that "I"—as "I"—endures within the experience of time. "I" am the one who engages process and change, but "I" am not identical with process and change.

So note well then, that by eternal we do not mean, a large amount of time, as when Andrew Marvell says:

> And yonder all before us lie
> Deserts of vast eternity.

> ("To His Coy Mistress")

Here, "vast" is a concept misleading us about transcendence. Just as infinite is distinct from space, no matter how vast the space; so eternity does not imply a vast amount of time, but simply means, distinct from time.

Neither is transcendent eternity to be thought of as endless time in the sense that a circle is endless, as Vaughan sees it here:

> I saw eternity the other night,
> Like a great ring of pure and endless light,
>
> ("The World")

Such a circle merely implies that all time is somehow gathered into a ring, a totality, and therefore goes on endlessly—the notion of "all time" automatically implies unchanging cyclic change, because there is no time left over into which to change. But there is nothing transcendent in this, as we are using the term. This is no more transcendent than for example an endless treadmill—our old friend the uroboros feeding on its growing tail, symbolizing the "eternal cycle, cyclic time" (Cooper 1978, 123).

This uroboric totality of time is related to the type of "time-lessness" which Jung pointed out was a characteristic of the unconscious. Jung says that in the unconscious, "past, present, and future are blended together" (1969a, 503). This is clearly a totality of time, which is quite a different concept from our notion of transcendence of time. In our terms, eternity and timelessness mean a distinctness from any notions of time at all, including the elimination or summation of time.

According to Plato, time is simply a copy or model of eternity, and thus obviously distinct; according to St. Augustine, God created time, so God is distinct from time; according to St. Thomas Aquinas (1947), "time and eternity are not the same thing" (*Summa Theologica*, Q. X, Fourth Article); according to some modern "Big-Bang" theory, spacetime came into being at the same moment as the rest of the universe, so time itself may conceivably (inconceivably) have some sort of beginning and end.

So transcendence of time does not mean simply shifting to a larger timeframe, nor is it the experience of Vaughan's endless ring of time, apparent when time is seen as a totality. Shifting to a larger timeframe is again, simply like becoming aware first of the street noise and then the ticking clock; sound is still sound, whether loud or soft, and time is still time, whether psychological, biological, or cosmic.

"I" rather is the one who can be aware of sound and of time. For example, we might ask Marvell and Vaughan above, "*Who* is aware of this vast eternity, this endless ring?" The answer: "I am—I who am distinct but not separate from this vast eternity, this endless ring." If this "who" can perceive time, perhaps even glimpse all time, then this "who" can be thought of logically as in but not of time.

Furthermore, at the very moment Marvell and Vaughan are having these experiences, we might ask them, "*When* are you having this experience of vastness and endlessness?" The inevitable answer will be, "Right now." So whether we experience time crawling, time accelerating, time constricting, or time expanding, we do all of this in the NOW. We are ever HERE, distinct but not separate from the flow of time. In the words of Ludwig Wittgenstein:

> If we take eternity to mean not infinite temporal duration but timelessness, then eternal life belongs to those who live in the present. (Wittgenstein 1974, 147)

So our use of eternal does not imply some distant forever, existing at the end of time. Rather, eternal is right here and now—it is us, in but not of time. Thus we have the familiar phrase, "The eternal now." Eternity is now, always, and we are it.

We may be absorbed in our regrets about the past, or be caught up in a wondrous vision of the future, but this simply shrouds the fact that we do all of this in the present. We can never really be anywhere else than when we are:

"NO MATTER WHEN I AM, I AM NOW."

It is precisely this eternal "in but not of time" which allows for continuity within the experience of time. "I" can be thought not to endure through time by virtue of being some sort of immutable structure, nor by virtue of being a continuous process, but because "I" is distinct from time, that is, eternal.

So too, we thus see how inseparable are transcendence and immanence. The ability to be distinct from time allows endurance in time, and so complete engagement in time. Transcendence of time can in no way be separated from immanence in time, for they are simply two sides of the same coin.

Again, remember that transcendence and eternity are here negating terms—they do not imply some sort of static substance existing through time. As T. S. Eliot (1943) says of the "still point," "But neither arrest nor movement. And do not call it fixity."

Words such as static and "fixity" imply a *thing* existing unaffected by other things, and this is not what is meant here. Rather, we are simply applying the principle of transcendence, that is, by eternity we mean that *every concept and experience of time is distinct from "I."*

## Transcendence as "One," Not "Wholeness"

As we begin to seriously examine ourselves, it becomes abundantly clear that our interior world is fraught with multiplicity. Here are strongly ambivalent feelings pulling in opposite directions, opposed needs competing for attention, and differing mental opinions in heated debate.

In addition, we may begin to recognize how different we feel, think, and behave in different spheres of life. For example, at work we may be dynamic and insensitive; at home with the family we may be weak, though sensitive; and visiting our parents we may feel and act like a small child.

It may even transpire that who we thought ourselves to be, disintegrates. Entering a life change, we may find we cannot do the things we used to do, that we are indecisive and unsure where formerly we were confident and "of one mind." Our whole personality may fall apart, and only gradually come back together again, as we come to form a new way of being in the world.

Looking at all such experiences of multiplicity, we must ask the question, "Who am I in all this? Who am I who can experience all this multiplicity? Who can experience wholeness, then disintegration, then wholeness again?" A possible answer is, of course, that since "I" seems to be able to observe, experience, and even act within multiplicity, "I" is distinct from multiplicity.

"I" can therefore be thought of as transcendent of multiplicity. This is obvious when we can observe chaotic fragmentation inside us. Here we are distinct, the *one* who feels the fragmentation. But we also learn we are distinct from any multiplicity which happens to be integrated into a whole—witness our ability to move through experiences in which the wholeness of our life disintegrates.[9]

This distinctness from multiplicity includes of course distinctness from duality. Transcendence is therefore to be distinguished from any sort of union of opposites, such as the alchemical "*coniunctio oppositorum*" referred to by Jung (1979, 31). It is not then the uroboros—"the united primordial parents; the Androgyne," which imply a synthesis of masculine and feminine ("*andros*" plus "*gyne*"). It is not to be confused with a supposed God-Goddess unity.[10] Transcendence is distinct from masculine, feminine, and from the whole created by their harmonious integration; neither is it that quality of "more than the sum of the parts" found in a whole.

Transcendence is distinct not only from masculine and feminine, but from all opposites, and from multiplicity itself. *It is by this very fact that it implies immanence within any multiplicity.* It is potentially able to participate in any and all opposites, multiplicities, and their unifications.

> *He is not one part of a plurality nor*
> *yet a total of parts. Indeed his oneness*
> *is not of this kind at all, for he does not*
> *share in unity nor have it for his possession.*
> —Pseudo-Dionysius

Thus too, transcendent being would not be considered merely receptive—merely consciousness (see chapter 3)—and therefore set over against an active "doing" to form a polarity of being-doing. Rather, here being is distinct from any such receptive-active polarity, and is therefore able to partake of either mode. Transcendent being can be immanent in activity, receptivity, or both.

We can look again to the uroboros for a demonstration of what we do *not* mean. The uroboros is a symbol of totality, of primordial unity, of undifferentiated wholeness. None of these concepts have to do with transcendence as we are describing it.

Transcendence implies a distinctness from any sort of union or summation of content, even if that content is all the mass, energy, space, and time of the entire cosmos. Thus transcendence is also distinct from any sort of patterning or ordering of content, such as implied by concepts like *ideal form* (Plato 1945); *archetype* (Jung 1968); *holism* (Smuts 1986); *holon* (Koestler 1967); *universal creative field* (Vargiu 1977); *implicate order* (Bohm 1980); or *morphic field* (Sheldrake 1981).

In other words, "I" is distinct from wholeness in the sense of an integration of parts, and from any abstract form of such a whole. Rather, "I" is *One* in the sense of being distinct from any multiplicity, unified or not, rarefied or palpable. *One* is here a transcendent term denying any notion of divisibility, as stated by St. Thomas Aquinas:

> *I answer that, One...* is only a negation of division: for *one* means undivided *being*. This is the very reason why *one* is the same as *being*. (Aquinas 1947, Q. XI, First Article)

And these words of St. Thomas seem echoed by humanistic-existential psychotherapist James Bugental:

> The *I*, as I conceive it, is irreducibly a unity and invariably a subject. It is, I postulate, the essential being. (Bugental 1981, 210)

Therefore, this irreducible unity, this undivided beingness of "I," is a negating term or anti-description (see the *via negativa*, appendix 1). Indivisible oneness is not meant to conjure up an image of a hard small atom which shall never be split. Rather, *one* means that *every concept and experience of multiplicity or wholeness is distinct from "I."* "I" is in but not of multiplicity, distinct but not separate from multiplicity:

"NO MATTER HOW FRAGMENTED OR WHOLE I AM,
I AM ONE."

# Immanence

Clearly, throughout our examination of transcendence, immanence has been with us every step of the way: transcendence of space implies the potential ability to be in all spaces; transcendence of time implies enduring existence within time; and transcendence of multiplicity implies an ability to engage multiplicity as well as wholeness.

By this very transcendence then, "I" can be actively involved in the space/time and mass/energy of any and all intrapsychic events. This of course is the principle behind the whole field of psychotherapy—that there is some subject in the inner world to whom inner events are objective and can be acted upon. For example, psychotherapy may involve experiencing that I am distinct from my feelings, that I do not need to be controlled by them, and that I can take responsibility for them.

The transcendence of "I" allows action in relation to psychic contents, the exploration of their depths and heights, and even taking an active part in integrating contents into increasingly meaningful expressions in the world. Since "I" always has the potential to experience disidentification, "I" ever carries the potential of increasing contact with the broad range of inner resources available to the human being.

# Immanence in Life Transitions

Inasmuch as the transcendence of "I" is hidden, changes in the status quo of one's life become extremely threatening, and this can limit one's immanent participation in them.

For example, we may find a particular role identification—such as mother, provider, or husband—becoming obsolete in the face of life changes. Often in these cases the particular personality integration serving that role begins to weaken and transform, in preparation for a new formation more appropriate to a new stage of life.

However, these types of changes will be inordinately anxiety-producing if we experience that we *are* the particular identification alone—the transformation will feel as if we are dying. Thus, this can lead to our desperate defense of the role, and in turn, to a resistance to life change. The confusion of "I" and the role can therefore cause fixation, as the normal transformations in human growth are blocked.

If however, we know the disidentification experience, we know the depth of our transcendence. In this case, we know we are distinct from the experience of different life stages or social roles, and are better able to stay present to them—experience immanence—as they change.

But remember that disidentification does not mean that we are in any way dissociated from such transitions and crises in our lives. It is not that these transitions take place before us like some motion picture projected on a screen "out there." Indeed, it means that we are *more* capable of experiencing the depths of pain, darkness, and psychological death-rebirth that such transitions often involve.

Far from implying a dissociation from experience, transcendence involves a faithfulness in allowing oneself to enter fully into deeper levels of experience. Indeed, a sense of "I" may here be thought of almost as analogous to faith—here we somehow, beyond what we may feel or think, allow ourselves to embrace fully the chaos and turmoil of existence.

Thus too, an experiential knowing of transcendence can lead us towards full engagement in any particular stage or role, because we know we cannot become stuck in it. We see this same principle often in psychotherapy, as when someone with a clear strong sense of "I" is able to plunge more deeply into an exploration of the unconscious—the sense of transcendence gives a sense of faithfulness which allows a deeper immanence, a "strength to be helpless."

So as one recognizes oneself as distinct but not separate from life transformations, one can begin to embrace such changes, perhaps even taking an active part in facilitating them, and in any case bring much more of oneself to them. In other words, as the experience of transcendence increases, so too does the experience of immanence.

Again, immanence is as fundamental to "I" as is transcendence. Transcendence implies immanence, and immanence implies transcendence—the two words merely represent two different perspectives on human being.

And of course, the experiencing aspect of immanence is what Assagioli called the *field of awareness*, and the dynamic aspect is what Assagioli called *will*.

## Immanence Means We "Are" Our Psyche-Soma

An important meaning of transcendent-immanent is that "I" is distinct but not separate from its individual unique location in physical temporal existence. That is, I exist in this specific existential moment, aware of these particular sensations, able to affect these particular events—and none of this is extrinsic to me.

While the transcendence of "I" means there is a distinction between any such particularities of experience and me, the immanent unique experiencing/acting of "I" means these particularities are in no way to be understood as separate from me.

The dualistic notion of "self-with-a-body/mind" has nothing to do with the discovery of I-amness, nor with disidentification. Assagioli himself relates the experience of "I" to the "essence of Being" approached by existential psychotherapists (Assagioli 1965, 113), and such therapists speak of Being as the experience of *presence* or "being there" (*Dasein*). According to Rollo May,

> The "there" [in "being there"] is moreover not just any place, but the particular "there" that is mine, the particular point *in time* as well as space of my existence at this given moment. (May 1958, 41)

The experience of existing in this specific place at this specific time is the experience of individual uniqueness, of eternity, derived from "I." "I am" immediately implies, "I am here and now, experiencing these particular sensations, feelings, and thoughts." As Gordon Globus (1980) would put it, while "I" is a dimensionless point, "I" nevertheless is coupled to a specific "address" (419) in spacetime (see appendix 2).

Observably, our individuality includes our unique moment in physical historical time, with its specific opportunities and limitations for self-expression. It is meaningless to think of "I" as some sort of pure abstract essence dissociated from concrete spacetime experience.

So it can be of help in theory and in practice to grasp transcendence-immanence: while "I" is distinct from the physical sensations, "I" cannot be understood as in any way separate from this particular psychosomatic here and now. The psyche-soma is a unique process/event in spacetime, and cannot be thought of empirically as some vehicle with "I" driving it about—this is dualism, whether Platonic, gnostic, theosophical, or patriarchal.

From the immanent point of view, we *are* our bodies. Let us again turn to T. S. Eliot (1943), as he uses negating terminology to speak our paradoxical physicality as "still points":

> At the still point of the turning world.
> Neither flesh *nor fleshless* ...
> ("Burnt Norton," emphasis added)

## The *imago Dei*

Insight into the transcendence-immanence of "I" gives rise to a question which takes us a step further in our exploration—"What could be the source of such transcendence-immanence?"

The understanding of transcendence developed above indicates that "I" is not composed of psycho-physical contents and processes, and thus is not a bit of content which has differentiated out of the psyche-soma. To so objectify "I" would be to fall into a materialistic monism.

Pondering the nature of immanence, on the other hand, neither can we assume "I" to be an incorporeal spark of spirit which has incarnated in psyche-soma. "I" has not fallen into matter from a far-off spiritual realm. To so abstract "I" would be to fall into the dualistic position.

In looking for the source of a transcendent-immanent "I," therefore, we must look not to psyche-soma nor to non-psyche-soma. So how might one conceptualize the source of such an improbable, paradoxical nature?

The source of transcendence-immanence, of course, can only be a deeper transcendence-immanence, a deeper transcendent-immanent Self. The transcendent-immanent "I" must be a reflection or image of a deeper transcendent-immanent Self. As we have seen, this is precisely how Assagioli thought of "I" and Self:

> The reflection ["I"] appears to be self-existent but has, in reality, no autonomous substantiality. It is, in other words, not a new and different light but a projection of its luminous source [Self]. (Assagioli 1965, 20)

"I" is therefore what can be called an image of Self, or an image of God, the *imago Dei*. The individual transcendent-immanent "I" is a reflection of a Universal Transcendent-Immanent "I am that I am."

> *And God created humankind in his image*
> —Genesis 3:27

> *Your Self is a copy made in the image of God.*
> —Jalalud-din Rumi, Sufi

Thus, human being is no more a spirit clothed with a psyche-soma than the Divine is a Universal Spirit clothed with the Universe. Rather, both are in but not of mass, energy, space, and time—in other words, transcendent-immanent.

So transcendence-immanence allows one to see through any materialistic conceptions of human being, as well as through any dualistic notions of human being. It further allows us to see into and through individual human being to the Source—Being. The following chapter comprises a careful look at both "I" and Self, given this understanding of transcendence-immanence.

*This unity of transcendence and immanence*
*is the mystery of mysteries.*
—Thomas Merton

# CHAPTER FIVE

# The Idealization of "I" and Self

*For many years I thought I was centered when
I was able to achieve a spiritual, flowing, idealistic state of
consciousness. I thought I had identified with my personal self
and even my Transpersonal Self. When I was into this state,
I felt a gap between the usual, daily me and this higher me.*
—"Ron," Graduate Student in Eastern Philosophy

The notion of transcendence-immanence serves to shed light on the nature of "I" and of disidentification. In doing so, it illuminates as well the difficulties created by the dualistic strain in psychosynthesis thought.

Primary among these difficulties are the idealization of "I" and Self, and the subsequent dissociation of "I" and Self from the unity of person and world. This chapter is an exploration of these idealizations and some of their effects on psychosynthesis theory.

## Idealization of Disidentification

Assagioli's dualistic "I *am not*" formulation of the disidentification experience is directly related to the idealization of disidentification and "I" in psychosynthesis.

One may unwittingly fall into this idealization simply by reading statements touting the benefits of the disidentification experience, such as this one by Assagioli:

> One can then—*at will*, and at any moment—disidentify from any overpowering emotion, annoying thought, inappropriate role, etc., and from the vantage point of the detached observer gain a clearer understanding of the situation, its meaning, its causes, and the most effective way to deal with it. (Assagioli 1973, 216, emphasis in original)

Assagioli's description may hold true for one particular person's disidentification experience at one specific point in time, and this statement does perhaps outline a very generalized though highly hypothetical direction of an increased realization of "I." But to confuse this generalized ideal state with the actual here-and-now experience of disidentification is misleading.

Disidentification may not in any way involve this ideal experience. Quite the contrary, it may involve a *more acute realization* that one is lost in an overpowering emotion, a *greater* feeling of helplessness vis-à-vis an annoying thought, and an *increased* confusion about what one is experiencing. These may be experiences from which we have been protected by a former secure identification, and now with disidentification, we begin to feel these things which were always present, though unconscious. In other words, increased transcendence means ipso facto increased immanence.

For example, consider the experience of a person with an analytical-thinking identification as described in "Observing vs. Thinking" in chapter 3. As she or he begins to experience disidentification from analytical thinking, the repressed feelings may begin to enter directly into awareness for the first time. Such a disidentification thus might initially be confusing and anxiety-provoking, as the emerging feelings disrupt the dissociated calm of the former identification.

In addition, these newly-discovered feelings may belong to one's inner child of the past who is carrying the helplessness, wounds, and anxiety of early childhood. Disidentification from the analytic mode would then involve an experienced loss of self-reliant control, as one opened to the hidden wounds of the past.

And deep in the experience of these wounds, one's disidentification experience may mean simply the ability to know oneself as distinct, but not separate, from overwhelming dependency and helplessness; and the experience of one's will may deepen to become a profound existential acceptance of this depth of human weakness.

At the very bottom of such abyss experiences, there is at times a strength of faith which allows even the experience of self-consciousness and will to disappear, as a person moves through the experience of *non-being* to a fuller experience of Being. Transcendence-immanence therefore implies not an escape from the suffering involved in experiences of psychological disintegration, but rather an ability to enter into them fully and to emerge on the other side.

So disidentification properly practiced opens us not only to a stable sense of identity and inner freedom, but to those layers of the psyche in which we are most wounded, most helpless. And because we are in but not of our wholeness and brokenness, disidentification may easily find us fully experiencing the latter as well as the former.

The point is that in authentic inner observation we do not attempt to control our experience, but merely seek to observe and be present to it—we cannot even demand that we *feel* disidentified when we experience disidentification! Rather, we must simply empty ourselves, let go of all expectations, and open to the truth of our inner world, for better or worse. And this letting go, a function of our distinctness from all content, means we become radically open to any and all experience—we discover our transcendence-immanence as "I"s.

## Identification with "Disidentification"

If we confuse disidentification with a particular mode of consciousness, such as that elaborated in Assagioli's description in the section above, we are not disidentifying at all, but instead *identifying with that particular mode of consciousness.* It is at this moment that disidentification becomes an attachment and belief rather than a lived experience. Here the seed of inflation and dissociation is planted.

To confuse any idealized state—indeed any state—with the here-and-now experience of disidentification can lead to our identifying with that experience as *the real me.* And what is lost is "I," experiencing whatever is actually taking place in the inner and outer worlds, for better or worse. Here we might paraphrase Lao Tzu (1968, 57)—" The name that can be named is not the constant name"—in the following way: "The disidentified state which can be named is not the true and constant disidentified state."

Here is Joseph Goldstein, a contemporary Western Buddhist teacher, describing nicely this radical disidentified openness to all experience:

> Mindfulness is an openness of mind to every part of ourselves, to the pleasure and the pain—to "the ten thousand joys and the ten thousand sorrows"—a willingness to experience all the different kinds of emotions and thoughts and sensations. (Goldstein 1988, 31)

If we do attach to a particularly meaningful experience of disidentification—whether freedom, or joy, or centeredness—we may in time form a "disidentified" identification. Like all other identifications, this dissociates us from any experience which is not coherent with the identification—in this case, any experience which seems "un-disidentified," such as feelings of helplessness or dependency, of compulsivity or pain.

For example, I may here become disdainful of what I call my Victim Subpersonality, an aspect of my personality which is not "centered, responsible, and disidentified." But as we have seen, if I *actually* experience disidentification, I may expand beyond my "centeredness" and begin to feel this helpless, lost, dependent part of myself *even more acutely.*

As practitioners of meditation and contemplation tell us, these practices properly applied are not avenues of escape, but lead one towards an openness to the reality of who and where we are—in other words, of disidentification. The psychotherapist James Finley says, "The contemplative attitude involves a weakening of one's defense mechanisms, not a strengthening of them" (1988). This is similar to Engler's statement that insight meditation functions in some ways like an "uncovering technique," as found in psychodynamic therapies (Engler 1986, 34).

But there is a still more advanced stage in the "disidentified" identification. Instead of becoming attached to a particularly profound or enjoyable experience of disidentification, we may attach to remaining beyond any and all contents of experience whatsoever. Here we attach to "contentlessness," and consider all experience—and the world itself—as illusory. Hui-Neng, the sixth patriarch of Zen, warns us about just such an "attachment to the void":

> In conversation with others, externally be detached from phenomena in the midst of phenomena; internally be detached from the void in the midst of the void. If you are entirely attached to the phenomenal, you would fall into perverted views. On the other hand, if you are entirely attached to the void, you would only sink deeper into your ignorance. (Hui-Neng 1975, 89)

Such attachment to the void involves the belief that, "I am not my experience of content and process" (that is, the "I *am not*" formulation), rather than, "I am distinct but not separate from my experience of content and process." The former is an over-emphasis on transcendence and an ignoring of immanence.

Such an imbalance in meditation may cause the practitioner to become fixated unknowingly at one level of experiencing, unable to move into new depths. Here one may sit in inner stillness, allowing all positive and negative contents of experience, and yet remain distant from the conditioning roots of that experience. One becomes subtly cut off from the deeper reaches of immanent being in the world; from plumbing the depths of childhood and one's family system; and from the possibility of working with this material.

Of course, this attachment to non-attachment can be very seductive, as this helps form the defense of dualistic denial. I can convince myself that I am somehow transcendent of my past conditioning and family system, and need not concern myself in an ongoing way with those types of painful issues—after all, "I am not that; I am pure self-consciousness and will."

But if we are to be truly disidentified and open to all we are—in immanence as well as transcendence—there must be an openness to the reality of our childhood wounding, and a grappling with how this affects our daily lives. Otherwise, our meditation practice leads us towards becoming attached to the void. For example, here is Jacob Barrington (a pseudonym), a Buddhist priest who entered Al-Anon, a 12-Step program for those affected by alcoholism:

> In the two years since I joined Al-Anon I've experienced more healing and personal transformation than in my 17 years of pre-Al-Anon Zen practice.... In all my years of sitting zazen, I got pretty good at forgetting the self, at letting go. Pleasant and painful memories, fear, nostalgia, anger, resentment, joy, worry, delight, jealousy, longing, sadness, would all arise in my mind as I sat, and I let them go with the greatest of ease. They didn't matter, I knew. They were only illusions. Ironically (and not coincidentally), however, this was exactly the message I had received from my parents growing up—that what I felt and thought and wanted didn't really matter. What I was doing in meditation wasn't letting go at all, it was repeating the denial I had learned as a child—and denial of my real self was the root of my sickness. (Barrington 1988, 44–46)

Note that Barrington considered the contents of his experience to be "illusions"—a strong indication of dualistic denial. Here the reality of content and process—the experience of immanence—is denied, as self is thought to be transcendent only. But again, we are so very transcendent that our immanence potentially extends to all our past history; therefore, as our experience of "I" deepens, we may ultimately need to be open to ancient wounds in our sense of identity. This encounter with the past (whether in or out of therapy) is especially true as one moves into conscious relationship with Self—that Being who is, as we shall see, immanent throughout our *entire* life experience.

So our ability to disidentify is quite the opposite of affirmation or dissociation, and will take us deeply into the roots and branches of our here-and-now experience. It is an ability to open to our depths as well as our heights, in a faithful letting go of the need to control. Furthermore, disidentification is far more than a technique or practice; it is an experience of our transcendence-immanence, a realization of "I."

## The Idealization of Self

One of the effects of the idealization of disidentification and "I" is that it may in turn lead to an idealization of Self. The reason for this is that, as we have noted, "I" is thought to be a reflection or projection of this deeper source of being, Self. Indeed, the "I"-experience is but a foreshadowing of the Self-experience:

> The experience of the point of self-awareness on the personality level is the first step toward the experience of the Self, or in existential terms, the essence of Being. (Assagioli 1965, 113)

Furthermore, the path of Self-realization comprises the lived ongoing relationship between "I" and Self, in which there is an increasingly conscious communion, and perhaps at times union, between "I" and this source of its existence.

Obviously then, if our notions of disidentification and "I" become idealized and dualistic, so too will our notions of Self. If the I-experience is the first step towards the Self-experience, then the inflation of "I" is but the first step into an even greater inflation in Self-realization.

When we think of "I" as some sort of disembodied otherworldly essence ("I *am not*"), then its source, Self, must logically be a blissfully transcendent being beyond the mundane vicissitudes of our daily lives. Here are statements in the psychosynthesis literature which illustrate this idealization of Self:

> ...the state of consciousness of the Self-realized individual...is a state of consciousness characterized by joy, serenity, inner security, a sense of calm power, clear understanding, and radiant love. (Assagioli 1977, 171)

> The Self, indeed, seems to be living in timelessness and freedom, beyond all problems and separations. (Ferrucci 1982, 159)

> When we transcend our everyday behavior and have a peak experience we are identified with the Higher Self. Peak moments occur for many when they are out in nature and experience a connectedness with all life around them. Others experience peaks when everything functions perfectly in performing a task: it seems that there is a natural knowing of exactly what to do at each moment and all decisions and moves are correct. (D. Russell 1982, 69)

> I was led in a meditation and inducted into a higher state of consciousness where I not only met, it was like I already was, my Higher Self. I felt like none of my cells were together...it was almost like there was so much space in my beingness that I felt like music. I felt more like the songs. I just felt light. I felt resonant. I was with a spiritual Presence and it was very profound. (King 1989, 50)

> As a result we achieve complete identification *as* the Self, and the realization of *Being*. The energy of the Self then pervades the remaining parts of our personality that still oppose it, transforming them, and integrating them with the rest into a harmonious, unified whole which becomes our willing instrument of expression in the world. (Firman and Vargiu 1977, 105)

Such statements confuse Self with the experience of spiritual or sublime qualities in peak experiences, for example, joy, freedom, connectedness, and light (qualities of the superconscious). The Firman and Vargiu quotation confuses Self not so much with superconscious qualities, as with the expression of such qualities in the world via an integrated personality.

But all of these quotations present us with a vision of Self as some wonderfully blissful entity who lives in another transcendent realm. And we are portrayed either as leaving mundane reality in order to reach up to this heavenly realm, or as experiencing this heaven as it forges our mundane realm into harmony and unity. But either way, dualism is rampant.

To claim that the above statements represent the *experience* of Self, is similar to saying, "Happiness is my true self, and sadness is my false self," or "Only when I am beyond problems am I my true self." But the fact is that you are "you" whether happy or sad; whether in the thick of problems or not; whether on a peak or in an abyss.

As we have seen, disidentification, a realization of transcendent-immanent "I," does not necessarily imply some sort of centered contentment. Quite the contrary, it may just as easily lead to the uncovering of hidden painful experiences. Ergo, since transcendent-immanent "I" is a reflection of transcendent-immanent Self, it follows that Self-realization does not necessarily imply bliss or joy either.

Self, like "I," is not to be associated with any particular state of consciousness at all. Self is transcendent of any state of consciousness, and therefore can be immanent in any and all states—Self can experience bliss or agony, unity or disintegration.

None of the quotations above acknowledge that an experience of Self may easily involve plunging into anxiety or isolation. Self is pictured as somehow above all such suffering. However, transcendent-immanent Self would very much experience such broken aspects of human life. In fact, our experience of isolation and pain may not mean we have distanced from Self at all, but quite the contrary, that we are joining Self in a radical openness to the depths of human suffering.

## The Broken Egg

Probably the most obvious example of the dissociative idealization of Self in psychosynthesis can be seen in Assagioli's fundamental oval-shaped diagram of the psyche, often referred to as the *Egg Diagram* (Assagioli 1965, 17; Assagioli 1973, 14):

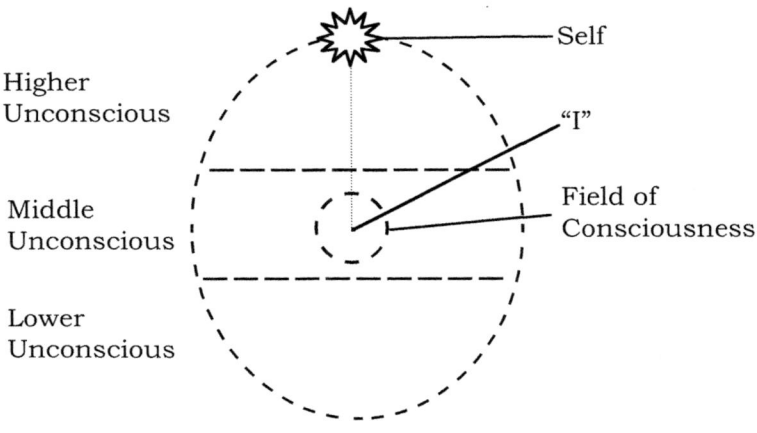

*Figure 5.1*

The Egg Diagram illustrates Self as existing in only one particular stratum of the psyche—the higher unconscious or superconscious. According to Assagioli, this particular area is the realm of phenomena such as "contemplation, illumination, and ecstasy" (Assagioli 1965, 17–18), and he states explicitly that, "the Transpersonal Self... operates from the superconscious levels of the psyche" (Assagioli 1973, 113).

However, this portrayal of Self makes it appear to be far removed from the lower unconscious, the realm of "phobias, obsessions, and compulsive urges" (Assagioli 1965, 17). This is a psychic stratum associated with childhood, and thus is the appropriate material for psychoanalytic technique (21).

Placing Self in the higher unconscious indicates a splitting of higher and lower unconscious in psychosynthesis thought and practice, with a strong propensity to give much less attention to the lower conscious.

*A veil exists between the world above
and the realms that are below; and shadow
came into being beneath the veil;
and that shadow became matter.*
—Gnostic Text

Thus, as Will Friedman (1984) and others have pointed out, psychosynthesis theory has been largely isolated from the continuing developments in psychoanalytic thought. But more than this, the theory has until very recently failed to grapple with the depth of human pain and brokenness as seen in serious mental illness, childhood abuse, and addictions, for example. To my knowledge, even today there are no fully developed psychosynthesis theories of the personality disorders, neuroses and psychoses, or even of early childhood development.[11]

But the portrayal of Self as remote from the lower unconscious confuses transcendence with "far away." Self is thought of as transcendent in the sense of, "It's way up there in the higher unconscious."

And from the point of view of "I," what then is Self-realization but an otherworldly journey into the superconscious? The notion of Self-realization becomes dominated by the image of a climb up the vertical dotted line on the Egg Diagram, "I" ascending to Self:

What has to be achieved is to expand the personal consciousness into that of the Self; to reach up, following the thread or ray to the star...(Assagioli 1965, 24)

Such images support the idea that Self-realization is a journey into the superconscious, when in fact it may be—even more so—a journey into the brokenness of childhood and the lower unconscious. This notion of Self-realization can thus become tantamount to dualistic denial.

## Self of Abyss, Plain, and Peak

However, Self need not be idealized, and we can see Self as simply a more profound transcendence-immanence than "I." Just as "I" can experience distinct-but-not-separateness from the flow of immediate experience, so Self can be thought of as experiencing distinct-but-not-separateness from *any and all content and layers of the psyche.* This distinctness would allow Self to experience immanence throughout the *entire* psyche-soma, rather than to be stored safely away in the superconscious.

Here is psychosynthesis psychotherapist and teacher Martha Crampton approaching this insight:

> An interesting point is that as the individual's field of consciousness expands more into the "heights," he or she is thereby enabled to descend further into the "depths," when there is a need to do so. (Crampton 1981, 714)

This ability to include the heights as well as the depths points to a Self who is transcendent of both of these, and therefore able to be fully immanent in them both. (As Frank Haronian pointed out to me, Martha Crampton's statement might even be strengthened to read that at many points in Self-realization, awareness of the heights leads *inexorably* to awareness of the depths and vice versa—see the discussion of "induction" in appendix 3.)

The Jewish tradition contains a similar insight, as the psalmist sings to God:

> If I go up to the heavens, you are there;
> If I sink to the nether world, you are present there.
>
> (Psalm 139)

Assagioli himself, although perhaps unknowingly, also approaches the insight that Self exists fully in the abyss of non-being as well as on the peaks of being. He does so when he acknowledges the image of Christ as an appropriate symbol of Self:

> Of the personified symbols of the spiritual Self, that of the Inner Christ ... (Assagioli 1965, 206)

If, as Assagioli believes (and Jung as well), the Christ-image can symbolize Self, then Self does indeed embrace the depths as well as the heights—for that is precisely what is embodied in the symbol of Christ. For the Christian, Christ is God not only of joyful resurrection, but of painful crucifixion as well; the two experiences are indissolubly linked in the person of Jesus Christ.

> *God became a human being, a baby.*
> *God was hungry. God was tired.*
> *God suffered and died. God is there with us.*
> —Archbishop Desmond Tutu

So in psychosynthesis, we need not think that Self is "up there" in the heaven of the higher unconscious. Nor is it helpful to think of the higher unconscious as transcendent. *Self* is transcendent and so may be immanent anywhere, any time, within the psyche-soma. One cannot assume an exclusive link between Self and one or another specific type of experience. In this sense, Self is not only at the top of the Egg Diagram, but in the middle and in the bottom as well.

Transcendence-immanence implies therefore that Self is all-conscious, is omniscient. That is, the levels of the unconscious outlined by the Egg Diagram are relative to "I" only, and not to Self. These levels represent contents of which "I"—not Self—is unaware.

Therefore, oddly enough, *transcendent-immanent Self has no unconscious.* This is because transcendent-immanent Self would be conscious of all the different levels at the same time. The term *unconscious* then denotes areas of consciousness which are so vast or complex that "I" cannot remain self-conscious in relation to them; the individual experience of self-consciousness and will is simply overwhelmed and lost in such immense awareness. Only Self has the intensity of transcendence-immanence to remain self-conscious and willing within such all-encompassing awareness.

Self can therefore be thought of as ever-present and potentially active whether one is experiencing a traumatic memory from the lower unconscious, a peak experience in the higher unconscious, or a combination of the two. Self is always there.

But as we shall see shortly, even more to the point is that Self is completely present in every daily minute-to-minute event of our lives. Self is not a far-off mysterious presence we only glimpse in peaks and abysses. Self is immanent in every second of our lives, and conscious contact with Self is therefore potential every moment.

Let us note carefully, however, that this immanence of Self throughout the psyche-soma is not to be confused with the idea that Self *is* the totality of psychosomatic contents—this would be an attempt to cure dualism with monism. Rather, Self as transcendent-immanent is in, but not of, all such contents.

In spite of the position of Self at the top of the Egg Diagram, we can understand that Self-realization is not simply a matter of attaining spiritual experiences; it is not a mere ascent into the superconscious, an activity which can be just as narrow and ego-serving as any other.

Neither is Self-realization a linear process in which one first works out neurotic issues of the past and lower unconscious; then proceeds to the more existential issues of the present and middle unconscious; and only then finally attains the illumination of the higher unconscious.

Such simple linearity ignores the fact that Self is ever-present. It is not that we work through our childhood trauma and only then finally attain Self-realization. Self is always present, and indeed, one may actually at times have a deeper relationship to Self while facing the pain of a traumatic childhood memory, rather than the joy of the superconscious.

So we are not implying here a propensity in Self for either agony or ecstasy, higher or lower, sublime or mundane. We are simply positing that the transcendence-immanence of Self means that Self-realization may involve either, neither, or both, of these poles at any time. Self-realization is not linked to any particular state of consciousness at all, and so is open to any and all of them.

If Self is immanent throughout the psyche-soma, then a living ongoing relationship with Self may take one into any and all levels of psychosomatic experience. Thus Self-realization asks of us a breathtaking openness to any and all possible life experiences, depending on where our relationship to Self leads us.

Such openness of course implies a letting go of all attempts to control Self-realization, whether by ascent into the superconscious; attaining some sort of absolute disidentification; doing good deeds in service of others; gaining esoteric knowledge and experience; or seeking powerful cathartic lower unconscious experiences.

Self-realization implies an openness and responsiveness to the minute-by-minute vocation or "call" of a greater will (see Assagioli 1973, 114–15). And a faithful following of such a call might just lead one into an experience of any layer of the psyche at all—not to mention into any life adventure at all!

Thus, among other things, the notion of Self as transcendent-immanent reveals that we must surrender our attempts to control Self-realization. We may here give up the desperate struggle to grab an "ideal" Self, and simply begin relating to Self in our daily lives, referring all our thoughts and actions to this Deeper Source.

## Idealization and Unity

Perhaps the Self-idealization most closely connected to psycho-synthesis conceptually, is the idea that the experience of unity or wholeness is intrinsic to Self-realization. As we have seen however, transcendence-immanence is distinct from wholeness or unity, so transcendent-immanent Self must be distinct from these as well. This distinctness from unity accounts for the fact that Self, along with "I," can be completely present in the utmost depths of fragmentation, as well as in unitive experiences.

Thus any concept of Self as connected necessarily to unity or wholeness constitutes an idealization of Self. Once again I can use my own words to illustrate a Self-idealization which makes use of the concept of unity:

> As a result we achieve complete identification *as* the Self, and the realization of *Being*. The energy of the Self then pervades the remaining parts of our personality that still oppose it, transforming them, and integrating them with the rest into a harmonious, unified whole which becomes our willing instrument of expression in the world. (Firman and Vargiu 1980, 105)

And joining Vargiu and myself in this Self-idealization is Ferrucci:

> But as we move toward the Self, unity replaces multiplicity. The psychological life becomes harmonized as the diversity of its parts fuses into a synthesis. (Ferrucci 1982, 134)

But as we have seen in our study of "I," realizing deeper identity may just as easily entail experiencing more fragmentation, as it may entail experiencing more wholeness. And if "I" is distinct from any disintegration/integration of parts, this would seem to hold true for the source of "I" as well. Self too, then, can be understood as distinct from any multiplicity-unity continuum, and as potentially present at any point on such a continuum.

For example, some of the most profound moments of Self-realization may occur deep in the fragmentation and chaos of life transitions, far from any sense of a "unified whole" or a fusion into a synthesis. Often it is in these very times of "hitting bottom," when the habitual patterns of our lives disintegrate, that space is created for a deeper communion with Self. Such a "dark night of the soul" (see St. John of the Cross, 1979), can lead to a profoundly transformed life, one lived at a deeper level of meaning than ever before.

Self-realization may also involve a distancing from, or conflict with, relationships which are revealed as unhealthy and/or abusive in the light of deeper insight. Here is that peaceful man, Jesus:

> "Do not suppose that my mission on earth is to spread peace. My mission is to spread, not peace, but division. I have come to set a man at odds with his father, a daughter with her mother, a daughter-in-law with her mother-in-law: in short, to make a man's enemies those of his own household." (Matthew 10:34)

Such division is precisely what many experience in Self-realization today. As we begin to address the wounding received from dysfunctional families and social systems, we often find ourselves at odds with those systems. On their part, the systems may seek to maintain the pretense of health by invoking an idealization of themselves, a facade of peaceful unity which masks dysfunction and injustice. But Self-realization will often involve recognizing the evils of the system, a "breaking silence" about it, and if the system does not change, facing the necessary division and conflict prophesied by Jesus in the quotation above.

Furthermore, ongoing Self-realization need not necessarily involve a healing of our personal psychological and spiritual brokenness. We may not in this process necessarily attain a harmonious integration of our personalities. From the point of view of Self, healing may not in some cases mean the knitting up of our wounds, but instead learning to live authentic lives with severe unhealed fragmentation and wounding. Self-realization does not necessarily imply personal integration and self-actualization.

As we have said too, neither then is Self to be understood as a union of opposites, whether the opposites are height-depth, yin-yang, or masculine-feminine, or any other *coincidentia oppositorum*. Like "I," Self is One—transcendent of any multiplicity, whether duality, triplicity, quaternity, or more. Self is distinct but not separate from opposites, and too, from a union of them in which "the sum is greater than its parts." Self is not *more than* anything. Self is no-thing, and so can be immanent in any thing.

So Self is not to be confused with Jung's "all-embracing totality" (1979, 223), that is, with the uroboros (see chapter 4). Self is not that primitive unity imputed to infancy, that undifferentiated "oceanic feeling" (Freud 1961, 11–12) or *"participation mystique"* (Jung 1969a, 221n) in which there is little or no awareness of self–other distinctions. Such a primitive undifferentiated unity is not a unity at all, because at the very least it excludes the experience of I-amness. (By the way, such a unity seems *not* a characteristic of infancy.[12])

Having said all of this about the concept of unity however, let us remember that unity vis-à-vis Self is only an idealization when this unity does not include fragmentation and conflict *as well as* wholeness and harmony.

But a unity which includes fragmentation as well as whole-ness would not imply the usual harmonious synthesis of parts; it would refer instead to Self's ability to be immanent in any type of experience, whether that experience is of brokenness or of wholeness. In such a unity, individual elements are not unified by virtue of coming together (although they may come together as a by-product), but are unified insofar as each has a direct relation-ship with the same, one, Self.

> He is one and he dispenses his oneness
> to every part of the universe as well as to its totality,
> to the single as well as to the multiple.
> —Pseudo-Dionysius

There is more thinking to be done along these lines in psycho-synthesis, because most often synthesis is thought to imply parts coming together into a harmonious whole. But the thrust of our current study is precisely that psychosynthesis, at least in terms of Self-realization, may not involve parts coming together in this way at all.

Perhaps the term *psycho-synthesis* can be thought to denote the process of synthesis or union based upon a relationship to Self, with no necessary implication of specific psychological or social unification at all. Again, it is the personal I-Self relationship here which is forefront. One may tread the way of disintegration or wholeness at different times in Self-realization—it all depends on where the relationship leads.

We may think of psychosynthesis then, as the process by which we develop an ongoing relationship and at times commu-nion with Self. This relationship with Self may in turn at times allow the experience of union or connection with all things— whether or not we and those things are fragmented or whole, in harmony or conflict.

Thus, this union is not a far-off goal at the end of an evolution-ary process which will establish a harmonious planetary or cosmic synthesis. This is a type of union which exists *now*, right in the midst of current personal and world crises.[13]

## Idealization and Timelessness

Self-idealization rears its head too when we believe that Self lives in timelessness while the personality lives in time. This is a dualistic splitting of reality into realms of time and timelessness (perhaps indicating an underlying conceptual split between immanence and transcendence). But just as it is meaningless to think of "I" as in any way separate from spacetime, so too with Self.

Self can be thought of as an example of Globus' "analytical singularity" (1980, 418–19), which does not require two domains, but only one (see appendix 2). Self does not live in a timeless world, set over against the world of time. Self is eternal, in but not of time, and so is utterly present in the spacetime of this world.

As we saw above, the eternity of "I" means a continuity and action within the flow of personal time. Thus, the eternity of deeper Self logically means continuity and action within an even *greater* span of time.

An eternal Self would not exist in another, timeless realm, but quite the contrary, within a much *broader* time-span than that experienced by "I." Thus for example, Self can be thought to be somehow conscious and willing within our lives as a whole, as if the phenomenological world of Self comprises all the events in our lives at the same moment.

Omnipresent, immanent in our lives by virtue of transcendence, Self is nevertheless distinct from this totality of our lifetime—as we saw earlier, this is not the timelessness of the uroboros, that timelessness created when all time is collected into a totality. The timelessness of Self is eternal, transcendent-immanent. That is, it is a timelessness distinct from any notion of time or no-time.

This eternal presence of Self helps account for Assagioli's equating the will of Self with a direction or vocation operating throughout one's entire life (see Assagioli 1973, 113–15). By virtue of this *transpersonal will*, Self can be ever-present throughout life, inviting us into deeper experiences of being at each step on the way, guiding us more and more in finding our unique contributions to the world at large.

As such, Self could not then be conveniently tucked away in the compartments of special times and special places, divorced from our daily lives. Rather, here is the potential to relate to Self every second of our day, no matter how boring, irritating, or mundane our day may be.

Here we find the advice to practice *mindfulness* as a way of life, or St. Paul's admonition never to cease praying. Brother Lawrence, in the seventeenth century, was known for what he called "the practice of the presence of God":

> The time of business... is no different from the time of prayer. I possess God as tranquilly in the noise and clatter of my kitchen, where sometimes several people ask me different things at the same time, as if I were on my knees before the Blessed Sacrament. (Brother Lawrence 1985, 145)

So there is a potential I-Self relationship throughout the spacetime of our entire lives. The most common daily choices, from how to use our money and leisure, to where to live and what to wear, can be the stuff of our ongoing dialogue with Self. This is not to say that one need consult Self for advice and permission in every second of the day, but that there is no human experience, however seemingly mundane or insignificant, in which there cannot be a meaningful relationship with Self. There is no compartment of spacetime in our lives which is "out of bounds" for Self.

The transcendence-immanence of Self in spacetime means too that Self is not limited to our own private inner worlds. Rather, we may look for Self reaching to us through other people and in the events of our lives. A chance word from a friend may ring true to our depths, giving us the answer to a problem with which we have been struggling. Or we may find ourselves happening upon a book or person at just the right time to guide us through the next step on our journey. We need not only close our eyes in meditation to contact Self; we may also open our eyes, and open them wide, to the rich matrix of relationship around us.

In short, Self's more intense experience of transcendence vis-à-vis time means a greater experience of immanence within time. Again we see how transcendence and immanence are but two sides of the same coin. This more intense transcendence-immanence does not imply another timeless world at all, but quite the contrary, that *Self is even more present in our world than we experience ourselves to be.*

# CHAPTER SIX

# Transcending the Levels
# of Consciousness

*Just as there is a personal will ... so there is a*
*Transpersonal Will. ... It is its action which is felt*
*by the personal self, or "I," as a "pull" or "call."*
—Roberto Assagioli

With the concept of "I" and Self as transcendent-immanent, it becomes clear that they and their relationship are distinct but not separate from all states of consciousness—whether painful or pleasant, mundane or sublime, boring or ecstatic. This understanding can therefore assist us in becoming more present to ourselves and others throughout all the tremendously varied vicissitudes of life experience.

However, when we actually encounter the wide range of the many types of consciousness in ourselves or others, it can be confusing at times to sort out where "I" and Self are in all of this. One may even be led into equating Self with higher states of consciousness and "I" with lower states, and then into thinking of Self-realization as a matter of moving up from lower to higher states of consciousness.

In this chapter, we will attempt to show how the I-Self relationship can be distinguished from all the many changing human experiences, all the many levels of consciousness, whether the lowest or the highest. As a part of this, we shall also critique the idea that Self is a totality or whole whose substance has differentiated or emanated to form these various levels of consciousness.

## Maslow's Experience

We can begin by examining the nature of those experiences most frequently called transcendent, namely, *peak experiences*. As an example of such, we will take a personal peak experience reported by Abraham Maslow himself, the originator of the term. Note that in describing this experience, Maslow uses the terms, "transcendence," "infinity," and "eternity" in ways at variance with our usage.

> *Transcendence* of time. For example, my experience of being bored in an academic procession and feeling slightly ridiculous in cap and gown, and suddenly slipping over into being a symbol under the aspect of *eternity* rather than just a bored and irritated individual in the moment and in the specific place. My vision or imagining was that the academic procession stretched way, way out into the future, far, far away, further than I could see, and it had Socrates at its head, and the implication was, I suppose, that many of the people far ahead had been there and in previous generations, and that I was a successor and follower of all the great academics and professors and intellectuals. Then the vision was also of the procession stretching out behind me into a dim, hazy *infinity* where there were people not yet born who would join the academic procession... (Maslow 1971, 269–70, emphasis added)

This experience, though apparently comparatively short and not tremendously overwhelming, has characteristics of many altered states of awareness encountered in peak, unitive, and mystical experiences (in psychosynthesis terms, this is a clear experience of the higher unconscious or superconscious). There is here an expanded experience of time and space, as one uncovers a surprising depth of meaning behind the immediate mundane moment.

In variance with our use of the term, Maslow calls this experience "transcendence," meaning in fact, beyond one's usual space-time experience. He also uses "eternity" and "infinity" here to

mean perhaps, unending time and endless space. All these meanings do not carry the notion of distinctness from spacetime, but
simply imply an expanded view of spacetime.

One may in peak experiences even experience a vision of all
mass, energy, space, and time—the entire cosmos—at a glance.
This state has been mentioned by many (for example, Bucke 1967;
Jung 1963; Maslow 1971) and can be called *cosmic consciousness*. In speaking of cosmic consciousness, Maslow states, again
in variance with our usage, "The ultimate limit here is the holistic
perceiving of the cosmos as a unity. This is the ultimate transcendence..." (Maslow 1971, 274). And elsewhere, in describing his
notion of transcendence:

> Also useful would be Bucke's use of cosmic conscious-
> ness. This is a special phenomenological state in which
> the person somehow perceives the whole cosmos or at
> least the unity and integration of it and everything in
> it, including his Self. (277)

Too, here is William Blake's description of such a unitive experience:

> To see a World in a Grain of Sand,
> And a Heaven in a Wild Flower,
> Hold Infinity in the palm of your hand,
> And Eternity in an hour.
>
> ("Auguries of Innocence")

But none of the above has to do with transcendence, eternity, or infinity as we have been thinking of them here. We are
reserving these terms not for contents of experience or states of
consciousness, cosmic or not, but for the *subject who experiences these*.

However valuable such peak experiences are, they can be
confusing, and can challenge us in tracking our sense of identity
or that of another person. For example, I might identify with the
vision, mistaking it for myself—"Who I really am is this transcendent self, and this mundane life is not as real."

Upon so valuing this higher state of consciousness, I may then begin to devote much time and effort to keeping it alive—it is my true self—until finally I may begin to minimize the importance of more mundane human existence, with its daily routine, interpersonal struggles, and so forth. (Such an attempt at apparent enlightenment can lead to dualistic denial and to the *crisis of duality*. See Firman and Vargiu 1980, 108-09.)

Conversely, there may be quite an opposite identity confusion in such peak experiences. Instead of feeling a pleasant expansion, one might become anxious in the face of such overwhelming grandeur. Being caught up in such a vision might seem to threaten one's identity and ability to function. Here there can be a devaluation not of the mundane experience of spacetime, but of the expanded state.

One might in this second case re-identify with the safety of daily routine, and attempt to repress the greater vision—"That was strange; hope I'm not going crazy." (Such an overall orientation in growth can lead eventually to the *crisis of meaning*. See Firman and Vargiu 1980, 99-102)

But in both attraction and repulsion to peak experiences, there is a split between a transcendence" up there" and an immanence "down here." Whether we are attracted to one or the other, there is still here a duality, an implicit splitting of identity between these two states. In Maslow's experience of the procession, he might wonder for example, "Am I really a symbol under eternity, or am I really this bored irritated professor? Who am I?"

## Staying Present to "I"

However, if we apply the notion of transcendence-immanence to Maslow's experience of the "universal" academic procession, we can stay with "I," that is, we can keep our focus on the living, willing person named Abraham Maslow. First, Maslow's term for his experience, "transcendence of time," would not be used at all. The experience would not be seen as transcendent, but as an experience of expanded spacetime.

And we know that transcendence-immanence involves a distinction but not separation from spacetime, so "I" must here be distinct but not separate from *both* the boring experience *and* the expanded state. It thus becomes clear that Maslow can potentially realize disidentification from both of these experiences.

What we see is that Maslow has simply experienced an expansion of his awareness from a constricted spacetime to a broader spacetime, remaining in but not of either one. Therefore, the shift from his boring moment to the grand vision is no different in its dynamics from an expansion of awareness beyond the sound of the nearby ticking clock to a broader awareness of the traffic noise outside my window, or from a feeling of inverted anger to a feeling of expansive joy—it is an alteration of the contents in the field of awareness.

Furthermore, since "I" is *one*—that is, transcendent of multiplicity—we know there are not two "I"s here, but only one. It is not that I have two selves, one experiencing the boredom and one experiencing the expansion. It is not a question of my lower self and my higher self.

Rather, since I remain *one*, what has happened in this experience is that I have shifted between two different states of consciousness. Furthermore, as I realize this I become more free to respond to the meaning of both experiences; neither one need be devalued or ignored.

If of course I have an idealized notion of Self, I might confuse this greater vision with an experience of Self. Thus, Self becomes "my transcendent Self up there." But experiences such as these need no notion of a greater Self at all. Here "I" is simply shifting between two states of consciousness—"I" is, as it were, merely viewing reality from a valley, and then from a mountain top.

Working with Maslow's experiences of the mundane and the sublime, one might ask in effect, "And who is aware of this shift from the boring experience to the meaningful expanded experience? Who is this 'I' who experienced both these states?" (I am not of course suggesting necessarily the clinical use of this type of specific phraseology, but rather indicating a therapeutic direction.)

Such a line of inquiry would open the opportunity for an increased experience of transcendence-immanence. As one began to experience disidentification from both states of consciousness, one might realize the ability to feel *both* the mundane boredom *and* the exalted perspective at the same time (as well as the pain, perhaps, arising from the dissonance between the two). Too, one might eventually explore new ways of bringing these two dimensions together in the actions of daily living.

And thus we will find "I" right where and when "I" always is—transcendent-immanent, infinite and eternal, in the here and now. I am distinct but not separate from my bored experience in which spacetime seems to crawl, but as well, from my sublime experience in which spacetime expands out to include the cosmos. I am in but not of my level of consciousness, cosmic or otherwise, and I can experience this in the present moment.

## "I" as Distinct from Levels of Consciousness

Again we see the importance of discriminating between "I" and consciousness. One might for example take Maslow's experience and develop a model of levels of consciousness leading from the mundane and boring to the sublime and expansive, and confuse this with the experience of identity, of I-amness. But "I" is *one*, so there are no levels, no dimensions, no multiplicity in "I." There are levels, dimensions, and multiplicity, however, in the psyche-soma, for example, subpersonalities, sensing, feeling, thinking, peak and abyss experiences, and other states of consciousness as well.

Assuming that identity has levels within it is a bit like riding in an elevator and assuming that each floor in the building is a different "you," rather than that the same "you" is simply visiting the different levels. This mistake can lead to the notion that I have a Floor #1 self (or I), a Floor #2 self (or I), a Floor #3 self (or I), and so on, until there is a confusing array of selves or "I"s running about, not to mention that I may begin to prefer a particular floor as the real me and neglect the other floors.

A confusion in theory between identity and consciousness can therefore generate an infinite supply of selves because a self becomes simply any state of consciousness or awareness which I can experience. Thus for example, I can have a body self; an emotional self; a mental self; a centered self; a creative self; an angry self; an eating self; and so on, ad infinitum. And what is hidden by all of this is the question, "Who is the 'self' moving among these different 'selves'? Who is the 'I' moving among these different 'I's?"

One can find this confusion at times subtly slipping into psychosynthesis concepts of identity too, when we say things such as, "When I identify with my 'I,'" or, "When I get in touch with my personal self." But this is a splitting, because here we are left with two important questions: "Who is the 'who' who identifies with 'I'? Who is the 'who' who *has* a personal self?" Are there two "I"s running around here? The psychosynthesis answer is: No, there is only one "I" here, which is moving among different states or alterations of consciousness.

This inviolate oneness of self-reflective being may be a reason why Assagioli and others in psychosynthesis have for the most part reserved the term *self*—whether personal self, Higher Self, or Universal Self—to apply solely to self-conscious being, to identity, to I-amness.

Following this convention, whenever *self* is used in psychosynthesis we can know we are not talking about states of consciousness, but about the one who experiences these. Given the ease with which I-amness is confused with consciousness, one hopes that this usage of *self* remains a firm practice within psychosynthesis.

None of what we have said regarding levels of consciousness should be construed in any way as dismissing work such as that done by Ken Wilber (1977) and others in categorizing different levels of consciousness. It is simply that human being is not to be confused with such states. Even Wilber, who outlines an elaborate "spectrum of consciousness," states:

> Since the Self was both the *ground* of every stage of development and the *goal* of every stage of development, it is perfectly acceptable to say that the Self was present all along, "guiding," "pulling," and "directing" development ... (Wilber 1980, 25)

Self is therefore distinct from such stages or levels, or "Self" could not be "present all along" as a distinct center of volition within the different levels.

Note however that transcendence-immanence means that Self is not some Formless Consciousness or Universal Energy in which all else swims as in an ocean. The presence of Self is not analogous to an ocean which is present in this sea and that sea, a whole which is present in this part and in that part—Self is *not* a whole. It is not that a part of Self fills this level, part that level, and so on—there are no parts to Self.

So Self does not include all the levels as a higher level includes all the lower levels. Self is not the summation of the lower levels, not a unity of the various states of consciousness, not even that "more" as in "more than the sum of the parts." And in turn, the various levels are not multiple parts of Self.

Rather, because Self is transcendent of all such multiplicities, Self can be somehow *completely* immanent within each and every level. Self is transcendent-immanent Being, eternally One, a center distinct from states of consciousness, and thus can be *entirely present and fully active at any level.*

> *God is everywhere and everywhere entire.*
> —Meister Eckhart

And as a reflection of Self, "I" directly participates in this distinctness—that is, the integrity of one's transcendent-immanent oneness remains intact, no matter what "floor" on a spectrum of consciousness one is visiting. "I" and Self, and their relationship, are distinct from any particular state of consciousness.

We need not then view Self as perched atop a ladder of identity, while "I" is down below, separated from Self via these levels. The transcendent-immanent nature of "I" and Self means that the relationship and even union between the two is possible *at whatever level of consciousness one happens to be.* And unless this is kept clear, our notion of human being may be confused and split by such spectrums.

Therefore, while using the notion of levels, one must keep firmly in mind that they form spectrums of *consciousness* or *identification*—they are not to be thought of as spectrums of *being* or *identity.*

## Emanating the "Scale of Being"

In this discussion of levels of consciousness we are discovering the difficulties for psychology in another traditional Neoplatonic-Gnostic notion: *emanation*. This is a concept which can arise whenever we seek to develop a spectrum of consciousness, and one which can have a strong impact on the understanding and praxis of Self-realization. Here too, transcendence-immanence can guide us.

The theory of emanation holds that all being is emanated from God, from the Pleroma, or psychologically, from Self (emanate is from *emanare*, to flow out). Thus, being is seen here as flowing out from God/Self and trickling down through various descending levels of being. This is akin to the common notion in psychology that the ego is a differentiation of the primal unity of self, or even the id.

Here is Stephan Hoeller, a contemporary self-proclaimed Gnostic, from his *Jung and the Lost Gospels:*

> The fullness (*Pleroma*) ["authentic Godhead"] is ... a fullness of being from whence individuality and manifest existence emerge by way of subtraction and not by way of a *creatio ex nihilo* (creation out of nothing). Emanation rather than creation is the law of manifestation, certainly in the realm of the psyche and in all likelihood in the sphere of cosmic manifestation also. The unitary primal nature of the psyche differentiates and descends into ever-deeper conditions of alienation from its original source of light and power. (Hoeller 1989, 112)

(Hoeller refers his readers to the Theosophist H. P. Blavatsky for more on this theory.)[14]

However, if we think of being as emanated down levels in this way, each level implies more or less being, more or less closeness to the "fullness," God, or Self. Here we are faced with the prospect of struggling up through this scale of being in order to attain full being in God—in other words, we need to attain higher levels of consciousness to draw closer to God/Self.

What can happen in this scheme then is that spiritual authority begins to reside in these higher states of consciousness rather than in Self—after all, Self is way up on top, so one must logically embrace higher and higher states in order to "get there." However, here one is not responding necessarily to the will of Self at all, but only to the levels of consciousness higher on the hierarchy.

Higher states of consciousness may or may not have to do with discerning the will of Self. Indeed, these states of consciousness can be a source of what Chogyam Trungpa (1987) called "spiritual materialism," in which spiritual awareness is misunderstood and/ or misused, and so leads one astray, or as Maslow (1971) stated, they can be "traps," the individual "tempted to seek them … and to value them exclusively, as the only, or at the least the highest goods of life …" (344). Placing authority only in one's higher experiences may lead as easily, if not more easily, *away* from Self-realization as towards it.

It also seems to follow from this scale-of-being idea, that those with more consciousness have ipso facto more being and more closeness to God, while those below are less spiritual than the hierarchically superior. Here again we can recognize the roots of gnostic elitism (see "More Conscious Than Thou," in chapter 3).

> *Jesus said, "I shall choose you—*
> *one out of a thousand and two out of ten thousand."*
> —Gnostic Text

In such a hierarchical system, God or Self is distant, sitting at the top of all these many levels of being, and the most holy are those who have climbed into these higher states to be with God. (In such systems, the notion of transcendence seems to be contaminated by a conception of spatiality as "far away.")

However, if human being is transcendent-immanent as we have outlined, it is distinct from these levels of consciousness, and cannot be dependent on them for existence. Transcendent-immanent "I" cannot therefore be a product of these levels, but must be created as a direct reflection of transcendent-immanent Self.

Being does not then, flow down the "waterfalls" of the many levels, but is created by a direct unmediated act of Self—remember, Assagioli's terms are the more immediate "projection" or "reflection" for the creation of "I" by Self. Assagioli seems here in agreement with the thought of Pseudo-Dionysius (or "Denys"), as outlined by Andrew Louth:

> Emanation, in a Neoplatonic sense, is a doctrine about the derivation of *being*: Being derives from the One, but in the stream of emanated beings, each being receives from the one above it ...
> Denys ... rejects any idea that being is (as it were) passed down this scale of being: all beings are created immediately by God. The scale of being and this sense of dependence only has significance in the matter of *illumination*: light and knowledge ... (Louth 1989, 85)

We, with Assagioli and Pseudo-Dionysius, do not reject such a hierarchical scale of consciousness; we simply reject it as a scale of being or identity. Such a scale can only outline levels of insight and "illumination," that is, consciousness.

## The I-Self Relationship

But perhaps the most serious problem with applying the idea of emanation is that it obscures the intimate and profound transcendent-immanent relationship between "I" and Self.

Emanation implies that "I" (for example, Hoeller's "individuality") flows out of the "unitary primal nature of the psyche," and this by "subtraction." Here we have a notion of "I" as a differentiation of a primordial unity, flowing out from Self like a stream flows from a lake, a branch grows from a tree, or a spark escapes from a fire. But there are at least two major difficulties with this idea.

First of all, if a particular emanation approaches its primal source, there is nothing to stop it from again merging into that source and losing its individual uniqueness. A stream, branch, or spark whose substance returns to its source loses its existence as a unique stream, branch, or spark.

Thus, one would need to be careful in approaching a Self which was in fact a psychic totality. Such a *totality-Self* would be equivalent to the entire psyche, that is, at least all the areas mapped by Assagioli's diagram of the psyche (see the Egg Diagram in chapter 5). Thus to unite with a totality-Self would be to unite with all the contents of the psyche—it would be the simultaneous experiencing of childhood rage, infantile memories, spiritual bliss, primary process imagery, and all sensations, emotions, and thought.

Such an experience would be so chaotic and overwhelming that one would not be able to remain self-conscious; one can lose self-consciousness when caught up in simple daydreaming, so how much more so if one were caught up in all possible psychic content and processes at once?

In all prudence then, it seems obvious that we should not completely trust such a totality-Self nor seek profound intimacy with it. It would also seem irresponsible if not actually self-destructive to surrender one's life and will to such an oceanic totality. In other words, the notions of emanation and totality-Self present an image of Self which impedes the development of an intimate I-Self relationship. (We explore this totality-Self concept further as *Abraxas* in appendix 3.)

As we have seen however, transcendent-immanent Self is quite distinct from any such totality of the psyche. Transcendent-immanent Self is Deeper Being, the universal personal "I am who I am" who creates individual personal "I" in Self's image. And since "I" is the reflection of Self, "I" and Self are from this point of view *always* in union. Far from overwhelming individual self-consciousness, this I-Self union is actually the very source of individual self-consciousness itself (we shall return to this point shortly).

A second major problem with the idea that "I" flows out from Self is that we lose any notion of "I" as an actual image of Self. A stream is not an image of the lake; a tree branch is not an image of the tree; a spark is not an image of the fire—each is the outflowing of the "stuff" of its source. But if "I" is a reflection of Self, we can understand "I" not as an outcropping or part of Self, but as an actual image or likeness of Self.

An analogy here might be that Self reflects "I" as a candle flame reflects its image in a mirror. "I" is like this reflected image of the flame, containing a complete representation of the reflecting source—Self—but existing in fewer dimensions.

Following this analogy, Self does not then emanate a part of its own substance to form "I," but instead creates "I," yes, virtually out of nothing (*creatio ex nihilo*). In other words, "I" is kept from immediate non-existence by the abiding creative will of Self.

We can perhaps think of it this way. If we cut off a stream, branch, or spark from their respective sources, they will not immediately cease to exist, but only gradually lose their forms; they have some independent subsistence apart from their sources. But a reflection of a candle flame cut off from the flame will *instantly* lapse into non-existence; as Assagioli said, "The reflection ["I"] appears to be self-existent but has, in reality, *no autonomous substantiality*" (Assagioli 1965, 20, emphasis added).

The notion of created image implies then that "I" is ever directly dependent, ever kept from immediate non-existence, by the creative source of Self. Parts of us may bridle at such dependence, fear this as powerlessness, and feel anxious about the closeness of non-existence, but it does appear that only the will of Self stands between "I" and sudden *nihilo*.

So transcendent-immanent Self is not an uroboric totality out of which "I" flows by subtraction, like a rivulet of primordial substance. "I" is a reflection, a direct, living image of a greater "I am that I am." The *imago Dei* is just that, an *imago*.

## The I-Self Unity

The created *imago* concept of "I" again points us to the nature of the union of "I" and Self—this is the union of image and reflecting source. My image in a mirror, for example, is completely dependent on me, and by this fact it is completely unified with me. But this unity is not a function of my emanating a bit of my substance, a spark of myself, onto the mirror and then reabsorbing this. Rather, it is a unity fundamentally and unalterably present by virtue of the image's dependence on me for its very existence.

Furthermore, unity in this model involves the mapping of my three-dimensional shape onto the two-dimensional mirror; it involves my reflected image acting like me at its own level of existence. So this is a union which does not absorb my mirror image, but actually depends on my image retaining its individual form in the mirror.

If then I decide on my own to climb up the ladder of consciousness to reach Self, it may easily be my will and not the will of Self. Self may want me to be where I am and who I am—an image of "I am that I am" with a particular part to play in creation. Our union in this way will be much more intimate than absorption; I shall be united in my likeness to Self as a dynamic center of consciousness and will.

> *The only way in which one spirit can*
> *become another without ceasing to be itself,*
> *is by way of perfect resemblance to this other.*
> —Etienne Gilson

We can press our mirror analogy even further in illustrating the nature of the I-Self union. The more my mirror image is responsive to me, the better the likeness to me, and thus the greater the realization of our unity. So to the extent that my mirror image fully realizes it is dependent on me for its existence, and does not pretend it is unlike me, the less interference there is in our relationship.

And the less interference there is, the clearer that image becomes and the more I am united with it. In other words, the more the image surrenders—that is, acknowledges the dependency which already exists—the more brightly and clearly it shines, and the more alike we are seen to be.

So by this model, my union with Self is not a fusion into totality, but a responsiveness to Self which allows me to realize increasingly my likeness to Self at my own level, in other words, to realize increasingly my I-amness in the here and now.

The more I am responsive to Self, that is, the more I surrender to Self—which is simply acknowledging the total dependency which already exists—then ipso facto the more I realize I am "I."

And since the reflected image, "I," shines more clearly as it better reflects the greater "I am that I am," here image and source are united in likeness to each other. (And remember that this intensification of "I" can engage one in any state of consciousness; see our discussion of disidentification in chapter 3.)

The union of "I" and Self is thus founded on the fact that individual human being is the result of a direct and ongoing act of creation by Deeper Being—the relationship of created and creator. This direct creation means that individual human I-amness is at its core surrendered to, receptive to, dependent upon, and *thus inextricably united to*, Deeper Being, Self.

> *There is something in the soul so closely*
> *akin to God that it is already one with him*
> *and need never be united to him.*
> —Meister Eckhart

Paradoxically then, as I realize and accept this absolute dependence on Self, I realize unique individuality, that is, the image becomes clearer, I-amness blossoms. Contrariwise, to the extent that I am unresponsive to Self, then to that extent I do not image "I am that I am," and so my sense of I-amness is diminished.

In short, we have a paradox in which surrender to Self does not ultimately diminish the sense of independence, but over time increases it. Here the experience of independence is born from dependence, power from powerlessness, victory from surrender. This is not an idealized independence; it is based upon acknowledging our ongoing dependence. We can call this phenomenon then, the *dependent-independent paradox*.

> *God desires our independence—which we attain when,*
> *ceasing to strive for it ourselves, we "fall" back into God.*
> —Dag Hammarskjöld

This dependent-independent paradox of the I-Self union has been realized quite practically on a daily basis by millions of men and women world-wide:

> The more we become willing to depend upon a Higher
> Power, the more independent we actually are. There-
> fore dependency, as A.A. practices it, is really a means
> of gaining true independence of the spirit. (*Twelve
> Steps and Twelve Traditions* 1953, 36)

And of course, since Being is transcendent-immanent and not simply one pole in a being-doing polarity, such surrender to Self does not imply passivity. Self is distinct from any such polarity, and thus we may even find ourselves challenged to let go of our passivity and inaction in such a surrender!

If we do then elect to employ Assagioli's principle of "reflection" or *imago*, rather than emanation for the creation of "I," it follows that one's relationship with Self is profoundly immediate. This relationship need not be mediated by any hierarchy of consciousness at all, but ultimately works itself out directly and intimately between "I" and Self, between created and creator.

In and through this creative I-Self axis, each human being has direct unmediated access to Being, independent of consciousness, hierarchy, multiplicity, or totality. In other words, there is here a transcendent-immanent union with Self. (Note however, that this does not eliminate the need for a supportive context in which to realize this union, the need for a community which can reflect or mirror one's I-amness; see "Larger Spiritual-Moral Contexts" and "I to I" in chapter 7.)

So what this entire discussion means practically is this: no matter what our level of consciousness, we may still have an immediate and profound relationship with Self, and thus with each other and the world at large. Indeed, it is much more a matter of *recognizing* our ever-present and inescapable relationship with, dependence on, and union with Self, in whatever state we find ourselves.

Furthermore, recognizing my ongoing dependence on Self may encourage me to risk trusting Self more in my life. Self is not a blind unconscious totality, not an uroboric ocean in which I risk losing my individuality like a drop in the ocean—indeed, my individuality *depends* on Self. Self is consciously and willfully *giving* me my individuality and my freedom, my consciousness and will—giving me, "me." Self is not seeking to imprison or overwhelm me, but to allow me to realize my uniqueness, freedom, and vocation in the world.

And I can enter into an ongoing relationship with Self now, in every moment of my day, and may—with no necessary change in consciousness and with no climbing up the ladder—learn to act completely in union with the will of Self, and thus move towards right relationship with others and the world.

Self-realization implies fundamentally then the discovery of my vocation, my way to be with and for others in the world, in an ongoing unification of my will with the will of Self. Again, here is Louth describing the thought of Pseudo-Dionysius:

> The creature's response to God is not to draw near to God by ascending the hierarchy, but to identity itself with God's will ... by fulfilling its role in the created order ... (Louth 1989, 107)

Self-realization is therefore not a matter of ascending the scale of being in order to achieve a special gnosis, a secret knowledge, an exalted state of consciousness. *Self-realization is not a matter of moving up through the levels of consciousness, but a matter of choosing for or against Self at whatever level we are.*

Self-realization involves the business of finding one's vocation, one's part to play in the scheme of things. Here we ask not for higher consciousness (although that may be a by-product), but simply that we discover that Deeper Will, that invitation in our lives to unfold our unique gifts and talents—our unique *imago*—for the benefit of ourselves and the world.

---

*And yet in all that immensity there is only one*
*possible place for each one of us at any given moment,*
*the one we are led to by unflagging fidelity to*
*the natural and supernatural duties of life.*
—Teilhard de Chardin

---

# CHAPTER SEVEN

# Transcendence-Immanence and Therapy

> *Sometimes our light goes out but is*
> *blown again into flame by an encounter*
> *with another human being. Each of us*
> *owes the deepest thanks to those who*
> *have rekindled this inner light.*
> —Albert Schweitzer

We have used the notion of transcendence-immanence to examine many of the idealizations of "I" and Self, and to distinguish their relationship from levels of consciousness. We can now turn to a consideration of how our understanding of "I" and Self impinges more directly upon the dynamics of the clinical situation. We shall also note how Self-realization ultimately moves beyond the purview of any sort of transpersonal psychotherapy at all.

## Transcendence-Immanence and Therapy

As we have seen, the concept of transcendence-immanence allows us to track the I-Self relationship as it weaves in and out among various states of consciousness. Transcendence-immanence can therefore be useful clinically in helping to understand and integrate higher states of consciousness glimpsed in peak experiences.

For example, an important task in integrating a peak experience would be not to mistakenly identify the person's true self with either the peak experience or the more mundane experience. This will allow the freedom to engage each of these dimensions of experience, as well as address the relationship between the two.

In working with someone trying to integrate such experiences, we might find ourselves first grappling with the psychological reactions to such a profound spiritual insight. We might explore compulsions which block the living out of this newly-discovered vision; or the anxiety of ongoing communication with this sublime realm; or the fear of working to change social structures to reflect this vision. We may even find ourselves sitting with the person as his or her entire sense of self and world disintegrates under the impact of such an experience, patiently being present to the search for a new wholeness.

All such work will involve some exploration of the childhood experiences which underpin these reactions, as well as developing practical strategies to cope with these as they are healed. As the childhood and family-system roots of the patterns are uncovered and worked through, there will be less tendency to split the mundane from the visionary, personality integration from spiritual development.

As we noted in chapter 2, this healing of the split between the mundane and visionary may be mistakenly couched in terms such as "learning to incarnate," "embodiment," or "choosing to manifest in matter." These terms are dualistic, because they imply a discarnate soul learning somehow to "come down" into physical reality.

More holistically, we would say that what is healed here is a dissociation between two dimensions of experience which are in reality united already. We are not souls learning to incarnate in a body, but transcendent-immanent "I"s. That is, we are in but not of both the sublime and mundane dimensions from the very beginning, although we are in the process of gradually realizing this ever-present reality. Thus at any particular time, our Self-realization may find us walking a path of personality integration, spiritual development, or both.

Furthermore, this splitting of the two dimensions often will be found to revolve around unresolved issues from childhood. As one experiences the wonder and beauty of the content of the superconscious, and then in this light begins to recognize the reality of one's childhood, one begins to see much more vividly the dysfunction, trauma, or abuse intrinsic to most families.

An increased sensitivity to the profundity of human nature produces a more refined understanding of what constitutes abuse, neglect, and trauma, and this leads to uncovering hitherto hidden childhood wounds, shame, and rage. As the dawning sense of "what might have been" begins to confront the "what actually was" in our early life, even the best childhood can reveal itself to be wounding. New heights imply new depths.

> *The height of a peak is a measure*
> *of the depths of the abysses it overtops.*
> —Teilhard de Chardin

Thus, new levels of higher unconscious experience imply an uncovering of new depths of lower unconscious experience— just what one would expect if Self were transcendent-immanent throughout the entire psyche, rather than locked safely away in the superconscious. (We shall call this phenomenon *induction* in appendix 3.)

*The path of Self-realization is found only through an openness to both the higher and lower unconscious.*

Clearly then, one is never finished engaging childhood issues until such time as all the further reaches of human potential are exhausted—that is, for all practical purposes, never. An increased sense of potential means an increased confrontation with the psychological patterns which obstruct that potential; and the roots of those patterns lead inexorably deeper and deeper into an increased ability to see, feel, and heal the wounds of childhood.

Whether or not these wounds need to be formally addressed in psychotherapy is another matter of course. We have no reports which indicate Buddha and Jesus, for example, ever saw psychotherapists! However, it is safe to say that such people did not repress their personal history, and lived their lives in an openness to the truth and transformation of earlier layers of their psychological formation.

## Self-Realization and Therapy

If we understand that the true foundation of human identity is not to be found in the peak experience nor in the mundane experience, we may see the importance of developing an I-Self relationship as a context by which to interpret and work with both types of experience.

A primary concern in therapy here is to assist the person in responding to Self. Perhaps through guided imagery, discussion, and/or a referral to the client's religion or larger spiritual-moral context (see "Larger Spiritual-Moral Contexts" in this chapter), one would plumb for the direction to be taken in the psychological work. Here there can be a cooperation between spiritual direction and psychotherapy, as one seeks to align with the will or call of Self within the context of psychological work.

Attempting to follow the deeper direction of Self, one may go in any direction at all. For example, the therapy might move into a more detailed discussion of the nature of the spiritual insight, of what it means in the context of the person's values, and of what practical steps might be involved in responding to the insight.

On the other hand, the therapy might take a lower unconscious direction as childhood issues emerge in response to the peak experience—perhaps feelings of worthlessness vis-à-vis the profundity of the vision, or a feeling of rage at self or others for not living up to this vision. Here analysis and transference work might be indicated.

And of course *both* of these directions may easily occur and include many other types of work, from hypnosis, to body work, to family-systems therapy. The point is that therapy can support, and take place within, the larger context of meaning a person has in life. Peak experiences, and indeed abyss experiences, can thus become not identifications, but meanings by which we live. Hereby either, or both, personality integration and spiritual development may be supported, all within the larger process of Self-realization.

This type of work, in which one seeks to integrate relatively overt superconscious experiences, is called *spiritual* or *transpersonal psychosynthesis* by Assagioli. He distinguishes this from *personal psychosynthesis* in which there is little or no obvious superconscious experiencing, and which focuses more on the middle and lower unconscious (see for example, Assagioli 1965, 55; and Assagioli 1973, 121).

So in such therapeutic process, one does not focus solely upon attaining a particular state of consciousness. The context of any such work is the developing relationship with Self, a relationship which can become an ongoing transformative axis of one's life. Whether we call this following one's destiny, responding to one's vocation, or facilitating the unfoldment of one's authentic personhood, it is an attempt to respond to the deepest direction in a person's life, in and through the presenting issues.

According to Assagioli, the chief characteristic in the realization of Self is "the realization of individuality and universality" (Assagioli 1965, 87). But this does not mean necessarily that one attains a synthesis of individual and universal *consciousness* in Self-realization, in the sense of experiencing cosmic consciousness or the like. As we have outlined, Self-realization implies an alignment of the will of "I" with the will of Self, and thus has no necessary connection with any particular state of consciousness, nor even with any specific state of psychological health or disease.

> *Let the Will of the Self guide and direct my life.*
> —Roberto Assagioli

For example, responding to one's vocation—that is, aligning the will of "I" with the will of Self—may include the following "states of consciousness," among unlimited others: choosing to do the right thing when feeling like doing the wrong thing; fearlessly examining behavior in the light of conscience; grieving the loss of someone dearly loved; struggling with childhood wounding; suffering during a demonstration of civil disobedience; or even dying for one's beliefs.

Such experiences very quickly dispel any notion of Self-realization as necessarily involving merely cosmic or universal consciousness, although these latter may be included as well. Tough decisions and painful events are experiences of "individuality and universality" too, insofar as they are an alignment of the will of "I" and the will of Self. (Clarity regarding the meaning of "individuality and universality" is crucial in the avoidance of psychological inflation by superconscious experiences; we devote appendix 4 to this important subject.)

Indeed, depending on the specific circumstances, an authentic response to Self may be hindered or helped by *any* particular type of consciousness, whether agonizing, humdrum, or ecstatic. I may for instance find that my ongoing immersion in either spiritual joy or existential pain—however true such experiences may be—may constitute an avoidance of the life experiences and commitments into which I am being invited at a deeper level. Agony and ecstasy, boredom and happiness, all have the potential for obstructing or facilitating one's ability to respond to deeper will.

So the therapeutic task regarding spiritual experiencing cannot be defined by the attainment of any particular state of consciousness. Rather, the central concern here is to facilitate the ongoing response to vocation, to Self. Here one enters into a relationship with Self, with all the risks, mystery, and unpredictability of any relationship.

However, since Self is transcendent-immanent and thus ever-present, this direction can be discerned by the trained therapist/ guide in even the most seemingly "non-spiritual" clients. No superconscious experiencing need be present at all. Self-realization is not simply for those on top of a particular pyramid of enlightenment, and indeed, takes place in *any* authentic I-Thou encounter, *whether or not it is overtly spiritual.*

The abiding pull to Self-realization can be seen in the client who is simply aware that life relationships are not working, or who is struggling against addictions and compulsions, or who senses there is something more to life—be that simply less pain or more fulfillment. If Self-realization is transcendent-immanent, a client need not present with overtly spiritual issues or existential questions of meaning. The person seeking help may simply be following the direction in themselves towards an increasing sense of who he or she truly is in the world. Sensing this direction, and responding to it, is the stuff of Self-realization in therapy. *Thus, Self-realization in therapy may include either or both personal and spiritual psychosynthesis.*

## Dualistic Denial and Therapy

If Self-realization is not to be equated with either personal or spiritual psychosynthesis, the therapist must be ready to move along either of these dimensions depending on the changing direction of the I-Self relationship. One might for example begin with integrating a peak experience, but then not deal with the superconscious at all, as childhood issues are addressed.

A great service can be offered by the therapist here, as she or he validates whatever issues are foreground for the client. There is no need to bring in the superconscious as an indication that Self-realization is happening. The superconscious may even constitute a distraction from solid personal growth.

The practical effect of this is that the therapist must be ready to work moment-by-moment with what is presented, with the actual changing existential situation of the person. One must listen acutely in an attempt to clarify, engage, and facilitate the lived subjective experience of the client, whatever that may be.

The danger for a dualistic psychosynthesis is that it can very easily move into the superconscious without truly dealing with the actual depth of distress presented by the client—"After all, is not the idea to move up the levels of consciousness? Does not such pain, after all, have more to do with my psyche-soma than with my true self? It may be right and good to work on these neurotic childhood issues, but let us get through with personal psychosynthesis and move into the real existential and spiritual issues of spiritual psychosynthesis."

In dualism, it is difficult, for example, to sit with someone in their rage at their parents and not move fairly soon towards forgiveness; it is difficult to see clearly the full scope of wounding, the possible parental abuse, and the aspects of irredeemable loss in such rage and grief. But as author and therapist Melodie Beattie states:

> Forgiving and forgetting feed our denial system. We need to think about, remember, understand, and make good decisions about what we are forgiving ... forgiveness is closely tied into the acceptance or grief process.

> We cannot forgive someone for doing something if we
> have not fully accepted what this person has done.
> (Beattie 1987, 197)

Dualism works against such full acceptance, because all
wounds are not to "me," but to my body, feelings, and mind: "I
can feel sorry for these vehicles of my personality, and even feel
their pain, but it is wrong to believe these wounds are to my *self*, to
*me*." Dualism will maintain it is a mistake to believe these wounds
are an integral part of my life and of human life in general.

In dualistic denial, forgiveness amounts to ignoring the true
nature and degree of one's brokenness, and developing an idealized
spiritual self-image fed by an ability to say, "I forgive." Such words
of forgiveness may indeed bring a true superconscious inflow of
peace and love, but unless they are based on an uncovering of the
actual breadth and depth of wounding, these words can only remain
superficial. In such behavior, one can see a gaping chasm growing between the higher and lower unconscious—my beliefs and my
words take me into the superconscious, and my core wounds are left
below. This may pass for healing, but clearly it is not.

It is difficult in dualism not to evoke the superconscious in an
unhealthy way in an attempt to help people with their suffering. In
dualism, we put superconscious bandages on the pain; never look
into the actual and ugly nature of the pain; and never discover
how, why, and by whom this pain was inflicted. And if any experiences of rage or despair last for very long, dualism will hold that
the person is resisting spiritual growth. Dualism would suspect
there must be some secondary gain involved, some attachment,
some subpersonality holding on, or otherwise such issues would
be resolved.

This is not to say that such expansions of context beyond the
concrete presenting issues—that is movements into the superconscious—are not valid and useful. However, in a dualistic system
they are unconsciously used to avoid the depths of pain and suffering embedded in the human condition, especially if those issues
are still unresolved for the therapist. (And as we stated in chapter 2, even cathartic psychological work may be done while still
conditioned by these unconscious dualistic beliefs.)

This disruption of the therapeutic process fueled by ideological belief can take place with any type of therapy, of course. The self-psychologist Douglas Detrick has called this type of dynamic, *ideological countertransference*, in which the "therapist, in effect, becomes the tacit representative of a particular group, and cure then becomes unconsciously equated with the acceptance of the group's values and goals" (Detrick 1986, 303).

This might be seen in psychosynthesis therapy as the client engages in intense experiencing of the various layers of the unconscious. As this work proceeds from the depths of the lower unconscious to the heights of the superconscious, the client feels accepted and valued as one who is traveling this spiritual journey "to the Self." Such work of course can completely miss the more central ongoing issues facing the client.

Through the use of symbolic visualizations and guided imagery especially, a dualistic psychosynthesis can encourage an involvement with psychospiritual energies which precludes an ongoing engagement with the specific debilitating effects of past wounding. Psychosynthesis thereby becomes a shared aesthetic of symbolic experience and energetic adventures on the "path to the Self."

This type of ideological countertransference will remain a clear and present danger to psychosynthesis unless the dualism is filtered from the system. (And of course, even a non-dualistic system can have its own type of ideological countertransference, but it will come from a different quarter; see Detrick 1986, 303.)

In any case, dualistic denial in therapy can be sharply contrasted from both personal and (non-dualistic) transpersonal psychosynthesis, and from the larger process of Self-realization. Let us sum up this section by making these very contrasts.

First of all, dualism may seek to assuage profound depths of despair, loss, and rage with the soothing balm of the superconscious, or it may simply affirm that the person is separate from these experiences. It will engender subtle and not-so-subtle criticism of anyone who takes "too long" with such issues. It will lead us to attempt to handle tough psychological issues such as grief, suicide, addiction, and depression by a facile reliance upon superconscious experiencing to somehow show us the way through.

Personal psychosynthesis, on the other hand, entails a being-with the person in these depths, making no demands that the person relinquish the experience until ready. Here we can be with the client (to the extent we can be with these issues in ourselves), nonintrusively facilitating an exploration of the experience and meaning of the client's actual subjective experience. We are facilitator and guide in this process, as foundational childhood issues are mobilized and worked through within the context of the client-therapist relationship. Here a good solid training is needed in a clinical and developmental theory which understands the symptoms and the healing of past psychological wounding.

Then the work of spiritual psychosynthesis revolves around the exploration and understanding of the spiritual dimension and its relationship to the person's psychological dynamics. One may work on psychological issues with the intention of living a life based on one's highest spiritual and religious values, while fully engaging the unavoidable wounds of living. Here client and therapist alike may engage that deepest of mysteries: how the beauty and goodness of life may co-exist with apparent senseless suffering and death. Responsible therapy here includes recognizing when the client's spirituality is taking him or her beyond the scope of psychotherapy, and that a need is emerging for a larger spiritual-moral context in which to live and work (see "Larger Spiritual-Moral Contexts" in this chapter).

Finally, we can note that the dynamics of personal and transpersonal psychosynthesis do *not* together constitute what we are calling Self-realization. These two types of work serve only to outline the general parameters of the overall journey of Self-realization. Self-realization in therapy is facilitated by the ability of both client and therapist to respond to the direction of a Deeper Will as it expresses itself within the interpersonal relationship. This ability to respond to this direction is fed by the commitment, by both therapist and client, to struggle towards authenticity in their lives no matter at what cost to personal pride or cherished beliefs. A therapist seeking to serve Self-realization must stand ready to facilitate, or to refer, no matter where the life impulse of the client may lead.

## Peak Experiences—Healthy or Unhealthy?

While psychosynthesis and transpersonal psychology accept peak experiences as healthy (depending on how they are integrated), some psychotherapeutic approaches may attempt to ignore such experiences altogether, or treat them as symptoms. For example, an experience of unitive consciousness or vision might be seen as merely an instance of ego decompensation. Such an approach will view the person in these experiences as being caught up into an unreal, idealized euphoria, a mere reverie or a dependency daydream, which may eventually loosen his or her grip on everyday reality and personal responsibility.

Indeed, powerful superconscious experiencing does often in fact entail a diminished sense of self-consciousness. That is, fully caught up in such a vision, it would be difficult to know oneself as a unique individual with the ability to act responsibly in the here and now. For example, one can easily imagine Maslow, caught up in his vision of the teachers marching through history (see chapter 6), smartly bumping into another professor as the procession stopped suddenly!

This fact is borne out by an edition of the *Comprehensive Textbook of Psychiatry* (Freedman and Kaplan 1967, 893), which rightly lists cosmic consciousness as a "dissociative reaction." (But of course, it should have listed experiences such as sexual and aesthetic ecstasies as well.)

It is quite correct to note that "I" can be caught up in psychic contents, and that this is dynamically the same whether the contents are a wave of anger or an insight into cosmic unity. Here is a priest discovering that one's sense of identity can be caught up by the mundane as well as the sublime:

> ...I experienced a powerful sense of the love of God entering into me...I definitely experienced—not once, but a dozen times at least—that my identity did not even exist during these religious experiences.
>
> Now, this is where I get into trouble talking with people. People say, "Yes, yes—the ego vanishes. The ordinary self disappears into the love of Christ"—or

something along these lines. Crap! At least, as far as
my own life is concerned ... crap! I can't ever explain,
I gave up trying to explain, that the identity disappeared in the same way it disappeared when I rammed
into that Buick. The same way it disappeared and was
disappearing a hundred times a day in every petty
annoyance or emotional outburst. (In Needleman
1980, 77)

Although the contents of the two types of experiences—
"the love of God" and "emotional outburst"—are certainly
quite different, and can be differentiated on a spectrum of
consciousness, *either can diminish an articulated sense of
individuality*.

Of course the fact that a sense of self-consciousness is momentarily obscured is no reason to denigrate cosmic consciousness
any more than it is to denigrate sexual orgasm or aesthetic reverie;
all can be meaningful and enriching experiences when integrated
into one's life, as indeed can a psychotic break or a struggle with
addiction (it is another story, however, if any of these dominate
one's life).

On the other hand, some spiritual and religious orientations
might ignore the psychological issues involved in integrating
peak experiences within the concrete realities of daily life. Such
approaches consider the sublime as more real, and the mundane
is viewed as an illusion and a trap—the dualistic attitude. Thus,
one here attempts to remain permanently in that more profound
realm, and perhaps seeks to "serve" others by helping them to do
likewise.

However, if "I" is transcendent-immanent, it is clear that
the sphere of its existence can include both the secular and the
sublime, and that *either* dimension can produce contents sufficient
to attenuate a sense of individual personal identity. Childhood
pain; spiritual joy; anger at a reckless motorist; fear of speaking
in a group; excitement at making a good presentation—all potentially can overcome a sense of articulated I-amness existing in the
here and now.

Thus, the psychiatric textbook was correct in classifying cosmic consciousness as a dissociation, but we must realize that it is also a dissociation to identify simply with the somatic and psychological. This latter identification dissociates one from the sublime. *Either* can be a dissociation which chronically obscures "I," and perhaps as well the ability of "I" to respond to Self.

Implicit in what we are saying here is that regarding Self-realization one cannot know whether any particular state of consciousness is regressive or progressive for any given person simply by the quality or content of the experienced state (as Ken Wilber's concept (1980) of the *prepersonal/transpersonal fallacy* attempts to do).

It is quite true that lower unconscious and higher unconscious experiences are very different, and that neither is reducible to the other. However, actual regression or progression in any experience can only be discerned by noting whether or not the experience leads one eventually into, or out of, relationship to Self. Either higher or lower experiences can constitute obstacles to that relationship.

This means, among other things, that we should be wary of any sort of spectrum of consciousness which posits a hierarchy of Self-realization leading, for example, up out of psychosis, through borderline and narcissistic states, and finally to self-actualization and Self-realization. Self-realization is distinct from personal integration, and is theoretically as possible for someone with schizophrenia as it is for a "self-actualizer." Again, our touchstone is not patterns of development or states of consciousness, but the I-Self relationship.

Thus, whether we are dealing with a psychotic episode (regression to the prepersonal) or a peak experience (progression to the transpersonal), either experience can be progressive if it moves us towards relationship with Self. From this point of view, the tasks of psychotherapist and spiritual director are substantially the same, although theory and practice, content and context, differ. In both cases, the task is to help the client understand and integrate life experiences, so that she or he can move towards a more intimate relationship with Deeper Being.

## Peak Experiences—What Do They Mean?

But if the notion of a transcendent-immanent Self means that we cannot assume any particular state of consciousness represents contact with Self; and a peak experience does not necessarily imply the working of Self; and *any* type of experience may function as a help or hindrance in responding to the invitations of Self—then how are we to understand and act upon higher superconscious experiences?

Does Maslow's vision of the academic procession, for example, mean he is being called to transform academic processions? Or is this an invitation to work towards improving higher education? Or is it perhaps a dangerous distraction, a potential step into an unreal romance about academia into which he may draw others?

However meaningful superconscious experiences are, the question remains: what is the will of Self in this? And then, "How am I to respond?" By virtue of my transcendent-immanence, I can elect to move towards or away from the will of Self, no matter what my state of consciousness.

Self-realization cannot, therefore, be separated from a consideration of morality, of our actions vis-à-vis Self. We are talking here about how we use our will, how we align our will with a deeper will or not, and what specific and concrete choices we make in our lives. Self-realization is profoundly a matter of the morality and immorality of our lives.

So note that by *morality* we do not mean simply following external rules, but rather an engagement with conscience, with the discernment of the goodness and badness of choices, in light of the will of Self. (We reserve the term *ethics* to indicate choices with respect to philosophical systems—which may or may not be moral for a particular person.) Self-realization then, is far more a matter of my morality, of my choices and how I live my life, than of what consciousness I have. It has to do with my response to Self who, in Wilber's words, is "present all along, 'guiding,' 'pulling,' and 'directing'" (Wilber 1980, 25).

Higher states of consciousness do not automatically increase the ability to make moral choices. Spiritually-based morality—

how I use my will vis-à-vis Self—depends not on the quality and intensity of my experiences of spiritual realities, but on my wise interpretation of, and action upon, these experiences. Even a valid peak experience, wrongly interpreted, may lead to destructive choices.

And of course, given our all-too-human limitations, it is quite easy to wrongly interpret spiritual experiences. For example, overflowing with the love and goodness of all creation, I may easily make myself believe that sexuality is so good and sacred that it should be shared with all—and so rationalize my promiscuity and sexual addiction. Or I may experience that our spiritual nature is so very transcendent of physical reality that it does not matter in any ultimate way whether I commit murder or suicide. Spiritual experiences—whether of unity, love, joy, or whatever—do not necessarily carry an obvious moral import, with specific guidance for one's will.

> *We are all one.*
> —Charles Manson
> Cult murderer

By the way, we have heard much about how our modern technological revolution has outdistanced our moral ability to handle such awesome power. But our *inner* technological revolution—for example behavior modification, hypnosis, cybernetics, techniques for altered states of consciousness, and so on—can just as easily outdistance our moral abilities with, we believe, potentially far more disastrous results.

One reason that higher states of consciousness are distinct from morality is that the I-Self relationship is transcendent-immanent, and thus not ultimately controlled by consciousness. No matter what our consciousness, we have some amount of free will distinct from that consciousness. We have choices in relationship to our experience at any level of consciousness, and indeed, we even have the potential freedom to change our state of consciousness itself. Even when functioning at the highest, most universal state of consciousness, transcendent-immanent "I" is still free to choose to do good or ill.

Here we again see the paramount importance of will, existing at every stage of development. True, every stage imposes its limitations on consciousness and will. But even at each stage of moral development, one has some semblance of will, and may make good or bad choices within the limitations of that stage. Whether one's conscience is rigid or flexible, limited or universal, undeveloped or developed, there are always good and bad choices. This follows from the notion of transcendence-immanence—the I-Self relationship is ever distinct, though not separate, from the specific contents of any stage of development.

If we rigorously apply the concept of transcendence-immanence to core human identity, it is even theoretically possible that we always have a choice about something. That is, at whatever stage of development we find ourselves, there are some contents, however minute, which are responsive to our will.

Thus for example there would still be choices available to someone in a dissociative or comatose state, in a fugue or psychotic state, and even perhaps in the very earliest stages of life within the womb. It appears however that the possibility of choice in some of these circumstances would be difficult to research, because the contents responsive to will in these apparently "non-I" states would be extremely subtle. (Although researcher Daniel Stern (1985, 6) has indeed recognized that even "prior to self-awareness and language," the infant demonstrates some sense of "agency" and of "having intentions in mind.")

For all practical purposes, the I-Self relationship is distinct from, though present within, whatever stage of development we find ourselves. This relationship is transcendent-immanent throughout all the spacetime of our lives, and we are therefore choosing for or against Self at every time and place. Any little girl or boy may choose to disregard their developing sense of truth; any adult may choose to violate individual rights; and any enlightened sage may still make evil choices.

Thus it is important to remember that we human beings will always be susceptible to pride and bad choices, no matter what stage of development we have reached or what state of consciousness we have attained. According to the notion of transcendence-immanence, it seems we never evolve beyond the ability to do good or evil, to choose for or against Self. In other words, *we always have some amount of free will*. That will is, after all, one of the abiding gifts of Self.

Self-realization is therefore not limited to one level of consciousness, nor one sphere of life, nor one time of life. Self-realization occurs throughout our lives and cannot be separated from the choices by which we create our lives. The alignment of the will of "I" with the will of Self—that is, morality—is ever an issue. Here is one woman's description of her encounter with, and alignment to, a deeper sense of truth in her life—which resulted in a peak experience:

> Since entering analysis and dealing with the roots of my suffering, I began to see, and feel the grief for, not only what had been done to me, but how I myself had harmed others.
>
> There was one particular moment when I realized that I had never loved. But when I realized I'd never loved, I felt forgiven. I had always felt deep down that I was deeply bad, but now my ultimate badness had been seen and forgiven.
>
> And there was something more about original sin. Original sin is not about being bad or rotten, it's something about never having truly loved.
>
> In this moment I suddenly felt connected to everything around me … there was no separation. I looked at the dirt on the window which I usually would clean immediately, and had no desire to wipe it away. I felt now totally part of everything. I felt in that moment I was a true daughter of the universe. It was amazing. It really was quite extraordinary.

Note that this profound experience of herself and the world derived from a willingness to see and accept a deeper sense of truth, as well as to take responsibility for it. This honest acceptance of one's moral faults seems akin also to what Anna Freud called "true morality" (Freud 1992, 119), a genuine coming to terms with one's deepest values.

In any case, this acceptance of human limitation is quite different from—indeed completely opposed too—a chronic sense of badness and worthlessness. Here is simply a recognition of the deviation of one's own will from a deeper, more true will, and in that same instant, the realization of a connection and belongingness to all things.

Since Self-realization is a movement towards a more consistent alignment with the will of Self, this process will ever involve us in confronting the times in our lives when we did *not* respond to Self as we might have (as did the woman above). Movement towards Self thus implies feeling healthy guilt and shame for our ill choices, and leads us towards making amends for these. An ongoing I-Self relationship creates a more abiding appreciation for what is right, and this sense of rightness illuminates our past actions and calls us to take responsibility for them (see our discussion of induction in appendix 3). Here is Benedict Groeschel, a Franciscan priest, author, and professor of pastoral psychology:

> If one is growing, there are ever new horizons and challenges. Yesterday's good works may be seen as today's ego-trips. Yesterday's imperfections may be today's sins of ingratitude or negligence. Even more surprisingly, previous acts of trust may suddenly appear as flagrant presumption or self-deception. (Groeschel 1988, 104)

Reality-based guilt and shame are therefore not dysfunctional artifacts to be eliminated, but helpful guides to Self-realization. Abraham Maslow and John Bradshaw, among others, have sought to differentiate such healthy guilt and shame from the unhealthy variety. As I have elaborated in course material (circa 1977), in psychosynthesis terms healthy or "existential" guilt is a function of a dissonance between the will of "I" and the will of Self; while healthy shame is a dissonance between the self-consciousness of "I" and the self-consciousness of Self. But that is another book.

## Larger Spiritual-Moral Contexts

Given the connection of morality and Self-realization, a context for Self-realization will need to provide support for the examination and development of conscience; it will need to be a matrix which nurtures the ongoing discernment of, and response to, the will of Self.

Thus it makes sense that at some point in Self-realization, one may feel moved to engage a spiritual-moral context which is not based solely upon one's own private spiritual experiences nor upon any psychological theory. It is not after all the task of any psychology, transpersonal or not, to provide a system of values and a moral framework for the living of a life.

So there may come a time when Self-realization bursts the bounds of transpersonal psychology, and a need surfaces for some broader context by which conscience itself may be illuminated and developed. Here Self-realization asks for a context beyond psychotherapy by which to interpret and act wisely on spiritual insights, and indeed, by which to live one's life.

Such periods in therapy occur, for example, when the client is experiencing an important spiritual awakening. Here there is strong superconscious inflow, accompanied by new insights, new perceptions, and a need to make sense out of a world now reborn. If the client does not already possess a larger context for understanding and living a deeply-felt and committed spirituality, it is strongly indicated that the therapist or guide explore the possible need for such a larger context.

A spiritual awakening like this in a client should not simply be handled within the context of the therapeutic process. Such Self-realization will affect all areas of the client's life, and this for many years to come. The wise therapist will thus understand the growing need in the client to connect to a wider community, a more profound wisdom, and a more precise guidance for choices.

Addressing the need for a larger spiritual-moral context requires humility from the transpersonal therapist, a recognition of the limitations of one's role and one's system. But as such a context develops, the client's struggle with ongoing spiritual-moral decisions can be referred to trusted people who are versed in the orientation which the client finds meaningful—just as one refers matters of medicine and law to a trusted physician and lawyer. Such people might be formally religious or non-religious; an Alcoholics Anonymous sponsor or wise crone; or simply an informal support group dealing with similar issues. The important thing is that the therapist recognize and address the need for a wider philosophical worldview and ongoing spiritual practice in Self-realization than can ever be provided by transpersonal psychology alone.

Lastly, let us say that if transpersonal therapists do not possess a sensitivity to the need to explore larger spiritual-moral contexts for Self-realization, the client's burgeoning need for such a supportive matrix may remain unrecognized and sublimated. And to the extent that this occurs, any spiritually-open therapeutic process then runs the risk of becoming distorted to meet these unconscious needs. In this way psychosynthesis, or any other transpersonal psychology, may easily be led away from the business of psychology and down a slippery slope towards becoming a default spiritual-moral system by which people attempt to live their lives.

## "I" to "I"

In moving towards the close of these chapters, let us reiterate a most important reason to seek clarity in understanding the transcendence-immanence of "I." This reason is that such understanding just may allow us better to perceive, to understand, and to be present to, the unique personhood of the individual human being.

You see, a problem with psychotherapy or spiritual guidance is that they invariably involve one in the archetypal/mythological; in the world of childhood trauma; in the vast array of different states of consciousness; and in the intricacies of family and social systems. Thus, in working with these many levels of content and process, one may begin to lose track of the unique individual person who exists within all of this.

For client and therapist alike, the person may be objectified into an archetype or neurosis; a myth or compulsion; a particular level of consciousness; a number or type in a particular typology;

or a cog in an intrapsychic or social system. And what is lost is the mysterious unique being we each are, living in the here and now, seeking meaning in the daily struggles and joys of human existence.

> *From the third century on there had been little*
> *or no recognition of individual personality.*
> *The real person, with his unique characteristics,*
> *had been obliterated by the Platonic concern with ideal types.*
> —Norman Cantor, *Medieval History*

But if "I" is transcendent-immanent, we are ever ourselves, ready to be discovered. Whether archetypal or neurotic, sinning or saintly, fragmented or whole, I remain unchangeably "I," a unique being with a unique belongingness in life. Thus, the gifted guide is one who can dare to look beyond all the patterns of psychology and spirituality, to see and reflect this mystery with his or her own mystery. When this is done successfully, there can be an answering response in the other, the calling forth of "I" by "I."

Thus, "good-enough" therapy and spiritual direction involve a looking from beyond all, through all, within all, to the unique "I" who is present in that unique moment. Here is Rollo May quoting the existential therapist Ludwig Binswanger:

> ... to wake or rekindle that divine "spark" in the patient which only true communication from existence to existence can bring forth and which alone possesses, with its light and warmth, also the fundamental power that makes any therapy work—the power to liberate a person from the blind isolation, the *idios kosmos* of Heraclitus, from a mere vegetating in his body, his dreams, his private wishes, his conceit and his presumptions, and to ready him for a life of *koinonia*, of genuine community. (May 1983, 157–58)

Binswanger's "existence to existence," or Martin Buber's (1970) "I-Thou," is akin to what we would call "I to I." This is the "fundamental power that makes any therapy work." Here is an encounter which rekindles the light of "I," allowing the experience of "I" to emerge.

In such authentic encounter, the therapist is not engaged in an "I-it" relationship. The therapist is not identified with doing or not doing something to the client, with placing implicit or explicit expectations on the other. Rather, here is someone daring to be with someone else in the mystery of the moment, giving permission for the other to be as well.

And as Rollo May points out elsewhere (May 1983, 159), this beingness in clinical orientation does not eliminate the need to know therapeutic technique and theory. It is simply that such authenticity in relationship provides the foundation or context for all interventions. Authenticity is necessary but not sufficient for good-enough psychotherapy and spiritual direction.

This I-to-I encounter is also the essence of parenting. In fundamental ways, good-enough parenting is quite similar to good-enough therapy and spiritual guidance. In parenting too there is a calling forth of mystery by mystery, transcendence-immanence calling to transcendence-immanence, beyond, yet utilizing, technique and theoretical understanding. Here is the psychoanalyst Alice Miller:

> ...the mother gazes at the baby in her arms, and baby gazes at his mother's face and finds himself therein... provided that the mother is really looking at the unique, small, helpless being and not projecting her own introjects onto the child, nor her own expectations, fears, and plans for the child. In that case, the child would not find himself in his mother's face but rather the mother's own predicaments. This child would remain without a mirror, and for the rest of his life would be seeking this mirror in vain. (Miller 1981, 32)

At the beginning of this passage, we can recognize a mother who is experiencing disidentification, who is not enmeshed in her own need to control or manipulate. She is walking the way of transcendence—she is contemplating, "just sitting." She is not identified with her own wants, hopes, fears, and expectations, but is able instead to look from somewhere distinct from them (although they may still be present).

Here the child is seen and mirrored, and the I-amness of the child is thereby called forth. On the other hand, if the mother was identified with her expectations and demands, she would only mirror those. In that case, instead of receiving a sense of "I am I," the child might for example receive a sense of identity such as, "I am the one who will take away my mother's loneliness," or "I am the one who will give meaning to my parents' lives." This is how the "false self" (Winnicott 1987) develops; here the child is not blossoming as the natural "true self" (Winnicott 1987), but becoming what the environment demands.

If however parents can walk a transcendent path, experiencing disidentification from their own needs, there immediately flows an immanent ability to call the I-amness of the child into realization. Too, this ability would pervade all the practical tasks of parenting, from discipline to feeding—all can be informed by the I-to-I relationship which is beyond, yet within, all of this. Parental contemplation is not to be dissociated from parental action in the world—that is, action, responsibility, and guidance are included in this relationship.

And these principles of parenting are quite applicable to the therapeutic situation. We can listen to Winnicott as he makes an explicit connection between such I-to-I parenting and I-to-I psychotherapy:

> This glimpse of the baby's and child's seeing the self in the mother's face, and afterwards in a mirror, gives a way of looking at analysis and at the psychotherapeutic task. Psychotherapy is not making clever and apt interpretations; by and large it is a long-term giving the patient back what the patient brings. It is a complex derivative of the face that reflects what is there to be seen. I like to think of my work this way, and to think that if I do this well enough the patient will find his or her own self, and will be able to exist and to feel real. Feeling real is more than existing; it is finding a way

to exist as oneself, and to relate to objects as oneself, and to have a self into which to retreat for relaxation.

But I would not like to give the impression that I think this task of reflecting what the patient brings is easy. It is not easy, and it is emotionally exhausting. But we get our rewards. Even when our patients do not get cured they are grateful to us for seeing them as they are, and this gives us a satisfaction of a deep kind. (Winnicott 1988, 137–38)

So there is something in this mirroring which kindles the realization of "I." Winnicott's words, "even when our patients do not get cured," indicate a depth of relatedness which transcends the attainment of any particular notion of mental health. Here is the blossoming of a sense of transcendent-immanent "I." That is, with no marked ascent up the hierarchical levels of personality integration, the patient still may be able to find "his or her own self" and "a way to exist as oneself." "I" is transcendent-immanent within personality integration.

In a discussion of psychosynthesis therapy, Frank Haronian calls this type of relating, "a momentary meeting at the interface of I and Thou in the here and now" (Haronian 1976, 29). He continues:

Ego needs are not operative. Self meets self, and these disinterested aspects of each individual merge for a moment in a sense of union and brotherhood [and/or sisterhood]. (ibid.)

We can see transcendence in his words "disinterested aspects," implying detachment/disidentification, and a meeting in this fertile void.

Haronian too, with May, makes it clear that this encounter does not merely involve receptivity to the client, but may include quite animated participation in the relationship as well (see Haronian 1975). This "self meets self," or being meets being, is beyond the active-receptive polarity and thus is able to partake of both, that is, it is not of, though it is within, all action and non-action.

As we noted earlier, "being" is not here one pole in a being-doing polarity. "Being" is transcendent-immanent, able to be in, but not of, doing and/or not-doing, action and/or receptivity.

> *Heaven and earth do nothing*
> *Yet there is nothing they do not do.*
> —Chuang Tzu

Using many of Winnicott's same words regarding parenting (from the Alice Miller quotation above), we might say that I-to-I relating forms as the therapist is really looking at the unique being of the client, and not projecting his or her own introjects, expectations, fears, and plans onto the client. Otherwise, the client will not find himself or herself reflected in the therapist's gaze, but rather find there only the therapist's own predicaments. The client will remain without a mirror, and will continue seeking this mirror in vain.

In psychosynthesis, the "predicament" of the therapist might well be the unconscious dualism which pervades the system. The therapist might be looking at the client not as transcendent-immanent "I," but as a transcendent soul who is incarnated in matter. In this case, instead of experiencing, "I am I, whatever I am experiencing," the client will feel the covert pressure to become for example, "one who is not attached to suffering and pain"; or, "a person who does a good piece of deep work and grounds it well"; or, "a disidentified and responsible 'I'." The therapist is then not inviting the client into authentic relationship, but is instead offering the client a new role to play.

Even though this type of inauthentic client-therapist relationship obscures I-to-I relationship, insightful and meaningful psychological work can still be performed here—one may integrate subpersonalities, work with dreams and archetypal images, abreact deep feelings from childhood, and have true experiences of free and non-attached disidentification. Indeed, because one can do all of this while missing the above hidden motivations, such work can easily mask these deeper issues. As Will Friedman, co-founder of the Psychosynthesis Institute of New York, has pointed out:

Too often for example, the client goes along with a psychosynthesis intrapsychic technique *for trans-ference reasons* (e.g. to please the therapist/parent figure), and therefore the technique may look good in the execution but fail to effect any real change in core patterns. Or the client may be resistant to using the technique, which psychosynthesists may conceive of as lack of "will alignment"—which is true enough—but pay too little attention to the interpersonal (trans-ference) issues of power, control, fear, and so on which may be at the heart of what is happening. (Friedman 1988, 50)

So even when doing "a good piece of work," the client can be caught in transference, the therapist can be caught in countertrans-ference, and so the hidden agendas will remain beyond the reach of both. Due to the unconscious issues of the therapist, the client is not here invited into I-to-I relationship, but is merely developing a new false self which allows a joining with the therapist in a new dysfunctional system.

## Transference and Countertransference

In moving towards a transcendent-immanent I-to-I relationship in therapy then, one needs to remain sensitive to the influence of transference and countertransference. These dynamics operate at a deep childhood level of the unconscious and very often can only emerge within the interpersonal relationship of client and therapist.

Of course the emergence of transference dynamics is precisely what very often needs to occur in depth individual psychotherapy. They can then be recognized, appreciated as deeply-felt issues from the past, and gradually addressed—unless of course the system of therapy does not fully respect the ever-present interper-sonal nature of those childhood layers of the unconscious.

For example, a dualistic system which has an idealized image of "I" might assume that in disidentification, the client is so tran-scendent that interpersonal issues such as transference need not—

or should not—become an ongoing issue. Here it will be assumed that the client can fairly quickly work through the dilemmas of the past using subpersonality techniques or intrapsychic work such as imagery and catharsis—modes of therapeutic work which focus *away* from the interpersonal, and towards the client as an independent self-sufficient entity. In this case the therapist communicates to the client, in effect, "Do not feel your childhood issues in relationship to me, or do so only briefly, and then realize these are merely the function of a subpersonality, of your own inner world—you are in reality an independent self-reliant 'I'."

That very attitude may be a reason why Victoria Tackett urged fellow psychosynthesis practitioners practitioners not to treat childhood wounding as "merely an unruly victim subpersonality to be integrated" (Tackett 1988, 29). Such a depth is not to be considered a child subpersonality, because wounding at this profound contextual level will mean that *all* parts of the personality will be affected, including the deeper immanent *experience* of "I am" (this might be considered wounding to the core personality).

When Self-realization then leads a person to experience this core level of wounding and healing, that person may not be able to step back on command, to take responsibility for the child subpersonality, and to realize a centered sense of self. These periods of vulnerable experiencing need to emerge and be held carefully within the interpersonal relationship with the therapist, because the client is simply not able to access independence and power. Or rather, the client is exhibiting the "strength to be helpless"—true disidentification is taking him or her out of a self-reliant false self towards feeling and healing the true self which lies wounded beneath.

But if the therapist relies only upon a model of subpersonalities from which an idealized "I" may fairly quickly step back, and/or upon work which stays exclusively intrapsychic, the therapist will be helpless to facilitate this process. In avoiding the interpersonal therapeutic matrix, the therapist cannot mirror the client's I-experience as it intensifies gradually over time to include earlier life experiences, nor can mirror a genuine disidentification from a more superficial independence. Instead, the therapist may actually become an obstacle to Self-realization.

In the worst cases reported to me, the therapist may even develop a covert attitude of anger and blame toward the client who is "too dependent," or "too attached to a victim or rebellious subpersonality." Then, if the client attempts to point out this countertransference, she or he is simply enjoined to own the projection and to work with it either as a subpersonality, or symbolically in imagery. In this way some clients may be re-victimized, undergoing a similar abuse to that received in their childhood environment.

To the extent psychosynthesis therapy does not root out its dualism and idealization of "I," it may therefore easily find itself missing the deeper conundrums of childhood experience. It may become oblivious to the ongoing playing out of these dynamics in human relationship, and thus inadvertently prevent the client from becoming conscious of these hidden dynamics in themselves and in their lives. The client will thereby be prevented from realizing I-to-I relationship within the therapeutic situation. We would agree again with Will Friedman:

> However, while from the standpoint of Psychosynthesis, psychoanalysis can be criticized for an overreliance and overemphasis on transference, I think many psychosynthesis practitioners are limited because they under-emphasize the importance of interpersonal dynamics in therapy. My observation is that many of the binds that psychosynthesists run into in their work can be attributed to not paying close enough attention to transference and counter-transference. (Friedman 1988, 50)

Paradoxically, such under-emphasis of transference actually fosters transference. That is, since deeper childhood layers of the unconscious are not allowed to emerge fully into the light of the interpersonal therapeutic milieu, they remain underground, operating to condition the process from behind the scenes. Here one may never discover the extent to which a client is, for example, being a "good client" (or a "bad one") out of buried childhood needs. Client and guide may eventually form an unassailable collusion dedicated to the proposition that they both are ever independent, responsible, powerful "I"s who are beyond the limitations of their personal psychology. In short, the therapeutic process may become subverted by dualistic denial. "I am not my psyche-soma, so you had better not be your psyche-soma."

There are at least two important ways for a therapist to prevent countertransference from violating the therapeutic process (and one cannot ever totally avoid this). The first is to undergo training and clinical supervision within a system which respects, understands, and knows how to work with early childhood dynamics as they emerge interpersonally.

The second and more important way is for the therapist to maintain an ongoing program of self-exploration and personal transformation which reaches to the deepest layers of one's own childhood conditioning. One way of thinking about such work would be that it is entering treatment for one's *codependency*—that syndrome in which a person becomes attached to controlling the behavior of another due to early childhood wounding.

The discovery of codependency is part of what in chapter 2 we called the "Recovery Revolution," by which a new depth of wounding and of healing is burgeoning within our collective consciousness. This increasing awareness has led many to realize that people in the helping professions are to a large extent codependent. Here is Anne Wilson Schaef in her book, *Co-Dependence*:

> I firmly believe, in fact—as many others have suggested (among them, Sharon Wegscheider-Cruse, Jael Greenleaf, Charles Whitfield, to name a few)— that *most mental health professionals are untreated co-dependents* who are actively practicing their disease in their work in a way that helps neither them nor their clients. (Schaef 1986, 4, emphasis added)

So recognizing and working with one's codependency might be one important way to approach a process of ongoing work which can act as a preventative measure against the ill effects of countertransference.

In any case, in order to develop a sensitivity to the underlying dynamics of transference and countertransference, one is well-advised to work on oneself within an approach which understands the pervasive effects of childhood experience well beyond the reach of extant psychosynthesis theory. Such ongoing depth work should not be, for example, reduced to the notion of simply disidentifying from one's "rescuer" or "helper" subpersonality—this again would be dualism subverting the process.

Let us emphasize here that by our discussion of transference and countertransference, we have not meant to say that these are the main weak points in psychosynthesis theory. Their lack of theoretical development in psychosynthesis simply indicates again the major difficulty with psychosynthesis we have been pointing to throughout—a dualism which dissociates human being from many important dimensions of humanness.

## Distinguishing Theory from Practice

Note carefully that the above critique of psychosynthesis says nothing about any particular practitioner within the field of psychosynthesis. For example, any given therapist may be well acquainted with the pervasive nature of childhood dynamics, and may be addressing these very competently within the therapeutic process. The point here is simply that if psychosynthesis therapists are doing this, it is in spite of published psychosynthesis theory—they are utilizing training received from other approaches or have developed their own private psychosynthesis theory.

We have made this distinction between theory and practitioner before (see note 11). The point we are making in the preceding section is that there is nothing in psychosynthesis *theory* which recognizes the tremendous centrality of childhood issues throughout the entire range of the human life-span. For example, the system offers no refined normative developmental theory; no theory of the difficulties and trauma encountered in early development; no systems approach to family dynamics; and not much beyond the valuable but relatively superficial theory of subpersonalities for working with the effects of early trauma.

While it is quite true that individual practitioners often make up for these deficiencies by employing other approaches, psychosynthesis itself does not offer understandings of many of these important dimensions of the human being—dimensions which seem fundamental to any serious psychological theory.

But if we assume that central understandings of the human person are always to be provided by other approaches, and only imported into psychosynthesis at the level of the individual clinician, what is psychosynthesis itself then but a spiritual ideology disconnected from psychological experience? Here again we come face-to-face with the dualism of psychosynthesis, a dualism which separates psychosynthesis theory from many of the existential complexities of human being.

And this separation can—in theory—lead to a subversion of genuine spirituality by unresolved early issues. It can—in theory—lead to an idealized spirituality which is fundamentally ungrounded in one's family of origin, personal life history, and existential life situation. Note that these criticisms of psychosynthesis are the very ones we heard from practitioners at the outset of this book (see "Dualistic Denial and Psychosynthesis," chapter 2).

If psychosynthesis theory finds itself finally unable to break its dualism in order to include central dimensions of humanness in an integral and serious way, the nature of "I" and Self, as well as the process of Self-realization, will continue to elude it. In contrast to Assagioli's statement in an interview with *Psychology Today* (Keen, 1974), we would then be forced to conclude that psychosynthesis is not limited because it is "too extensive, too comprehensive," but because it is *not extensive or comprehensive enough*.

## In Sum

It seems we have ended where we started, with a critique of the past, and therefore, a possible promise for the future. To the extent psychosynthesis can liberate itself from its dualism, and succeeds in avoiding monism, it may become free to recognize the transcendent-immanent nature of the unique individual human being engaging all the various experiences of life. The concept of

"I" can then become not some ideal centered state separate from psyche-soma, but rather the unique, living, willing, human being who can experience any and all that life has to offer.

And to the extent psychosynthesis recognizes that Self does not simply exist in the superconscious but is transcendent-immanent, the human relationship to Self may be seen to abide throughout all life experiences. One can know it is not necessary to ascend a scale of personal integration or spectrum of consciousness to relate to Self, but that one can do so at any time, in any place.

Whether I am engaging ongoing transference issues in therapy; struggling with compulsions or addictions; exploring my family system; walking through darkness and disintegration; ascending the breath-taking heights of the sublime; or simply moving steadily and faithfully through the daily demands of human life—throughout it all, I am "I" in relationship to a deeper "I am that I am."

# "I" in Religious Traditions

*This is not a pantheistic submersion*
*or a loss of self in "nature" or "the One."*
*It is not a withdrawal into one's spiritual*
*essence and a denial of matter and of the*
*world ... but that my "identity" be sought*
*not in that **separation** from all that is,*
*but in oneness with all that is.*
—Thomas Merton

Two ancient religious traditions or spiritual paths seem to illuminate the nature of disidentification and "I" as we have been discussing them. Each path or way describes a different avenue by which human being may approach experiential communion with Universal or Divine Being.

The *via negativa*, or "way of negation" speaks to the transcendence of "I," the ability to experience ourselves as distinct from the changing processes within the psyche-soma; while the *via positiva*, or "positive way," speaks to the immanence of "I," the experience that we know ourselves as intimately united with psyche-soma and the world around us.

Taken together, these two ways assume that deepest human being is in but not of, distinct but not separate from, the changing contents and processes of life experience.

## The *Via Negativa*

Here is the psychosynthesis thinker James Vargiu describing an approach to Self which we would say holds true for "I" as well:

> But the transcendent nature of the Self [and of "I"] places it beyond the power of understanding of the concrete mind, and consequently beyond the possibility of describing it with words. The only recourse is to describe what the Self is not. This approach has been very popular in the East, where it is called "the way of negation." (Vargiu 1973, 7)

This way of negation is of course well-known in Western spirituality as well. Such an approach was obvious in the work of Pseudo-Dionysius in the fifth or sixth century:

> For this would be really to see and to know: to praise the Transcendent One in a transcending way, namely through the denial of all beings. We would be like sculptors who set out to carve a statue. They remove every obstacle to the pure view of the hidden image, and simply by this act of clearing aside they show up the beauty which is hidden. (Pseudo-Dionysius 1987, 138)

The way of negation, or *via negativa*, can be traced through the Christian contemplative tradition, as represented by the likes of Meister Eckhart, St. John of the Cross, and the unknown author of *The Cloud of Unknowing*. In the East, this orientation can be recognized in such traditions as early Taoism (Lao Tzu, Chuang Tzu), Zen Buddhism (shikantaza meditation), and Theravada Buddhism (vipassana meditation).

The premise implied by the *via negativa* is that contact with Supreme Reality (that is, speaking very generally, God, The Tao, Nirvana, Samadhi, and so forth) is transcendent, an experience beyond all things. In other words, such contact is only possible as distinct from any particular contents such as sensations, feelings, thoughts, desires, or images which make up the world of appearance:

> A buddha has overcome every kind of craving; although even he also has pleasant and unpleasant sensations, he is not ruled by them and remains innerly untouched by them. (Schuhmacher and Woerner 1989, 46)

> Here you should know that true detachment is nothing else than for the spirit to stand as immovable against whatever may chance to it of joy and sorrow, honor, shame and disgrace, as a mountain of lead stands before a little breath of wind. (Eckhart 1981, 288)

Contact with Reality is a state of distinctness from psychosomatic events such as "craving" and "sensations," involving a transcendence which leaves one "not ruled," "untouched," or "immovable" by such processes. One is in, but not of, these events.

And contact with this Transcendent Reality even transcends any experience of spacetime at all—here is Eckhart again:

> Nothing hinders the soul's knowledge of God as much as time and space, for time and space are fragments, whereas God is one!... If the soul is to see God, it must not look again on any temporal thing, for as long as the soul dwells on time or space or any image of them it may never know God. (Eckhart 1941, 131)

The problem is of course that since this experience is beyond all such usual subject-object spacetime ways of knowing, it is indescribable. Contact with this Reality can only be spoken about by referring to what it is not, that is, by negation. Here is the *via negativa* as expressed by Thomas Merton:

> Everything you say [about the contemplative experience] is misleading—unless you list every possible experience and say: "That is not what it is." "That is not what I am talking about." (Merton 1961, 284)

Let us look at the *via negativa* as it is applied first in theory and then in practice.

A) First, from a conceptual point of view, the *via negativa* seeks formulations which reflect this insight that Reality is transcendent and cannot be described. Any positive statement about the nature of this transcendence is held to be at best partial, and at worse completely illusory.

Thus if one does not simply lapse into silence, at the very least the discussion is limited to negating terms like uncaused, no-self, emptiness, and ineffable (see Meagher, 1979, 2501). This then, is the conceptual approach to Reality by way of negation (also called negative theology). Lao Tzu puts it well:

> The way that can be told
> Is not the constant way;
> The name that can be named
> Is not the constant name.
>
> (Lao Tzu 1968, 57)

B) A second application of the *via negativa* is in actual spiritual practice rather than theory. Here it is found in meditative contemplative methods which involve direct experiencing beyond all contents and processes, beyond space and time.

Such spiritual practices have been called *apophatic*, that is, "speech denying." By this is meant that no particular sensations, feelings, thoughts, words, or images should be confused with the actual experience of Reality, which is beyond all these, and cannot be communicated. Therefore, *via negativa* sages like Meister Eckhart may write of emptying oneself of all content in order to find God:

> And you must know that to be empty of all created things
> is to be full of God, and to be full of created things is to
> be empty of God. (Eckhart 1981, 288)

We can recognize disidentification in Eckhart's words. One here lets go, detaches, empties oneself of all possible contents of awareness in order to be open to God—an impossibility for a self who *is* such contents. This is selling all we own for the "pearl of great price" (Matthew 13:46).

> *A condition of complete simplicity*
> *(Costing not less than everything)*
> —T. S. Eliot

But here again, we must not confuse disidentification with dissociation; this apophatic emptying should not be confused with some sort of repression or dissociation of psychological contents.

Letting go of thoughts is not a blanking out of one's mind, nor is letting go of a desire the repression of that desire. The buddha in the Schuhmacher and Woerner quotation above still has "pleasant and unpleasant sensations" even though "he is not ruled by them and remains innerly untouched by them."

> Having the semblance of the qualities of all the senses,
>     (Yet) freed from all the senses,
> Unattached, and yet all-maintaining;
>     *Free from the Strands, yet experiencing the*
>     *Strands (of matter) ...*
>                         (*Bhagavad Gita* 1964, 66, emphasis added)

> For we are not discussing the mere lack of things; this lack will not divest the soul, if it craves for all these objects. We are dealing with the denudation of the soul's appetites and gratifications; this is what leaves it *free and empty of all things, even though it possesses them.* (John of the Cross 1979, 77, emphasis added)

The words of the *Bhagavad Gita*, "free ... yet experiencing," and St. John's, "free and empty ... even though it possesses them," imply only a distinction—not a separation—between "I" and objects of experience. We are not told to get rid of all contents of consciousness, but to realize that we are not identical to them. It is the identification with them, the attachment to them, which is addressed by the *via negativa*. And as we have seen, disidentification may be experienced even while contents are present in consciousness. Lao Tzu follows suit:

Hence always rid yourself of desires in order
    to observe its secrets;
But always allow yourself to have desires in order
    to observe its manifestations.
These two are the same
But diverge in name as they issue forth.

                    (Lao Tzu 1968, 57)

According to Lao Tzu, realizing one is distinct from desires is "the same" as having desires, that is, transcendence and immanence are one. These two concepts are contradictory notions which seek to model aspects of one paradoxical phenomenon.

Many applied spiritual practices of the *via negativa* are therefore apophatic, using no symbols or scripture, no thinking or imagery, no inner or outer activity (though such things may—and usually do—provide the context for the practice). Practices often involve a simple sitting and being with what arises rather than involvement with inner or outer activity. Here there is no striving, even for enlightenment or God, but rather a growing alertness to just what is.

For example, here is the Christian meditation teacher James Finley:

True prayer rises spontaneously in goal-less-ness. If when we sit in prayer we sit with no goal, then there is no place for either discouragement or spiritual pride to take hold. The very notions of progress or the lack of progress cease to have meaning when one is no longer going anywhere. When we "just sit" we enter into the way of goal-less-ness, the nondualistic way of simply being who we are in the reality of the present moment. (Finley 1984, 128)

So this is not a blanking out, but an alertness to the experience of "the reality of the present moment." However, such bare attention or wakefulness to existence is such that one does not become caught up in the particular contents of experience or alterations in consciousness (or at least, in the practice one gradually becomes aware of when one is caught in these). The Benedictine monk Cyprian Smith writes:

> The kind of meditation I am talking about here is not meditation *upon* anything or *about* anything; it consists simply of sitting still for a lengthy period and simply *watching* the various thoughts and emotions which arise in the mind; not trying to resist them, drive them out, or change them, but simply watching them without identifying with them or being engulfed by them. (Smith 1987, 47)

The *via negativa* can be seen too in the Zen Buddhist practice of *shikantaza* meditation, which means, "nothing but precisely sitting":

> According to Dogen Zenji, shikantaza—i.e., resting in a state of brightly alert attention that is free of thoughts, directed to no object, and attached to no particular content—is the highest or purest form of zazen ... (Schuhmacher and Woerner 1989, 321)

And here is the *via negativa* appearing in Engler's statement about the Theravada Buddhist practice of vipassana meditation in which he quotes Nyanaponika:

> In its contemporary form, Vipassana is described as training in mindfulness, choiceless awareness or bare attention. This is the practice of a "clear and single-minded awareness of what actually happens to us and in us at the successive moments of perception" (Nyanaponika, 1973:30). (Engler 1986, 20)

Again, one is acutely aware of psychosomatic contents and processes, but not caught up in them—that is, disidentification.

Apophatic spiritual practices plumb for Reality through disidentification. One detaches, allowing the moment to be as it is without grabbing hold of the passing experience, the "stream of consciousness" of William James (1918, 239). By this refusal to "grab," one is saying in effect, "No," to all content, whether these are sensations and feelings, images and thoughts, visions and ecstasies. One hereby learns to experience disidentification within any and all inner processes, and becomes increasingly open to that ineffable Beingness which is distinct from process.

## The *Via Positiva*

As we have noted, this disidentification experience means an increased sense of intimacy with the inner and outer worlds. So while we may be alarmed by such apophatic terms as detachment, indifference, disinterest, or non-attachment that are often used in the *via negativa*, we must remember the paradox that the more there is a sense of "I" as non-identical with specific experiences, the more one is freely open to any and all changing experience and potential for action. *Transcendence cannot be separated from immanence.*

For example Eckhart, a master of the *via negativa*, was by no means an advocate of world-denying passivity. He saw both God and humanity meaningfully active in the world:

> The more he regards everything as divine—more divine than it is of itself—the more God will be pleased with him. To be sure, this requires effort and love, a careful cultivation of the spiritual life, and a watchful, honest active oversight of all one's mental attitudes towards things and people. *It is not to be learned by world-flight, running away from things, turning solitary and going apart from the world.* Rather, one must learn an inner solitude, wherever or with whomsoever he may be. He must learn to penetrate things and find God there ... (Eckhart 1941, 9, emphasis added)

The *via negativa*, for all its transcendent talk, in no way denies immanent engagement in the world, for either human being or Deepest Being. In other words, the "No" of the *via negativa* is not in any way separate from the "Yes" of the *via positiva*—the "positive path" or "positive way of knowing."

The *via positiva* can be thought of as knowing Reality in and through the reality of the human and natural worlds. It is recognizing and embracing the relative/temporal as a creation or manifestation of the absolute/eternal. Let us examine how this approach is applied to research and theory, and then to the experiential and practical.

> *All nature expresses God.*
> —Hugh of St. Victor

A) First, from a conceptual point of view, the *via positiva* entails allowing affirmative statements about Reality, beyond the negating terms of the *via negativa*. The *via positiva* can for example, develop an understanding of qualities such as beauty, goodness, joy, and justice, as Divine attributes. This path seeks to talk about the "constant way," attempts to name the "constant name," always remembering that Transcendent Reality can never be grasped conceptually.

This approach is not stopped by words such as ineffable or mystery, and presses on in an attempt to describe what can be described about the Ultimate. Perhaps the entire field of transpersonal psychology can be seen as a *via positiva*, as it seeks to study afresh mystical and unitive experiences of all types.

Specific examples of modern psychological *via positiva* conceptual approaches would be Maslow's discerning universal values in his study of peak experiences (see "Fusions of Facts and Values," in Maslow 1971); and the study and evocation of transpersonal or superconscious qualities in psychosynthesis.

> *That Light whose smile kindles the Universe,*
> *That Beauty in which all things work and move.*
> —Shelley

B) Secondly, from the point of view of applied practice, the *via positiva* does not employ the "speech denial" of apophatic approaches, but instead utilizes approaches called "cataphatic." (That is, as opposed to the speech denial of the apophatic, the cataphatic employs speech, activity, content, and process.)

Cataphatic practices involve content and activity. We find such things as: ritual; art; architecture; active prayer; reflective-receptive meditation; imagery; study; reading scripture; service to others; social activism; life-long commitment; and even in some instances, psychotherapy. Here transcendence is known as immanence, and one's deepest non-attached sense of self blossoms in the world.

An excellent illustration of the *via positiva* is provided by the words and deeds of the twelfth-century Abbot Suger. Here was a devout man who was deeply influenced by the writings of Pseudo-Dionysius, the mysterious author who had outlined the *via negativa* and *via positiva* for Christian spirituality.

In addition to being a religious and an abbot, Suger was also a minister and advisor to the French king Louis VI, and even governed during the absence of the king. For the abbot, there was no dissonance between spirituality and a life of action in the world.

Abbot Suger had an abiding belief that the material world need not be an obstacle to approaching God, but that it can in fact be an avenue for approaching God. This is a central principle of the *via positiva*. He wrote, "The dull mind rises to truth through that which is material." (Suger 1973, 527) This was perhaps a difficult line for him to maintain, given he lived in an age of reform in which the greed, opulence, and wealth of many monasteries were coming under attack.

But Abbot Suger seemed to be able to make the distinction between the use of worldly goods to aggrandize the ego, and the use of these goods as doorways to God. He went ahead and applied this *via positiva* idea, against much adversity, to the reconstruction of the church of St. Denis.

He designed and supervised the building of a beautiful structure with ribbed vaulting; large perpendicular windows which allowed light to flow into the interior; and a stained-glass rose window over the entrance. This was his attempt to create a beauty which would facilitate a relationship with God for all who would enter the structure. Abbot Suger hereby gave birth to what became known as Gothic architecture! He writes:

When—out of my delight in the beauty of the house of God—the loveliness of the many-colored stones has called me away from external cares, and worthy meditation has induced me to reflect, transferring that which is material to that which is immaterial, on the diversity of the sacred virtues: then it seems to me that I see myself dwelling, as it were, in some strange region of the universe which neither exists entirely in the slime of the earth nor entirely in the purity of Heaven; and that, by the Grace of God, I can be transported from this inferior to that higher world in an anagogical manner. (ibid.)

Any visitor moved by a Gothic cathedral can attest to the power of the *via positiva* affirmed by this twelfth-century abbot. Note from the passage that the positive path has not taken him out of the world, but rather into a place neither entirely worldly nor entirely un-worldly.

At the core of the *via positiva* is the notion that Spirit is present and active in the world: through the events of our daily lives; in our joys and sorrows; in the beauties of nature; in the most mundane physical objects which surround us. The *via positiva* contains the premise that Self is immanent, God is with us, that the Ultimate is pressing in on us in every moment of our existence.

And this intimate presence of Self is not merely a passive "being with," but is actively inviting us to engage the world, to live a life of continuous transformation of ourselves and our social structures. The *via positiva* implies that we are invited to respond to the vocation or "call" from Self in every minute of our lives.

> *Try, with God's help, to perceive the connection—*
> *even physical and natural—which binds your labour*
> *with the building of the kingdom of heaven.*
> —Teilhard de Chardin

Walking this path, we are images of God challenged to act with God in the world. In psychosynthesis terms, we are invited to align our personal will with the will of Self, and thereby facilitate the ongoing I-Self relationship we can call Self-realization.

## All Roads Lead to Self

But the austere apophatic language of the *via negativa* does at times seem to deny the cataphatic immanence of the *via positiva*, especially when the former seems to negate any experience of independent selfhood at all. Here is Thomas Merton:

> But if the truth is to make me free, I must also let go
> my hold upon myself, and not retain the semblance of
> a self which is an object of a "thing." I, too, must be
> no-thing. And when I am no-thing I am in the ALL,
> and Christ lives in me. (Merton 1964, 10)

Along these same lines, the *via negativa* might also tell us to surrender ourselves, to turn our will over to God, or to die to self—with no cataphatic talk at all. We might even be admonished to refuse completely any terminology which refers to the experience of self (see "Transcendence and No-thing-ness," chapter 4).

But properly understood, even such "selfless" terminology does not involve the actual loss of the experience of being a responsible agent in the world—or all people touting selflessness might simply retire to a mountain top and never be heard from again.

The term "selfless" might be translated as, "I am distinct from my ego concerns; I am distinct from the experience of isolation and separateness; I am distinct from any sense of myself as an object rather than a pure subject." (This is the defeat of what we call in the next appendix, the "narcissistic mistake"—the objectification of "I.")

Thus, the lives of the great mystics of East and West are quite often filled with purposeful action, whether as social reformers, missionaries, teachers, or authors. St. John of the Cross was a busy administrator and reformer; Meister Eckhart was a preacher, scholar, and teacher; and Chuang Tzu was a talented administrator and writer.

Even a cursory look at the mountain of literature written about apophatic spiritualities should be enough to convince us that these people are not talking about inaction, passivity, or the loss of true individuality. They can communicate a great deal about how it is that Reality is ultimately incommunicable!

So it would seem that personal responsibility and meaningful action in the world are in no way anathema to the deeper sense of self uncovered by the *via negativa*. Here is Eckhart:

> As I have often said, if a person were in such a rapturous state as St. Paul once entered, and he knew of a sick man who wanted a cup of soup, it would be far better to withdraw from the rapture for love's sake and serve him who is in need. (Eckhart 1941, 14)

Obviously, here is not a person who is selfless in the sense of losing one's boundaries in an ecstatic union with Reality. Rather, here is a selflessness which is free to give up even rapture. "I am distinct from my rapture."

An attachment to, an identification with, "a rapturous state" (or indeed any particular state of consciousness) would be every bit an obstacle for the *via negativa* as it would be for the *via positiva*. Attached to a state of rapture, I cut myself off from the experience of my distinctness from rapture, as well as from my ability to act well in the world. But experiencing disidentification from rapture allows me to have rapture without becoming attached—or addicted—to it.

All of this of course implies a self who is distinct from both rapture and action. Here is an empty self, a selfless self, or even a no-self if you wish, who can participate in either rapture or action as need be—one's transcendence allows free immanence. The *via negativa* is not separate from the *via positiva*.

So while we might hear of the selflessness of a Gandhi, a Mother Teresa, or a Martin Luther King, Jr., when we look at their lives, their selflessness is vastly different from any sort of inaction, passivity, or lack of personal power.

In all healthy spiritual practice, the disidentification experience is not separated from the expression or actualization of this deepening sense of "I" in a committed affirmation of life. If "I" is simultaneously transcendent and immanent, the *via negativa* simply addresses the former, while the *via positiva* addresses the latter. And both roads lead to contact with a transcendent-immanent Reality:

> God is therefore known in all things and as distinct from all things. He is known through knowledge and through unknowing. (Pseudo-Dionysius 1987, 108–109)

In sum, here is the Buddhist Loppon Lodro Dorje describing well a progression of—and identity of—these two basic paths of transcendence and immanence:

> In the Vajrayana tradition, there are three steps, crudely speaking. First is the dissolution of personal pride and the letting go of the reference point of personal ego. Then there is the notion of letting go of any conditioned experience whatsoever. Finally there is the level where you reappreciate the relative experience; in other words, the relative world is re-entered or brought back. This last stage corresponds to the notion of living in sacredness, or of transforming relative experience. So there is a process of going in—to union or dissolution—and then there is a coming out. Beyond that there is also the idea that *relative and absolute reality are together already, from the beginning*. (Dorje et al. 1987, 163, emphasis added)

# "I" in Psychology

> *As Narcissus bent over a clear pool for*
> *a drink and saw there his own reflection,*
> *on the moment he fell in love with it.*
> *"Now I know," he cried, "what others have*
> *suffered from me, for I burn with love of my*
> *own self—yet how can I reach that*
> *loveliness I see mirrored in the water?*
> *But I cannot leave it. Only death can set me free."*
> —Edith Hamilton

Attempting to track "I" in Western psychological theory is a bit like tracking a point of light as it illuminates first one object and then another—during which for the most part we see and describe the objects illuminated rather than the luminous spotlight.

It is rare that "I" is seen as distinct from that which it is identified, as a subject rather than an object. Instead, "I" is confused for example with organized cognition, purposeful behavior, the ability to relate to the outer world, or a tendency towards integration.

However, let us attempt to take a very brief look at some of Western psychology in which "I" can be discerned, however faintly. Our intention here is not to provide an exhaustive overview, but to invite the reader into a way of looking at psychological research by which the elusive "I" can be tracked.

## Freud and Ego Splitting

At the beginnings of modern Western psychology stands the giant
figure of Sigmund Freud, who did in fact discern a human subject
distinct from other elements of the psyche. This subject he called
"*Ich*" or "I." Here is Freud:

> Putting ourselves on the footing of everyday knowl-
> edge, we recognize in human beings a mental orga-
> nization which is interpolated between their sensory
> stimuli and the perception of their somatic needs on
> the one hand and their motor acts on the other, and
> which mediates between them for a particular purpose.
> We call this organization their *"Ich"* ["ego"; literally,
> "I"]. (Freud 1978, 17–18)

So while he is confusing "I" with a "mental organization,"
here nevertheless is the recognition of a center of responsiveness and power within the inner world, a center that is somehow
distinct from, and can act upon, that world.

While Freud's conception is tremendously important historically, it considers "*Ich*" as an object having mass and energy, an
object of awareness rather than the subjective experiencer. Freud
did however briefly recognize another possible way of thinking in
which the pure subjectness of "I" was affirmed:

> We wish to make the ego the matter of our enquiry, our
> very own ego. But is that possible? After all, the ego is
> in its very essence a subject; how can it be made into
> an object? (Freud 1965, 52)

Freud for a moment recognized the possibility of formulating the ego as something that is, "in its very essence a subject."
If he had stayed with this, he would have been focusing on "I"
as understood in psychosynthesis. "I" is in essence a subject,
because "I" is ever the experiencer rather than the object of experience, always the subject who is aware rather than the content of
awareness.

But Freud rejected this "essential subject" notion for human identity because, he says, the ego can split into parts, and thereby observe itself. Ego is not therefore essentially a subject. Immediately after the above passage, Freud continues:

> Well, there is no doubt that it can be. The ego can take itself as an object, can treat itself like other objects, can observe itself, criticize itself, and do Heaven knows what with itself. In this, one part of the ego is setting itself over against the rest. So the ego can be split; it splits itself during a number of its functions— temporarily at least. Its parts can come together again afterwards. (ibid.)

Now the ego is no longer the subject who observes, but the *object observed*. Ego has become a "thing" which can split into parts or which can be formed from parts. It has become a content of consciousness, not the subjective experiencer, and so the reality of "I" is missed.

But we would say Freud was correct in the first instance, and that his shift from ego-as-subject to ego-as-object does not eliminate the fact that there is still an essential subject here. Psychosynthesis would see through Freud's notion of a "splitting ego" to the undivided oneness of the subject beneath.

For Freud, ego is akin to a clay-like substance that can be pulled into pieces, one part the observer and one part the observed. One problem with this formulation of ego is that it covers many experiences which are in actuality very different ones: the ego can "take itself as an object, can treat itself like other objects, can observe itself, [and] can criticize itself." The single concept of "ego" fails to differentiate among all these types of experience.

For example, when "my ego splits," am I actually in the moment observing myself critically, or am I feeling that inner criticism directed at me from my internal judge? Am I inwardly shouting angrily at myself, or am I feeling guilty and ashamed? Freud's formulation does not clarify these questions, and the experiential difference between these positions is enormous—being critical is a very different experience from being criticized.[15]

On one hand, Freud's description of splitting the ego might refer to "I" receiving criticism. Here, I would be identified with a part of myself that feels guilty, ashamed, and worthless. Identified with this place in me, I would hear the words of my internal critic as he or she berated me. Here "ego" becomes that downtrodden part of myself with which I am identified, with the energy of blame being sent to me from my internal critic or judge. This represents an experience in which I am feeling bad and worthless, internally burdened and depressed by self-criticism. The critic is not felt to be "me" as much as some "other" within me.

But these very same dynamics of splitting may entail a very different experience, depending on where "I" is identified. I might for example be feeling angry with myself for having made some foolish mistake, and am inwardly (and/or outwardly) shouting at myself. In this case, I am identified not with the part of me who feels criticized, but with the part of me who criticizes, the one who feels not blamed, but blaming. This is a vastly different subjective experience from the former one, although the actual content and dynamics of the experience have not changed at all.

Here, I am identified with the critic, and can feel myself blaming. Whereas in the prior case the critical stance was felt to be other, now it is the criticized "ego" who is "other." (Ironically, I shall feel the impact of this criticism later, when my identification shifts from the "Top Dog" back to the "Under Dog," to use Fritz Perls' (1992) terms.)

If we only have the structures of "critic" and "ego," presumably split from the same ego-core, we miss entirely the difference between these two experiences—a difference accounted for only by tracking the pure subject who is able to move between these two positions. Freud's formulation does not help us discriminate between these experiences.

So the point of all this is that Freud's "ego" does not allow us to describe the true phenomenological nature of experience in the moment. And because of this, we miss "I"—the one who experiences in the here and now. The notion of "ego" obscures our view both of the variety of experience, and thus of the living, willing, subject of experience.

But if we posit an "I" who is essentially a subject and never an object, we can begin to understand various experiential possibilities. What this allows is crucial to psychotherapy and human relationships in general—*it allows one to understand and be with another person as she or he experiences these various possibilities.*

I will have much more ability to empathize with a person through all types of experiences if I do not simply lump them all into the one mechanistic notion of ego splitting. I will need to look carefully, ask questions, and listen well to discover what the other person's actual experience might be among all the different possibilities. The notion of "I" as subject seems therefore to have much more theoretical and clinical power than "I" understood as an object that can be split into pieces.

## Freud and the Narcissistic Mistake

This objectification of the subject is what we might call the *narcissistic mistake.* Narcissus was of course the chap who fell in love with his reflection in the water. But Narcissus' problem was not primarily the fact that he fell in love with his image; it was that he thought he could observe himself as an object—he thought he could split his ego! Narcissus saw a representation of himself, took it for himself, and thereby became trapped in the illusion that his self was something he could possess and love like an object. He did not realize that he was the one who was aware, and wasn't the contents of his awareness.

This narcissistic mistake, this assumption that "*Ich*" can be objectified and made into a content of awareness, therefore functions as a blind spot which prevents Freud from seeing clearly into the nature of the subjective "I."

And it is important to mark that Freud's assumption is indeed an assumption—it is an a priori belief which conditions his scientific impartiality. After all, why *not* consider "*Ich*" as pure subject, and find another way to account for the phenomena of self-observation and self-criticism? Others do not seem to have a problem with the pure subjectivity of "I." Here is psychologist Gaston Berger, as quoted by Assagioli:

If I wanted to speak more rigorously, I should then say
I am I, expressing in this unusual way the fact that the
I is always the subject. (Assagioli 1973, 262)

And humanistic-existential psychotherapist James Bugental,
responding to this very same ego-splitting passage by Freud
above, counters with his own view:

The *I*, as I conceive it, is irreducibly a unity and invariably a subject. It is, I postulate, the essential being.
(Bugental 1981, 201)

If we look at Freud's passage on ego splitting, we can see
that he presents no reason as to why the ego may not be thought
of as pure subject—except that it seemed able to split into parts.
But as we have seen, the experiences of supposed splitting (self-
criticism, and so forth) can be explained in far better ways—for
example, subpersonality theory (Vargiu 1974); ego states (Berne
1961); identity states (Tart 1986)—than with the idea that the ego
has divided into pieces. Something seems to have prevented Freud
from positing an essential subject.

Freud's blind spot may possibly derive from his commitment
to the Helmholtz philosophical school. This school held that, "No
other forces than the common physical chemical ones are active
within the organism" (Yankelovich 1970, 46).

Such a credo would therefore argue that all intrapsychic
dynamics are to be objectified, to be thought of as physical objects
or processes. This would quite effectively rule out any conceptions which attempted to describe the pure subject. From this
point of view it would be a foregone conclusion that ego should
be conceptualized as composed of content—"physical chemical" forces—rather than as a someone who eludes objectification.
Perhaps this is the source of Freud's narcissistic mistake, and the
reason "I" eluded him.

As in the case of Assagioli's gnostic-theosophical philosophy,
Freud's nineteenth-century positivism seems to have prevented
a full grasp of "I." But where Assagioli fell into dualism, Freud
slipped into psychological monism. (For an examination of

Freud's philosophical conditioning, see "Freud's Philosophical Commitment: The Helmholtz School" in Yankelovich 1970, 44–51.)

One suspects however, that if Freud had been familiar with some of the contemporary revolutionary concepts in physics, he would have pressed them into service to describe inner experience. Gordon Globus (1980), for one, does just this, drawing upon modern physics to reach towards quite a promising description of "I" as subject (see "Gordon Globus" later in this appendix).

In any case, Freud missed the subject, "I." His "*Ich*" became an object, a mass of content which could be pulled apart and stuck together like any other mass of content. He did not recognize that "I" can be understood as distinct from such content, as a subject and not an object.

Given Freud's blind spot, it is interesting to note the oft-mentioned fact that the actual practice of classical psychoanalysis does seem to involve disidentification. Here, the client is invited to free associate, that is, to observe and report objectively on what is occurring in the inner world—similar in some ways to contemplative prayer and insight meditation (this similarity is mentioned by Deikman 1982, 96–97; and Engler 1986, 34–35).

Free association directly implies that "I" is distinct but not separate from psychic contents such as sensations, feelings, thoughts, images, and memories which make up the stream of consciousness. Classical psychoanalytic technique, if not the theory, seems therefore to recognize implicitly a transcendent-immanent "I."

# C. G. Jung and the Transcendent-Immanent Function

C. G. Jung approaches our understanding of "I" most closely not in his concept of ego, but in his concept of the *transcendent function*. Jung sees the transcendent function at the very core of the process of healthy personality transformation, the process he calls *individuation*. Here he describes this transcendent function, which in some ways is reminiscent of Freud's ego splitting described above:

If we picture the conscious mind, with the ego as its centre, as being opposed to the unconscious, and if we now add to our mental picture the process of assimilating the unconscious, we can think of this assimilation as a kind of approximation of conscious and unconscious, *where the centre of the total personality no longer coincides with the ego*, but with a point midway between the conscious and unconscious. This would be the point of new equilibrium, a new centering of the total personality, a virtual centre which, on account of its focal position between conscious and unconscious, ensures for the personality a new and more solid foundation. (Jung 1966, 221, emphasis added)

In the beginning of this passage, Jung is describing a psychological situation in which the "centre of the total personality" is identified with the ego. Since this center will shortly demonstrate its ability to shift from this identification—disidentify—we are assuming that this center may be equivalent to what we are calling "I."

Jung goes on to say that the operation of the transcendent function is such that this "centre of the total personality no longer coincides with the ego." That is, this center can disidentify from the ego, and can move to a position midway between the conscious and unconscious.

So we have now a disidentification of "I" from its former identification, and thereby an increased ability to be aware of, and to integrate, formerly unconscious contents. One might imagine this evolving towards a new configuration made up of contents from the former ego and unconscious areas of the personality:

This would be the point of new equilibrium, a new centering of the total personality, a virtual centre which, on account of its focal position between conscious and unconscious, ensures for the personality a new and more solid foundation. (Jung 1966, 221)

As Jung saw, the transcendent function immediately implies the ability of the disidentified center to embrace much more of the inner and outer worlds. *Thus the transcendent function cannot be separated from what we might call the immanent function.*

Increased transcendence leads directly to increased immanence. Upon experiencing disidentification, one has a much broader range of psychological potential available, and will therefore have much more of oneself to bring to the business of living.

## Contemporary Psychology

The psychosynthesis view of "I" was echoed in more recent times by Abraham Maslow, whose ground-breaking study of human psychological health gave birth to Humanistic and Transpersonal Psychology. We can here see Maslow's insight into the transcendence of human identity (we note Maslow uses "he" generically):

> ... it makes similar sense to describe highest, most authentic identity as non-striving, non-needing, non-wishing—as having transcended ordinary needs and drives. He just is. (Maslow 1961, 258)

The transcendence of this "is-ness" or "being" is however in no way found to be dualistically disconnected from the world. Rather, Maslow notes that the person is more immanent, having "more 'free will' than at other times" (256). Maslow states:

> As he gets to be more purely and singly himself, he is more able to fuse with the world, with what was formerly not-self ... (255)

Very much in agreement with Maslow, the humanistic psychologist Clark Moustakas also posits transcendence-immanence, when he speaks first of what he calls the "being" aspect of self:

The individual self, or being, is an ultimate core of reality which remains unchanged throughout changes of its qualities or states. (Moustakas 1956, 272)

And then he adds the immanent concept of "becoming:"

The individual is engaged in leading his life in the present, with a forward thrust in the future. This is the concept of becoming, with its implications of change and transformation. (ibid.)

An interesting piece of research which considers "I" in some ways consistent with psychosynthesis, is the study of the "I-am-me experience" published in the *Review of Existential Psychology and Psychiatry* by Herbert Spiegelberg. He found that,

... the "I-am-me" experience ... precedes, as it were, any character or role. It is precisely the experience of one's non-coincidence with these "identifications" which leads to the awareness of the "I-am-me" in its most acute form. (Spiegelberg 1964, 9)

And much of existential psychotherapy, especially the work of Rollo May (1958, 1983), seems consistent with a non-dualistic psychosynthesis (an *existential* psychosynthesis?). The following is part of a case history presented by May to illustrate what he calls the "I am" experience. Note the progression through initial disidentification to a realization of "I." These are the words of his patient:

Later on that night I woke up and it came to me this way, "I accept the fact that I am an illegitimate child." *But* "I am not a child anymore." So it is, "I am illegitimate." That is not so either: "I was born illegitimate." Then what is left? What is left is this, "*I Am.*" This *act* of contact and acceptance with "I am," once gotten hold of, gave me (what I think was for me the first time) the experience "Since I Am, I have the right to be."

...It is my saying to Descartes, "I *Am, therefore* I think, I feel, I do." (May, 1958, 43)

Also, from a more "hard research" approach, the insights of Menninger Foundation biofeedback researchers Alyce and Elmer Green seem relevant here as well. Their research has apparently taken them along a *via negativa* to face the transcendence-immanence of human identity:

> What can be said as we work with these levels is: We are not merely what society says we are, as children, as adults, or as old people. That is the first level of field-independence: independence from what we perceive outside the skin. Further, we are not merely what our bodies say we are, not in the voluntary nervous system or in the involuntary nervous system. Not only are we not our emotions..., but we are also not our thoughts. The question remains, then: Who are we? (Green 1977, 193)

In addition, the term *true self* as found in D. W. Winnicott (1987), Alice Miller (1981), Charles Whitfield (1987), and John Bradshaw (1988), as well as Heinz Kohut's (1977) concept of *nuclear self* and Daniel Stern's (1985) concept of *emergent self*, all lead us beyond the Freudian ego, and in the direction of "I" as understood by psychosynthesis (although all appear to stop short of transcendence-immanence).

These authors see a core spontaneous self which when traumatized develops a false self, or defensive structures, involving such things as compulsions, codependency, addictions, and the feeling of living inauthentically.

## Gordon Globus

> *Psychiatry has, in general, little to say about "I."*
> —Gordon Globus

A very interesting conceptual approach to "I" is that of the psychiatrist Gordon Globus, who borrows the notion of "singularity" from contemporary cosmology and physics (for example, as found in the study of black holes).

Globus describes "I" as an "analytical singularity." This concept allows him to approach a discussion of transcendence which is consonant with modern physics:

> More formally put, a "singularity" in a domain is a region that is singular because the fundamental properties of the domain are absent, i.e., the ordinary rules governing the domain no longer apply. At an analytical singularity, there are not entities and there is no relatedness in space or time; the very manifold of spacetime breaks down. That "I" is "not a part of the world," is "indescribable," and "shrinks to a point without extension" does not force "I" to be illusory, for *these very characteristics describe an analytical singularity.* (Globus 1980, 419)

Here we see the *via negativa* in the words, "the fundamental properties of the domain are absent," and in the phrase, "not part of the world." This approach leads to a notion of distinctness from spacetime, to an indescribable dimensionless point called "I"—in our terms, transcendent "I." Again, this is all valid physics and mathematics.

But at the same time, as in the case of a black hole, the analytical singularity is engaged in spacetime at a specific individual location, called an "address" by Globus:

> ... "I" is coupled to an "address" at which the very analytic properties of that domain disappear ... (ibid.)

In other words, "I" is immanent. "I" does not belong to another, other-worldly domain, but to *this* domain. "I" as a singularity, as with a black hole, is not a concept which implies a dualistic transcendent order disconnected from the world. Rather, singularity simply describes something (a no-thing) occurring within the world itself. Globus hereby carefully avoids the dualistic mistake:

> ... "I" as analytical singularity does not commit us to ontological dualism because only one domain is required.

and:

> ... "I" is coupled to its world—"the world is my world"...(420)

Thus "I" is "in the world," by virtue of being coupled to an address, and because "only one domain is required" to describe it. And yet "I" is not "of the world," because, "the ordinary rules governing the domain no longer apply." It seems clear that Globus' application of singularity to "I" addresses both the transcendence and immanence of "I."

Such refined application of modern physics to psychological thought is a welcome and much-needed approach. Perhaps the current mapping of mind-boggling discoveries in the outer world may assist us in mapping mind-boggling aspects of the inner world, and vice versa. Such coherence of maps is possible however, only if inner and outer realities are related aspects of a single reality, and not dualistically separated realms.[16]

## Arthur Deikman

One of the most important thinkers on the subject of "I" is the psychiatrist and clinical professor Arthur Deikman. Deikman has long been known for his research on meditation (Deikman 1980), and has been a vociferous critic of his own profession when it attempts to interpret mystical experience as simply pathological (Deikman 1977).

To my knowledge, Deikman's *The Observing Self* (1982) is the only major work which clearly approaches the (non-dualistic) psychosynthesis insight into the nature of "I." Given this, we shall here critique his notion of the observing self, so that the psychosynthesis reader might discern "I" within Deikman's framework. Here is Deikman:

> The observing self is the transparent center, that which is aware. This fourth self [observing self] is most personal of all, prior to thought, feeling, and action, for it experiences these functions. No matter what takes place, no matter what we experience, nothing is as central as the self that observes. In the face of this phenomenon, Descartes' starting point, "I think, therefore, I am," must yield to the more basic position, "I am aware; therefore I am." (Deikman 1982, 94)

Deikman is quite clear that the observing self is of a very different order from psychic processes, even using the term "transcendent" for this self (95). He is a master at consistently recognizing the distinction between objects of awareness and awareness itself, and his writing here is lucid:

> In contrast [to the objects of awareness], however, the observing self has no elements, no features whatsoever. It is not a question of a searchlight illuminating one area while another is dark, but of the nature of the light itself. (102)

At the same time, Deikman does not make a distinction between "I" and awareness, saying, "We *are* awareness … it is the core experience of self" (103). In his searchlight metaphor above for example, he is saying that the observing self *is* the awareness—the "light"—which illuminates the objects of awareness, while itself remaining distinct from these objects. This is a major problem in his formulation, and the major difference between the psychosynthesis notion of "I" and that of the observing self.

Staying with his metaphor of the searchlight for a moment, we would very much agree that the light is distinct from the objects, but we would maintain that "I" is not the light, but the searchlight itself. Furthermore, we would say that the searchlight not only has the fundamental ability to shine light/awareness, but the equally fundamental ability to direct that light as well—"I" has will. (Deikman himself recognizes that increased experience of

the observing self allows "increased mastery," [110]; and "auton-
omy" [108].)

We might say in fact that "I" in this searchlight model is more
analogous to the person who can direct the searchlight, casting
light first on this object and then on that. We would therefore not
make the statement, "I am aware, therefore I am;" but affirm the
more basic proposition, "I am, therefore I can be aware and will."

Because Deikman identifies self with awareness, observing is not seen as a function of "I" but instead as a discrete self
among other selves. He thus speaks of four selves, the emotional,
thinking, functional, and observing selves—a confusing formulation that obscures the very different order, the transcendence, he
imputes to the observing self. (See "'I' as Distinct from Levels of
Consciousness," chapter 6.)

We would say rather that there is only one self—"I"—who can
have these various experiences of feeling, thinking, functioning,
and observing. One can see the need for this interpretation when
we read phrases of Deikman's such as, "able to locate ourselves in
the observer" (108) or, "identify with the observing self rather than
with the thoughts, emotions, and images" (145). What escapes
such phrases is the "who" who "locates in the observer"—who is
the one who is doing the locating? Who is the one who "identifies
with the observing self"?

It seems there is an unnoticed someone here, moving from the
experience of thoughts, emotions, and images, to the experience
of observation. We maintain that this invisible, elusive someone is
"I," distinct but not separate from the functions of consciousness
and will.

From a psychosynthesis point of view then, Deikman's observing self is actually a description of "I" experiencing disidentified
observation. However, inasmuch as self is deemed equivalent to
awareness, his conception misses the central position of will in
human identity.

In spite of—or with the inclusion of—the above critique,
we must say that Deikman's book would be required reading
for anyone interested in the topic of "I." Of particular interest
is his section entitled, "The Observing Self in Western Psychotherapy" (96–103), which shows how incomplete is our own

brief exploration of this subject here (although oddly enough, he unaccountably leaves psychosynthesis out of this survey).

In this survey section, Deikman takes up for example, Fritz Perls, Heinz Kohut, and the psychoanalytic concept of the observing ego. Here too he critiques Gordon Globus, saying that although Globus begins well, he ends up focused on the object self rather than on the true observing self.

## In Conclusion

It appears then that the above psychological researchers and clinicians are in agreement, to a greater or lesser degree, with the spiritual approaches mentioned in appendix 1. All seem to be saying in some way that the deeper nature of human identity is capable of experiencing itself as distinct from psychosomatic contents, while at the same time remaining fully engaged in these contents. Even Freud's narcissistic mistake includes a distinction between the ego and other psychic content.

Thus, deepest human being appears to some extent to be widely recognized—in East and West, in religion and psychology—as "in but not of," or "distinct but not separate from," the psyche-soma. In other words, we might consider ourselves to be essentially transcendent-immanent.

> *We can do all that, but we will still not know the essence of the self as differentiated from its manifestations.*
> —Heinz Kohut
>
> *And therefore I now give it finer names than I have ever given it before, and yet whatever names, whatever words we use, they are telling lies, and it is far above them.*
> —Meister Eckhart

# Good, Evil, and the I-Self Relationship

> *Today as never before it is important that
> human beings should not overlook the danger
> of the evil lurking within them. It is unfortunately
> only too real, which is why psychology must insist
> on the reality of evil and must reject any definition
> that regards it as insignificant or actually non-existent.*
> —C. G. Jung

Perhaps unlike other psychological approaches, which do not attempt to study the heights of spiritual experience, both psychosynthesis and transpersonal psychology in general have a need to grapple with the nature of human evil.

Is it holistic to think of Self as made up of both good and evil? Does there need to be a concept of evil will to balance Assagioli's concept of good will? Is it positive thinking to ignore human sin? How is it that men and women, experienced in higher states of consciousness, can still perform violent and immoral acts?

Questions such as these are crucial to any approach—religious or psychological—which is seeking to understand and work with the spiritual dimension of the human being. Here we shall briefly explore the question of good and evil from a psychological perspective, outlining principles such as induction, Abraxas, and *privatio boni*, which are helpful in clarifying the I-Self relationship in an encounter with suffering and evil.

We shall again draw on our understanding of transcendence-immanence as we do this.

## Induction

There is a common phenomenon in human growth which we have already alluded to in the body of this book ("Transcendence-Immanence and Therapy," chapter 7). This phenomenon is one in which we experience a movement towards a deeper I-Self relationship, and thereby become acutely and even painfully aware of the attitudes and behaviors which need transformation in order to actualize that deeper relationship.

In these cases of emerging negativity, is Self to be thought of as causing these reactions in the person? Does Self choose the suffering this often entails? Is this negativity part of the totality of Self? If so, is there not a dark side to Self—one I must be wary and distrustful of?

Obviously, the answers to such questions can be vital in the ongoing I-Self relationship, as these would have a great deal to do with how we perceive and relate to Self. So let us take a closer look at the actual phenomenon we are discussing.

Take the case of someone having a powerful vision like Abraham Maslow's (1971, 269–70), in which he saw himself as part of a vast procession of teachers, leading from the ancient past to the distant future (see "Maslow's Experience," chapter 6). Such a vision, however inspiring, may engender feelings of fear and worthlessness in a person. One might ask, "How can I ever live up to such a profound vision? I am unworthy to walk in such a noble procession of teachers." These feelings may become obstacles to acting upon the vision, and will most likely have childhood roots. Here the energy of the potential has flowed into the person and energized a childhood issue.

Another example of this phenomenon would be a person who reviews past behavior in the light of newly-discovered truth and a deeper sense of responsibility, and feels healthy guilt and shame for actions now perceived as wrong. This new sensitivity can then lead to taking responsibility for the effects of the past, and a healthy transformation of one's life may ensue. Here new potential has energized feelings of guilt and shame, albeit healthy ones, leading to a deeper sense of authenticity.

This phenomenon, by which emerging potential reveals obstacles, increases resistances, and illuminates issues, can be called, *induction*. Our usage of this term follows for the most part Aldous Huxley's use of the same term, which he describes in this way:

> It [induction] also takes place in the cortex, and is the physical basis of that ambivalence of sentiment which is so striking a feature of man's [and woman's] psychological life. Every positive begets its corresponding negative ... we find such things as a hatred that accompanies love, a derision begotten by respect and awe. (Huxley 1952, 187)

Our understanding of induction is akin to the physics principle of the same name, whereby energy flows from an electromagnetic field into a conductor. Speaking psychologically, we have energy from the field of the positive insight or choice flowing into the personality. As James Vargiu pointed out, this is also a model for understanding how energy flows from the "magnetic field" of the superconscious into the conscious personality (Vargiu 1977, 23).

Further, our use of induction includes the fact that this energy flowing in the psyche-soma energizes obstacles or resistances to that energy. The positive energy "heats up" the inner obstacles which need to be transformed in order to express the insight or choice (see Assagioli 1965, 43–49); and Maslow's concepts of the Jonah complex and "counter-valuing" (Maslow 1971, 35–40). Here is Assagioli describing what we would call induction:

> Sometimes it even happens that lower propensities and drives hitherto lying dormant in the unconscious, are vitalized by the inrush of higher energy, or stirred into a fury of opposition by the consecration of the awakening man ... (Assagioli 1965, 47)

Another example of induction would be a novice committing to a religious order and being plunged into a feeling of abject unworthiness (and possibly interpreting this as God's punishment for sins). Or a bride or bridegroom might find the upcoming marriage vows energizing latent fears of entrapment (and perhaps interpret this as the other person having conscious intentions to entrap). Or we might find ourselves feeling inferior and even resentful when meeting a person possessing qualities we admire (and attack the person for supposedly making us feel that way—an example of Huxley's, "a derision begotten by respect and awe"). In each case, the new potential illuminates a latent obstacle to its acceptance and possible actualization in our lives.

> *Life in God is not an escape from [sin],*
> *but the way to gain full insight concerning it.*
> *It is ... the experience of religious reality*
> *which forces the "Night Side" out into the light.*
> —Dag Hammarskjöld

Induction is a common aspect of human growth and of psychotherapy. How often a person will enter therapy suffering from a sudden onslaught of anxiety and inadequacy, and gradually discover a new sense of self in the world—a sense of self far healthier than that *before* the onset of the symptoms.

What has happened in these cases is that an unconscious potential for a new way of being has energized the symptom or negative reaction; the negativity is a direct response to the burgeoning positive potential. Upon then working through the painful reactions, one discovers the potential which inducted the reactions in the beginning. Induction also accounts for the often-noted fact that a spiritual discipline such as meditation often surfaces hitherto hidden psychological issues.

From the other direction, we may begin with a deep sense of our potential, of what we may be. In this case, induction quite often will only fully manifest as we entertain a concrete course of action based on our higher values, that is, as our will comes into play. As long as we merely focus upon the wonders of potential, dreams, and plans—that is, upon the level of "quality" dissociated from "event"—no resistance to actualization need arise.

As long as we avoid commitment, we are free for example to idealize our romantic partners or our spiritual community. We can do so up to the moment when we need to act in concert, to actually make choices together. At that point we begin to struggle with the power issues and the like which come with the concrete living out of commitments in life. It is only as we move towards acting on our values that obstacles are encountered in ourselves and others. This is one very important reason that idealization and dualistic denial are so seductive; here one may experience the wonder and beauty of the potential, adhere to one's most pure spiritual values, and never meet any resistance.

Many a marriage and spiritual community have foundered on the hidden rocks revealed by induction. Indeed, I suspect induction lies at the root of many a well-intentioned spiritual group which, while beginning with profound spiritual truths, became overwhelmed by inducted dynamics, and turned into a cult. On the other hand, induction can prevent us from risking any committed, wholehearted application of our values at all. And in still other cases, induction may lead us to adopt beliefs which spiritually rationalize our passivity and lack of commitment.

But let us look now at what can occur if the principle of induction is not clearly understood, and one begins to believe that Self is producing the negativity of the resistances. This of course has dire consequences for the I-Self relationship and Self-realization.

## Induction and Abraxas

Induction is important to understand because if movement towards Self energizes negative experiences in us, we may be tempted to think that Self is causing this negativity, or wants it to be there, or is responsible for its creation in some way.

However, all that is happening is that the realization of greater potential is illuminating pre-existing hidden obstacles. When we go out in the sunlight, and our imperfections are illuminated, it is unfair to blame the sun for these imperfections!

If we ignore induction, and *do* mistakenly interpret our negative experience as somehow chosen and created by Self, we then may consider Self not as transcendent-immanent, but as some totality

which includes both good and evil. We may think that Self is causing our pain and turmoil; is testing us; is manipulating or punishing
us; is judging and shaming us; or is harshly teaching us a lesson
for our own good. (Yahweh of the Hebrew Scriptures often suffers
from such misinterpretations, and these Scriptures should, I believe,
be read with the dynamic of induction firmly in mind.)

Here is that great early secretary of the United Nations, Dag
Hammarskjöld, speaking to precisely these misinterpretations, as
contrasted to the principle of induction:

> That piece of pagan anthropomorphism: the belief
> that, in order to educate us, God wishes us to suffer.
> How far from this is the assent to suffering when it
> strikes us because we have obeyed what we have seen
> to be God's will. (Hammarskjöld 1968, 164)

According to Hammarskjöld, the notion that there is a punishing Self is quite different from the idea that as we follow Self
we will energize resistances in ourselves and others. In the first
instance we have an abusive Self; in the second instance we have
a Self who is with us in our struggle to love more fully.

If we do misinterpret our suffering as chosen by Self, we drift
towards a notion of Self much like the abusive gnostic demiurge:
a blind, arrogant, punishing ruler of the cosmos who cannot be
trusted. Jung called this god, when seen as universal totality,
*Abraxas*, adapting the term from the Gnostic, Basilides:

> Hard to know is the deity of Abraxas. Its power is the
> greatest, because man perceiveth it not. From the sun
> he draweth the *summum bonum*; from the devil the
> *infimum malum*; but from Abraxas LIFE, altogether
> indefinite, the mother of good and evil. ...
>    Abraxas is the sun, and at the same time the eter-
> nally sucking gorge of the void, the belittling and
> dismembering devil. (Jung 1963, 383)

Here we have a notion of Self as a good-evil unity or a God-
Devil combination, and note too, this concept is equivalent to the

uroboros—a symbol for cosmic totality (see "Transcendence as Infinity," chapter 4). This is indeed a notion which conditions Jung's conception of Self:

> The self is defined psychologically as the psychic totality of the individual. ... Without the integration of evil there is no totality ...
> (Jung 1969a, 156)

Such thinking led Jung to add the devil to the Christian Trinity, envisioning the Godhead as a quaternity which included evil. According to Jung, "Murder, sudden death, war, sickness, crime, and every kind of abomination fall in with the unity of God" (175); and again, "We naturally boggle at the thought that good and evil are both contained in God ... " (196).

Of course Jung's good-evil notion of self and God is simply a personification or deification of unity, of the uroboros, and is far from any understanding of transcendent-immanent Being. As we have seen, transcendent-immanent Being is not to be confused with a totality of any sort, though we may experience an altered state of consciousness in which we apparently see all things, including evil, fitting into a single unity, into "The All."

This Abraxas image is very different from the psychosynthesis concept of Self, and seems to present an insurmountable obstacle to trusting Self—one would be foolhardy and/or masochistic to seek intimacy with such a Self, much less surrender to it. A good-evil Self is the very picture of the abusive alcoholic parent, loving one minute and raging the next. Such an Abraxas Self can be feared and placated, but never sought out in intimacy and love.

On one hand, the Abraxas concept can be taken to mean that we are morally superior to God/Self (as Jung maintained in *Answer to Job;* Jung 1969b). We thus seem encouraged here to stay aloof from this great stumbling power of Self, treating it with the respectful distance we might grant to a powerful beast of the field; that is, we respect and harness the power of the animal, but would never think of actually letting it into the house.

On the other hand, an Abraxas image of Self might quite logically encourage us to develop a mysticism of sin. Here we could

seek to unite with Self by doing ill, thus acting in union with the
dark side of Self—why not? If Self is choosing evil, then I, an
image of that Self, must learn to act with malicious destructive-
ness as well. By doing evil things, I may thereby draw closer to
Self. Or if Self is evil *and* good, perhaps I should be loving half
the time, and abusive the other half of the time!

> *I worked one case where a kid*
> *said he was both God and the Devil.*
> *That's something Manson would say.*
> —Tim Boyle, Police Officer,
> Satanism Investigator

In any case, it seems clear that a concept of Self as Abraxas
highly contaminates the I-Self relationship. If we consider
ourselves images of that Self, it may cause us to mistrust ourselves
or lead us down a dark path. Or we may distance ourselves from
Self, maintaining our own personal morality in the face of this
deeper, fickle lawlessness.

But we can instead remain clear that when negativity increases
in Self-realization, this negativity is not something created by
Self, but is surfacing as a result of induction. It is simply that a
potential for greater truth in our lives is painfully revealing the
hidden corners of untruth by which we have been living—and this
process, though painful, is not evil.

An example of mistaking induction for a supposed dark side
of God can be seen in a striking childhood experience of Jung's.
He was as a youth once profoundly disturbed by a daydream or
vision which terrified him:

> I saw before me the cathedral, the blue sky. God sits on
> His golden throne, high above the world—and from
> under the throne an enormous turd falls upon the spar-
> kling new roof, shatters it, and breaks the walls of the
> cathedral asunder. (Jung 1963, 39)

The young Jung thought that God was forcing this vision upon
him, and was thereby demanding him to commit the unforgivable

sin in witnessing such apparent blasphemy. He also thought that God's wanting him to sin here was analogous to God (supposedly) wanting Adam and Eve to sin—the duplicity of an Abraxas god.

However, there is no sin or evil represented in Jung's vision at all, at least not by the actions of Jung or God. The vision is in fact an excellent example of induction: God's turd shattering the cathedral is God's truth shattering the superficial and legalistic religiosity of Jung's elders.

Here, energy from the "field" of God was inducted into the resistant structure of the cathedral, destroying it. On the other hand, a structure which was open and receptive to the energy of God would have conducted the energy, allowed the energy to flow through it unhindered. In the latter case, no heating up and combustion would have occurred. But the resistance of the structure itself caused its downfall.

So Jung's vision represents no dark side to God, in the sense of evil. Quite the contrary, this is merely the light of truth dispelling a falsehood—a triumph of Good. The only evil represented here is the cathedral, symbolizing the disservice rendered to the community (or to Jung at least) by the prevailing religious practices of the day.

It is easy to think that any sort of destruction is automatically evil—the dark side—without looking at what is being destroyed and by what means. Understanding induction allows us to see that as we approach Reality our illusions heat up and may indeed burn up, but this is far from evil.

This burning which is created by induction has been called *purgation* in mystical literature. It is analogous to what can happen when a strong electrical current meets resistance—instead of conducting the electricity, the resistance absorbs the energy and builds up heat, until finally combustion takes place.

And of course if we are identified with the illusion, we will feel pain and even rage as the illusion is inducted, as it heats up and finally burns in the light (perhaps this is a psychological description of purgatory or hell). In such hellish turmoil, we may indeed claim that truth is evil, that the "dark side" of truth is destroying us. We have only to look at our historical abuse and murder of prophets to see how quickly we blame truth for attempting to dispel our illusions. However, it is actually our own refusal to acknowledge truth which is at fault here, and which in turn causes the pain and fear, the rage and revenge.

*What burns in hell is nothing.*
—Meister Eckhart

## Abraxas and Cosmic Consciousness

But the illusion of Abraxas may arise not so much from the operation of induction, but directly through our experiences of cosmic consciousness. The reason for this is that such an experience offers us an apparent view of the entire cosmos:

> To have a clear perception (rather than a purely abstract and verbal philosophical acceptance) that the universe is all of a piece and that one has his place in it—one is a part of it, one belongs to it—can be so profound and shaking an experience that it can change the person's character and his Weltanschauung [worldview] forever after. (Maslow 1970, 59)

But how can such a glorious realization lead to the two-faced Abraxas? Note that the experience presents itself as a vision of the entire universe. Everything is seen as a unity, and of course part of this unity is evil. That is the way the universe is. Therefore one may see in this unitary insight not only the good and the beautiful, but the malicious and cruel. Here, "All is One."

And if we then confuse this unitary perception—the uroboros—with transcendent-immanent Being, then unity literally becomes our idol. And the name of this graven image is: Abraxas. Both good and evil make up the unity. As Jung stated, "Murder, sudden death, war, sickness, crime, and every kind of abomination fall in with the unity of God [Abraxas]." Here is a passage from Maslow which illustrates this very dynamic:

> [People who have had peak experiences] become reconciled to evil. Evil itself is accepted and under-

stood and seen in its proper place in the whole, as belonging there, as unavoidable, as necessary, and, therefore, as proper. (Maslow 1970, 63)

But if evil is "necessary" and "proper," why not simply do evil? Why not work on developing evil will as well as good will? For example, the film *Manhunter* (1986) portrays a serial killer following exactly this type of logic. Since the suffering and cruelty in the world revealed to him that God had a supposed dark side, he felt he was simply acting in union with God as he murdered his victims. And one cannot fault this logic based merely upon an experience of cosmic consciousness—indeed, such an experience can be used to support such thinking.

Unfortunately too, this is not simply the stuff of cinema. Here is the late R. C. Zaehner, former professor of Eastern Religions and Ethics at Oxford University, pointing out the moral difficulties of the non-dualism (monism) of Abraxas:

> For most of its modern enthusiasts Eastern mysticism means either Zen or Neo-Vedanta, non-dualism as it is frequently called. This Aldous Huxley has called the "perennial philosophy," and at its heart lies the "coincidence of opposites" so dear to the heart of C. G. Jung. In the Absolute One all the opposites are fused into One, and evil is seen simply as an aspect of good: "justice *is* strife," as our own Heraclitus said. Or, in the words of Charles Manson ... "If God is One, what is bad?" R. M. Bucke the idealist Canadian doctor [author of *Cosmic Consciousness*], and Charles Manson, the unruffled murderer and master of murderers: curious company, you may think. Perhaps, but behind them lies an ancient Hindu tradition as old as the Upanishads and the Bhagavad-Gita. (Zaehner 1981, 35)

These may be disturbing words to us. But one can take issue with professor Zaehner only insofar as the specific traditions he mentions do in practice break away from a pure monism, from "All is One." Only in this way can they elaborate a spiritual-moral context by which to interpret and act wisely on unitive experiences. The point is that *any* monistic interpretation of Ultimate Reality is vulnerable to Abraxas, to finding itself finally unable to clearly distinguish between good and evil.

A monistic system would need to navigate the treacherous waters of Abraxas, and somehow make some distinction between good and evil, between what is right to do and what is wrong to do. I do not know enough to judge, but one might assume that most religious traditions do offer some such moral matrix within which spiritual experience can be safely nurtured and expressed.

But if there is indeed no spiritual-moral context, no community, no scripture or tradition to hold these powerful unitive experiences, then these life-changing experiences may indeed burst the bounds of morality—they may lead us to violate the potentially intimate communion of "I" and Self. Then we may hear ourselves proudly asserting, "Who is to say that *my* spiritual experience, the greatest insight of *my* life, is not The Absolute Truth?" We are extremely vulnerable to Abraxas in this attitude.

Abraxas awaits us when we avoid all spiritual-moral contexts because we fear they will be archaic and dogmatic; or when we wish to remain the sole interpreters of our private revelations; or when we want the "pure experience" unfettered by precise understanding, theological discernment, or behavioral consequences; or when we confuse the notions of ineffable and mystery with our own inability to articulate our higher experiences.

Part of the problem posed for psychosynthesis, and for humanistic and transpersonal psychology in general, is that they often claim to study the "pure experience" divorced from the traditional moral, social, and religious contexts in which they are usually found. Maslow for example spoke of the "core-religious experience:"

> This something common, this something which is left over after we peel away all the localisms, all the accidents of particular languages or particular philosophies, all the ethnocentric phrasings, all those elements which are *not* common, we may call the "core-religious experience" or the "transcendent experience." (Maslow 1970, 20)

But such a core-religious experience does not in fact exist. It is an intellectual abstraction. We cannot dualistically separate the experience from the historical moment and socio-cultural context in which it occurs. Such would be a notion of transcendence with no immanence.

Can one understand Buddha based simply on one moment under the Bodhi tree, without understanding the needs of his historical time; the purpose he followed in his life; and the social effects which flowed from his insight and actions? Can we understand Moses merely based on his moment at the burning bush, and ignore the powerful historical impact of this experience—an experience at a particular time and place, occurring to this particular man? I think not.

There is an historical import to such revelations, an import which cannot be separated from the experiences themselves. It is not that all historical ramifications of such experiences can be discounted as simply artifacts, encrustations, and degradations of the original experience. It is quite true that many historical "ripples" made by these revelations are indeed distortions, deviations from the intention of the original prophet. But it is also true that there are many other effects in which the original intent can still be discerned. And more than this, some of these ripples through spacetime reveal increasingly *more* about the original impulse than was appreciated in the prophet's own time.

Transcendence-immanence tells us we cannot separate such revelatory experiences from their historical context, and prevents us from believing that such dualistic thinking approaches a deeper reality. The idea that we can make such a separation suffers the same dualism contained in the statement, "I am not my body, feelings, and mind." Here we say instead, "I am not my historical space and time."

But we and our highest experiences are distinct but not separate from our individual, unique moment in history. There are common elements in these experiences which can indeed be studied, but there are also very many uncommon elements which are integral, and cannot be discarded without violating the meaning of the revelation.

Thus both transpersonal psychology and humanistic psychology must, in their study of peak experiencing, take into account the historical moment, the cultural-religious context, and the life story of the one having the experience. There is no other way to discover how it is that a unitive experience can quite easily produce either good or evil, a saint or serial killer. There is no other way to ascertain whether the experience was Self-realization or not. *The crucial data for such a discernment lie in the context, not in the experience.*

And too, let us carefully note that this discussion has direct clinical applications. If we fully understand that we cannot separate spirituality from its context, we as clinicians must also recognize that our clients' spiritual needs may include a need for a nurturing and guiding matrix, a spiritual tradition. As we have said, a developing spirituality in a client very often demands what we will call a "larger spiritual-moral context"—a context *beyond* the scope of psychology, transpersonal or not.

That is, transpersonal psychotherapy must know its limits, and when spirituality blossoms strongly in a client, it must be ready to acknowledge that the client has in some ways outgrown the therapeutic context. Otherwise, the psychology itself may begin a pretense of offering the structure and guidance only appropriate to religious traditions. When this happens, psychology ceases to be psychology, and begins to become a religion. (See "Larger Spiritual-Moral Contexts" in chapter 7.)

## *The Shadow, Evil, and* Privatio Boni

Now, having thrown the concepts of good and evil around a bit, perhaps it is time to talk about them more directly. First of all, let us be clear that throughout our discussion of evil here we are not talking about "integrating the shadow." According to Jung (1968, 20), the shadow simply comprises those unconscious contents standing in immediate opposition to the social persona and conscious ego (and shadow contents may be quite benign and even beneficial). And as Jungian analysts John Sanford (1987, 124–47) and Fritz Kunkel (in Sanford 1987) have pointed out, the shadow has nothing to do with evil. Evil resides not in the unconscious, *but in the ego*—that is, *it is a function of will.*

When we discuss evil we are not talking about psychosomatic contents which must be integrated in order to attain psychological wholeness. We are instead talking about the use of will to consciously do ill to oneself, others, or nature. Evil is not so much a matter of consciousness or unconsciousness, but is a matter of what we *do* with the consciousness or unconsciousness we have.

For example, I may uncover a murderous rage which I have been repressing my entire life, an aspect of my shadow. I can feel this rage, safely express it, trace its historical roots, and finally integrate it, transforming it perhaps into appropriate anger at injustices in the world. But none of that has anything at all to do with evil. Morality, the use of will, would only come into play as I for example struggled with the choice to actually kill someone from this rage or not. Only then am I engaging the question of good and evil. Good or evil are acts of will, consciously chosen; *they are not contents of the personality.*

If we look at Assagioli's concept of Self, we see clearly that Self is not to be thought of as choosing good one minute and evil the next. Self is not for him an Abraxas mixture of good and evil. For example, no psychosynthesis therapist assists a client in getting in touch with Self by suggesting an image of a wise-and-treacherous person, or a loving-and-hating person! And while Assagioli considered goodness as one of the few fundamental aspects of will (*the good will*—Assagioli 1973, 85–90), we never find exercises for developing the logical opposite—bad will. An oversight? We think not.

For Assagioli, Self is indeed Good, but in a transcendent-immanent sense—not as a pole to an opposite evil Self or to a dark side of Self. That is to say, Self does not cause evil, does not choose that bad things happen, and does not wish us to be alienated from Self, others, and the world.

True, it may be that our relationship with Self involves pain and suffering. Through induction, the deeper potential for truth and goodness may starkly reveal and even painfully destroy our false pride, our inflated dreams, our hypocrisy, and those portions of our lives based on these illusions. This is healthy purgation.

We may even, following our truth, become the victims of someone else's evil choices, and perhaps give up our lives in this struggle. But throughout, Self is here doing nothing more than offering us truth, inviting us to be who we truly are. We can, and indeed often do, refuse.

No, in psychosynthesis, evil would not be an opposite in the sense that masculine and feminine, or yin and yang, are opposites. These latter are opposites created by Being, chosen by Self, allowing the necessary dynamisms of life.

Rather, evil is unnecessary to life; some would say it is "the one thing unnecessary." Betrayal is not always necessary to establish individuality; war is not always necessary to peace; malicious deception and revenge are not always necessary so that we may appreciate integrity and forgiveness; evil is not the spice to an otherwise boring goodness. And even though good things often may come out of evil situations, this occurs *in spite* of evil, not because of it.

Speaking theologically, we believe Assagioli would not say, for example, that God chooses world war, genocide, epidemics, earthquakes, flood, and famine. These things do take place of course, and are included in the unity of our world, but *we need not deify that unity*. This is the idolatry of Abraxas. As we have seen, that unity is simply our own perception of the total cosmos, and does not necessarily include God or God's will at all. God is not simply all things, but a transcendent-immanent Being, in but not of all things.

Speaking psychologically, we may say that evil is the chosen absence of our relationship with Self. Evil is our unwillingness to surrender to Self, to acknowledge that fundamental dependency which already exists. We hereby choose to act as isolated individuals with no fundamental unity between us, others, and the world.

(And note that our choices for good or ill can be made at any level of consciousness at all, that is, we may do bad things while in cosmic consciousness, and we may elect to do the right thing even though we are full of hurt pride and revenge.)

Evil can therefore be seen as the absence of relationship to (Good) Self, or as this absence is known, a "privation of good" or the *privatio boni*. Here privation means that the fundamental reality of our deeply good ontological connection to Self is willfully ignored. This is therefore a privation, a lie, a non-thing, because it is not based on reality.

> *Evil cannot be known simply as evil, for its core is hollow,*
> *and can be neither recognized nor defined*
> *save by the surrounding good.*
> —St. Thomas Aquinas

*Privatio boni* does not imply then, as in Jung's description of his patient's attitude, that evil is "nothing, a trifling and fleeting diminution of good, like a cloud passing over the sun" (Jung 1982, xx). On the contrary, by ignoring our fundamental unity we abuse and kill each other every day, and that is very real, in no way a "nothing" or fleeting trifle.

The point is that we abuse and kill each other because we choose to act according to a lie, an illusion—we are not in truth fundamentally isolated beings, but reflected images of one Self. In Assagioli's words, "the isolated man [or woman] does not exist" (Assagioli 1973, 85).

Therefore acting from selfish isolation and non-relationship, although it causes very real effects—from the ecological crisis, to racism, to war—is nevertheless a choice for an illusion, an absence, a privation.

> *I define Satan as a real spirit of unreality.*
> —M. Scott Peck

Psychologically, it is this illusory isolation from Self (and thus from others and the world) which is the *privatio boni*. This lie about our identity can be called pride, the notion that I am the center of the universe. Pride is a nothing which causes quite real suffering. Perhaps the illusion of pride is akin to the illusion of ego discussed in Eastern religions. (*Privatio boni* thus may be a point of contact between East and West.)

*Privatio boni* also means that our fundamental unifying center, Self, is not choosing that we act from pride, from an iden-tification as selfish isolated individuals. As Assagioli maintains, the will of Self is beckoning us towards something quite differ-ent from that:

...the Spirit working upon and within all creation
is shaping it into order, harmony, and beauty, uniting all beings (some willing but the majority as yet
blind and rebellious) with each other through links of
love...(Assagioli 1965, 31)

So Self in psychosynthesis is not a yin-yang synthesis of good
and evil with a light and dark side, with an evil will and a good
will. First of all, Self is not a member of any polarity, because Self
is transcendent of any polarity. And second of all, Self is immanent
in the good-evil dichotomy not by choosing good and evil, but by
*supporting* the former truth and *dispelling* the latter lie. In psychosynthesis, human evil would not be seen as created and supported
by a supposed dark side of Self (a transcendent-immanent Self has
no "sides"!), but as arising from our own selfish actions, our own
holding onto our illusory isolation from our fundamental Unifying
Center—Self.

We therefore need not fear relationship to this Self. Here is not
a fickle totality-Self, not a blind abusive Abraxas Self, but a faithful Self, one that merely invites us to know the reality of our lives.
Too, this Self is not some amoral impersonal cosmic energy which
we can use like a cosmic dynamo for our own purposes; here is
transcendent-immanent Being, loving us, guiding us, and perhaps
most of all, respecting our free will.

To close our discussion here, let us reiterate that the importance of concepts such as induction, Abraxas, and *privatio boni*
is that they allow us to maintain clarity regarding transcendence-
immanence as applied to "I" and Self. This in turn can assist us in
recognizing and facilitating the developing I-Self relationship in
ourselves and others.

Clarity about the nature of evil is of crucial importance to any
transpersonal psychology, and especially to psychosynthesis. As
psychosynthesis struggles to heal its dualistic denial, and begins
to look at the nature of human evil, it must be on guard against any
sort of monism which would bring evil into the conception of Self.

*For several decades we psychologists looked upon the whole matter of sin and moral accountability as a great incubus and acclaimed our liberation from it as epoch-making. But at length we have discovered that to be "free" in this sense, i.e., to have the excuse of being "sick" rather than sinful, is to court the danger of also becoming lost. This danger is, I believe, betokened by the widespread interest in Existentialism which we are presently witnessing. In becoming amoral, ethically neutral, and "free," we have cut the very roots of our being; lost our deepest sense of self-hood and identity; and with neurotics themselves, find ourselves asking: "who **am** I?"*

—O. Hobart Mowrer

# Individuality
# and Universality

*That is to say, even the enlightened person
remains what he is, and is never more than
his own limited ego before the One who dwells
within him, whose form has no knowable boundaries,
who encompasses him on all sides,
fathomless as the abysms of the earth and vast as the sky.*
—C. G. Jung

Many times in Assagioli's writings we can find the idea that a union between "I" and Self is not only possible, but desirable:

... to reach up, following the thread or ray [on the Egg Diagram] to the star; to unite the lower with the higher Self. (Assagioli 1965, 24)

Self-realization, in this specific well-defined sense, means the momentary or more or less temporary identification or blending of the I-consciousness with the spiritual Self, in which the former, which is the reflection of the latter, becomes reunited, blended with the spiritual Self. (202)

...toward the unification of the personal center of consciousness, the "I" or ego, with the Transpersonal Self... (Assagioli 1973, 33)

...which culminates in the unification of the consciousness of the personal self, or "I," with that of the Transpersonal Self. (122)

However, we must not then allow this experience of I-Self union to grow into the idea that therefore, "I *am* my Higher Self." Assagioli's statements should not be taken to mean that one's essential identity is that of Self. Both Assagioli and Jung have warned against this danger:

...it is most important to recognize clearly, and to retain ever present in theory and in practice, the difference that exists between the Self in its essential nature...and the small ordinary personality, the little "self" or ego, of which we are normally conscious. The disregard of this vital distinction leads to absurd and dangerous consequences. (Assagioli 1965, 45)

...the great psychic danger which is always connected with individuation, or the development of the self, lies in the identification of ego-consciousness with the self. This produces an inflation which threatens consciousness with dissolution. (Jung 1968, 145)

So, although "I am *not* my Higher Self," it seems possible to recognize a positive and healthy union of "I" and Self. This union, as we have seen in chapter 6, is profound—the union of reflected image and reflecting source—and by virtue of it, "I" can be seen as not self-existent, and in some sense as non-existent (see "Transcendence and No-thing-ness," chapter 4).

However, it seems overstating the case to maintain that therefore there are "not really two selves," but *only* Self, as Assagioli does at one point (Assagioli 1965, 20). That statement is as close as Assagioli ever gets to monism, although it seems merely to be his attempt to describe the profound unity of "I" and Self as recognized in the quotations above.

By the way, maintaining clarity about this distinction between "I" and Self is not dualism, because there is only one domain and one ontological source. Too, it is only by recognizing this distinction that the true nature of the I-Self unity can be approached. As we saw in chapter 6, such a union is far more profound than the act of simply affirming one's identification with Self. Such an affirmation also reduces Self-realization to a private action of "I," ignoring the developing I-Self relationship.

This experiential reality of the I-Self distinction can however become obscured in psychosynthesis theory by a concept often used by Assagioli to describe Self. This is the concept that Self, "feels itself at the same time individual and universal" (87).

The reason this can be confusing is that the human being ("I") also can have experiences which may be described as "individuality and universality." Such a description can for example be applied to peak experiences of unitive or cosmic consciousness. Therefore, "I" can experience individuality-universality, and Self can experience individuality-universality. But are these actually different experiences? If so, how? Or are they the same experience? If so, does this mean that, "I am my Higher Self," after all? Or am I simply momentarily sharing in the consciousness of Self?

Ambiguity about the meaning of individuality-universality can therefore translate into a confusion between "I" and Self, leading potentially to the dangers mentioned above. How we understand this experience of individuality-universality thus becomes important in maintaining clarity about "I" and Self, and thus too, in describing the intimate healthy union of "I" and Self.

Also, a careful examination of the concept and the experience of individuality-universality can be helpful in providing much-needed clarification about the concepts of Higher Self and Universal Self as used in psychosynthesis theory.

We shall therefore devote the following pages to an examination of this concept of individuality-universality as it pertains to human experience, and again apply the principle of transcendence-immanence in guiding our way.

## Individual-Universal Consciousness

Assagioli was quite clear that the human being can, in a healthy way, experience universality. According to him, this occurs in moments of *"samadhi, prahna, satori,* ecstasies, cosmic consciousness, etc." (Assagioli 1973, 128). We might quote Maslow again on cosmic consciousness:

> Also useful would be [Richard] Bucke's use of cosmic consciousness. This is a special phenomeno-logical state in which the person somehow perceives the whole cosmos or at least the unity and integration of it and everything in it, including his Self. (Maslow 1971, 277)

This passage describes a person's vivid awareness of the unity of the universe—an experience of universality that does not submerge the individual self-consciousness of the person. Thus, this can quite rightly be called an experience of individuality and universality.

But how does this experience relate to Self, who according to Assagioli, also "feels itself at the same time individual and universal"? On one hand, we have "individual-universal" used to describe a state of consciousness attained by "I," and on the other hand, it is used to describe the nature of living, willing Self. Here the distinction between "I" and Self becomes blurred.

Let us carefully examine a passage in which Assagioli employs this individual-universal concept:

> The real distinguishing factor between the little self and the higher Self is that the little self is acutely aware of itself as a distinct separate individual, and a sense of solitude or of separation sometimes comes in the existential experience. In contrast, the experi-ence of the spiritual Self is a sense of freedom, of expansion, of communication with other Selves and with reality, and there is a sense of Universality. It

feels itself at the same time individual and universal. (Assagioli 1965, 87)

But we know that "I" can in fact experience universality, and is not limited to merely a "sense of solitude" and "separation." A sense of universality is exactly what one feels during an experience of cosmic consciousness; here "I" partakes of a larger, more universal reality, and experiences an integration with that reality. To identify "little self" or "I" with the experience of "separation," ignores the fact that "I" is transcendent-immanent and may experience separation *or* unity, solitude *or* relationship. As we have seen, "I" is distinct but not separate from states of consciousness.

We may also note in this passage that Self is idealized. Self is held to experience "freedom" and "expansion," which may or may not be the case. These words clearly describe a superconscious experience, but as we have seen, a transcendent-immanent Self is distinct but not separate from the superconscious. Such a Self pervades not only the superconscious, but all the other levels of the psyche as well. Thus, Self might experience anything at all, and in transcendence-immanence theory, *does* experience everything.

But we can see the limitations of Assagioli's words above most clearly as we discover we are still left with the question: If one shifts from an experience of separation to one of individuality-universality, *who shifted between these two experiences?* It cannot be the "little self" who only experiences separation, and it cannot be "the spiritual Self" who only experiences individuality-universality. So who is it that experienced *both* of these states?

Asking such questions allows us to look in the direction of true I-amness. And as we do, we can see that such a shift in experience is most clearly and simply described as a shift in the awareness of "I." *It is "I" who experiences first separation and then a universality in which individuality is not lost.* Thus it would seem much more accurate to talk about this movement from separation to unity, as "I" having an experience of universal or cosmic consciousness. Thus, we need no conception of a deeper Self here at all.

Assagioli's notion of individuality-universality may here be taken to be his attempt to point out, quite correctly, that one can realize a profound experience of unitive consciousness, and still maintain one's sense of personal identity, of individuality. This may be his way of guarding against a monism which would hold that individuality is an illusion to be lost in the "sea" of universality. Here is Assagioli quoting Lama Govinda (1970), with whom he agrees on this issue:

> Merely to "merge into the whole" like the "drop into the sea," without having realized that wholeness, is only a poetical way of accepting annihilation and evading the problem that the fact of our individuality poses. Why should the universe evolve individualized forms of life and consciousness if this were not consistent with or inherent in the very spirit or nature of the universe? (Assagioli 1973, 128)

Again it is clear that Assagioli was not a monist. Nevertheless, it can be misleading to use "individuality-universality" to denote this unitive state of consciousness, and then use the same term to describe Self. This confuses Self-realization—that can involve *any* sort of consciousness at all—with the personal experience of cosmic consciousness.

This confusion can therefore lead to all the problems we have discussed in earlier chapters. Most simply put, this confusion is one whereby I mistake experiences of cosmic consciousness for Self-realization. I then may devote myself to cultivating these peak experiences as my "true self." Here my vision of my deepest identity becomes inflated and idealized, and I will be doomed to believing that I can experience my true self only in these peak moments. This obviously can become a tangent in the overall process of Self-realization, as one moves into dualistic denial and begins to disown and or at least devalue the more mundane experiences characteristic of daily life.

In conclusion, if we use individuality-universality to denote a particular state of consciousness—cosmic consciousness—we should then avoid using this terminology as a description of Self.

The term may then be used simply to describe a particular type of experience, without pretending to say anything at all about the subject who has the experience (either "I" or Self could conceivably have such an experience).

We would still need to avoid the usage, "I am a synthesis of individuality and universality," because that equates human I-amness with a particular state of consciousness.

If, on the other hand, we wish to use individuality-universality to describe Self, we are not then speaking of any type of state of consciousness. We are now talking about living, willing, experiencing being. We are now pointing to an *Individual-Universal Self.*

## Individual-Universal Self

This idea of an Individual-Universal Self is indeed already an aspect of psychosynthesis theory, and therefore we have a strong incentive to maintain clarity about how we use the individual-universal formulation. To approach this issue, we must look fully at the fact that Assagioli postulated what he called, *Universal Self:*

> As we have seen, man's basic existential experience, when disidentified from all the various psychological elements, is the conscious "Being"—*is being a living self.* This is an aspect [or "reflection"] of the Universal Self or Being. (Assagioli 1973, 126)

He supports this idea of Universal Self by pointing to the experiential reports of a vast array of different people, saying that "the most enlightened men and women of all ages have given testimony" to this Reality (ibid.).

Assagioli also maintains that Universal Being, while ultimately beyond the powers of human comprehension, can be partially conceptualized by means of analogy. Thus he can posit the existence of Universal Will, and thus of Universal Self, by understanding these as analogous to personal will and personal self:

> Here again let us recognize that if there was not a
> Universal Will, man would possess something not
> existing in the universe, and therefore the microcosm
> would be superior to the macrocosm—indeed a ridicu-
> lous conceit! (Assagioli 1973, 130)

In our terms, given the mysterious transcendence-immanence of human being, this being cannot simply be a product of
psychosomatic or social processes; human being must ultimately
be a reflection of a deeper, universally Transcendent-Immanent
Source.

And of course, in psychological enquiry it does not matter
whether we believe in such a Source or not. That is, whether or not
we believe that Universal Self is an objective reality, it is nevertheless what Jung referred to as a psychological fact.

> God is an obvious psychic and non-physical fact, i.e.,
> a fact that can be established psychically but not phys-
> ically. (Jung 1969a, 464)

Thus, without engaging the theological issues of whether
Universal Self or God exists or not, we can with confidence state
that such a reality is a widely-observed aspect of healthy human
experience. We can then consider Universal Self to be an accurate mapping of human experience, with no need necessarily to
venture into the realm of religious belief.

So how does this notion of Universal Self relate to our
understanding of individuality-universality? It does so directly
and immediately, because Universal Self *is* individual as well
as universal. That is, there can only be one Universal Self or we
are not talking about true universality, but about something more
relative. Any sort of plural "universal selves" would still seem
to demand a more universal Self to give them their being. Thus
Universal Self is one, singular, unique, *individual*. (Assagioli, to
my knowledge, never spoke of Universal Self in the plural.)

And therein lies a danger of inflation. Following this understanding of individuality-universality, if I consider that "I am

Self," that "I am a synthesis of individuality and universality," then what I am saying in fact is, "I am Universal Self."

While it is very true that we may experience union with universality in cosmic consciousness, this is very different from saying, "I *am* Individual and Universal." This statement is not the statement of any type of relative self, but can only be the statement of a Universal Self. Many selves might perhaps experience a sense of universal consciousness, but only a Universal Self would experience true Individuality-Universality.

Thus, if we understand individual-universal as denoting true Individual-Universal Selfhood, a statement that "I am the Self" strongly risks the danger of inflation mentioned by Assagioli and Jung. While we may indeed experience a union with Self, and thereby a union with the individuality-universality of Self, this should not be interpreted as meaning that I *am* individual-universal, that I *am* Self. Only Self has a right to that statement.

So whether the phrase, "I am the Self," amounts to inflation through a confusion of I-amness with a higher state of consciousness, or whether it amounts to inflation through a confusion of human I-amness with Individual-Universal I-amness, it seems an inflationary statement when uttered by a human being. "I am the Self," may be as idealized and inflated as, "I am not my body, feelings, and mind."

## No Need for "Higher Self"

Given all of the above, we believe there is no need in psychosynthesis theory for the notion of a Higher or Transpersonal Self which experiences individuality and universality.

On one hand, if Higher Self refers to an experience of universal consciousness in which individual I-amness is not lost, it simply indicates a particular state of consciousness and not living, willing Being at all. Thus Higher Self is an inaccurate usage, and we believe should be dropped.

On the other hand, if Higher Self refers to actual Individual-Universal Being, then it is a redundant term—there is already a Universal Self in psychosynthesis theory which carries that meaning. Thus, the usage of Higher Self is unnecessary and confusing, and either it or Universal Self should be dropped.

But it seems more advisable to drop both "Higher" and "Universal," and to use the simple word, *Self*. This term can easily cover all the dynamics understood under the concepts of Higher Self and Universal Self.

For example, the older usage seemed to imply that the Higher Self was close to us, meeting us deep within; while the Universal Self was further away, out there in the universe somewhere. But if Self is understood as universally transcendent-immanent, it follows that Self can be present to all individuals, meeting them in the most interior intimacy of their inner beings; as well as present and active in the outer relationships and events of their lives; as well as conscious and willing throughout the entire universe.

Thus, for instance, Assagioli's most powerful way of describing the union of "I" and Self remains what it always has been: the alignment of the personal will with the will of Self (or to put it another way, a committed and loving relationship between "I" and Self).

The will of transcendent-immanent Self is universal in that it is experienced as acting in and through all things and not merely vis-à-vis myself; but this will is completely immanent and personal to me and my life as well. We do not, in other words, need a distinction between the will of the Higher Self and the will of Universal Self.

For example, note Assagioli's description of the experience of the will of the Higher Self:

> Accounts of religious experiences often speak of a "call" from God, or a "pull" from some Higher Power ... (Assagioli 1973, 114)

Compare that passage to his description of the experience of the will of the Universal Self:

> For those having a devotional nature or a religious conception of faith, it is the relationship and eventual unification of man's will with God's will. (Assagioli 1973, 130)

There seems to be no need to view these two passages as describing two different wills greater than the will of "I"—in both cases, "God" is inviting human being into intimate relationship. If we are talking about the will of a transcendent-immanent Self, it is not at all paradoxical that one can experience the most universal connection at the level of unique human being. (And in both cases it may be inflationary to consider one*self* the source of such higher will, rather than the one who can respond to it and thereby realize intimate union with it.)

One's individual call or vocation cannot but be the expression of a universal will, a will which calls us to play our part in the greater, universal whole. Could one be aligned with vocation and not with "God's will"? We think not. One's individual, personal story has its own unique part in the whole; and a full unfoldment of our own unique story finds its unique place in the Greater Story.

## One Self

Finally, if we elect to follow Assagioli's notion that Self is individual and universal, and use "Self" in the plural, we again run the same dangers of idealization and inflation. Assagioli does this for example in the phrase, "the experience of the spiritual Self is a sense ... of communication with *other Selves* " (Assagioli 1965, 87, emphasis added).

But plural "Selves" implies plural syntheses of individuality and universality. We are therefore again talking about either many private, individual experiences of universal consciousness, or many Individual-Universal Selves, in which case we are not talking about Universal Being at all.

It is quite true that we each can have our own unique personal relationship and individual union with Self, and can experience these deeply within us as well as through the people and events in our lives. But we need not therefore understand these as experiences of multiple private "Selves."

If we understand these experiences as not simply cosmic consciousness, but as relationship with actual Individual-Universal Being, it seems more precise to describe these moments as different experiences—each in its own way accurate and limited—of one Self. Such a singular Self would be the unique source of all "uniquenesses;" the one source of all "onenesses;" the individual source of all individuality.

So instead of saying for example, "I have my Self and you have your Self," we propose that a better mapping of human experience is to say something like, "The One Self has *us*." (The phrase, "my Higher Self," can take on a certain proprietary air, amounting to the individual ego claiming ownership of Individuality-Universality.)

This idea of one Self is useful in explaining the phenomenon that in developing an intimate relationship with Self, one often may find intimate relationship, and indeed unity, with other people and the world at large (and vice versa—one may discover Self in others and the world). This relatedness of all things makes sense if we posit a common universal fulcrum or pivot of this unity; otherwise there would seem to be no basis for such an experience.

Such a fulcrum is conceivable as a universally transcendent-immanent Self, a Self who is absolutely transcendent of the universe, and by that very fact, absolutely immanent throughout the universe—"Having pervaded the universe, I remain." And if this relatedness of all things is indeed founded in such a Self—the very source of I-amness—it is a relatedness which preserves the unique individual boundaries of both self and other. (But again, Self-realization may lead as well into profound realizations of isolation and disintegration—such is the profundity of transcendence-immanence engaged here.)

By this "one Self" hypothesis then, we can distinguish Self-realization generally from any sort of fundamental or final isolation and world-denial; from any final selfish absorption in one's own psychological or spiritual needs; and too, from any unhealthy dependency and self-sacrifice of the type now known as codependency. In this understanding of Self, we have therefore a possible psychological basis for understanding a synthesis of individual need and altruism, of personal growth and service to others.

## A Religious Postscript

Let us close this appendix by venturing some psychological comments about a few traditional religious ideas. We here follow a venerable tradition in psychology, from Freud's criticisms of religion in general; to Jung's commentaries on the Trinity or the Catholic Mass (among many other subjects); right up to present-day psychological speculations about scriptures such as the Adam and Eve story in Genesis.

Recall first that earlier in this book we undertook a careful examination of the empirical/phenomenological experience of "I." We saw that "I" has the ability to experience itself as distinct but not separate from psychosomatic processes, and therefore it seemed appropriate to conceive of "I" as transcendent-immanent. Positing a source for such human transcendence-immanence, we have come to the notion of a universally transcendent-immanent Self. This latter concept seems demanded by the nature of transcendent-immanent "I," and as well, seems to map accurately the age-old experience of Universal Spirit or Being. Let us apply these understandings briefly to some religious concepts.

First of all, our study finds itself inconsistent with theologies which identify Universal Being with the universe, with creation, with the cosmos (for example, pantheism and nature worship). The God of such conceptions can logically only produce an image or reflection—the human "I"—which is itself identical with content and process. If Universal Being is reducible to the universe, to "all things," then human being is reducible to all things of the psyche-soma. Here is the materialistic, "I am my body, feelings, and mind." This is a concept of immanence without transcendence.

By the same token, our study finds itself at variance with any religious conceptions which view Universal Being as dissociated or separate from the universe (for example, deism and Gnosticism). Such a God would produce an image or reflection which is itself dualistically separated from psychosomatic processes. Here, "I am not my body, feelings, and mind." This is a concept of transcendence without immanence.

And finally, our study is inconsistent with theological ideas which view Universal Being as any sort of synthesis of parts such as feminine-masculine, good-evil, or spirit-matter (for example, God-Goddess, Abraxas, or the Supreme Synthesis of holistic gnosticism). Such conceptions still imply a fundamental split in human and Universal Being, even though that split is seemingly closed by an intimate union of the opposites. This seems in effect to be the worship of an intellectual concept of unity—the concept of a "God-Universe whole"—rather than the worship of God. With such a God, the reflected "I" is therefore a totality made up of parts: "I am a synthesis of opposites, of good and evil, of spirit and matter, of...etc." This view can only represent transcendence and immanence as two different parts which come together into a composite whole.

However, our exploration in this book does seem in accord with conceptions which view Universal Being as universally transcendent-immanent, as distinct but not separate from the cosmos, as in but not of all things. Here transcendence and imma-nence are not two parts of a whole, but two views of the same single God.

The reflected image of such a God would therefore itself be transcendent-immanent, distinct but not separate from the content and process of psyche-soma and the world at large. This transcendent-immanent *imago* would of course be contingent, utterly dependent upon the creative act of the reflecting God for its being. As Assagioli states, "The reflection appears to be self-extent but has, in reality, no autonomous substantiality" (Assa-gioli 1965, 20).

Furthermore, in realizing an ongoing connection with this universally transcendent-immanent God, the human being would ultimately realize a deep sense of identity in the world, an iden-tity which is intimately and actively engaged with others and with the entire universe. And as we have seen above, human "I," as conceived of by non-dualistic psychosynthesis, does indeed seem to be precisely such an *imago Dei.*

*Me as abiding in all beings whoso*
*Reveres, adopting (the belief in) one-ness,*
*Tho abiding in any possible condition,*
*That disciplined man abides in Me.*
—Bhagavad Gita

# Working with
# Roberto Assagioli

*With understanding is born the recognition
that an individual "is as he is," and in a
certain sense has the right to be what he is.*
—Roberto Assagioli

When I worked with Roberto Assagioli, he was a small-framed 85-year-old with fine white hair and beard, twinkling eyes, and ready humor. His infectious smile and warm sincerity gradually put me at ease, though I was a bit awed to finally work with this colleague of Freud and Jung.

Sitting with him in his book-filled Tuscan study, he in his European smoking jacket and I in my California cords, I thought, "Maybe this is someone I can trust to understand me, who may be safe enough to let into the most private places within me." Such an unguarded opening of my inner life felt risky of course, but something about this quietly joyful, accepting man inspired a trust that allowed me to contemplate taking the risk. I felt in the presence of a respectful person, a compassionate person, a good person.

As we met over the following months and I continued to sense no traces of judgment or demand from him, the walls that guarded the citadel of my interior life gradually came down. He joined me there, inside those guarded gates, and stood by me as friend and confidant. Roberto was neither pushy nor passive, but simply fully alive with me, interested in my life, interested in my experience, interested in me.

Over the days, weeks, and months, I experienced such an empathic presence from him that I was able to forget about guarding myself and instead safely focus my attention on the precise nature of my unfolding experience. There was no need to defend here: he was not demanding that I think or feel more or less, not wedded to any technique, nor invested in giving me any particular type of experience.

If I was uninterested in a direction he suggested he would drop that with no hint of disappointment or judgment and find out where I wanted to go; he did not seem attached to his interventions nor to the pursuit of any particular result. Within such a pure empathic field I was freed to explore the depths and heights of my world unmolested, and the results amazed me.

During the time I worked with Roberto, long-buried emotions erupted to be felt, old wounds and sorrows emerged and were cleansed, my creativity flowed freely, my life history revealed new and fascinating meanings, and above all, I felt inwardly confirmed in my vocation as therapist, teacher, and writer.

Another fascinating dynamic of this work was that many important insights and emotional breakthroughs occurred even when I was not meeting with him. Traveling on a bus, walking the streets of the city, lying in bed awaiting sleep, the flow of deep feeling and thoughts continued. He was not only an external presence catalyzing the blossoming of my being, but an internal one as well; he was inside me, holding the space for the unfolding and transformation of my world. Even today, many years later, Roberto can still function as an inner presence in my life, alive with that same empathy, compassion, and joy.

Working with Roberto reminded me of my meditation practice in which I sat silent and still, mindfully open to the flow of my experience without becoming swept into that flow. Now it was as if he and I meditated together, not he in his own world and I in mine, *but both of us in my world.* And his joining of me in my world facilitated this same type of direct encounter with arising experience, but took me to much deeper levels.

Our communion brought an enhanced ability to engage all levels of my being, allowing deeply hidden layers of both higher and lower unconscious to emerge and be integrated. It was as if I had formerly meditated on only one floor of my being, but now empowered by his empathic holding, I had access to many different floors and could work with these in healing and growthful ways.

> *It is of the greatest importance that*
> *psychotherapists continue to study meditation.*
> —Roberto Assagioli

Another way of describing my relationship with Roberto is simply, "love." But this was a love operating independent of, yet manifest through, our personalities. This was an unconditional, spiritual love, perhaps what might be called compassion or agape. Held by this love, I was freed from my defenses and could allow any and all experiences to arise within me—and so they did, with surprising power.

And all this healing and growth occurred by having someone standing close by me in love, as near as my own feelings and thoughts, who would look with me at the terrain of my private inner universe. Roberto wrote of empathy, "It means approaching him or her with sympathy, with respect, even wonder, as a 'Thou' and thus establishing a deeper inner relationship" (Assagioli 1973, 89).

But what was this mysterious ability to stand so very close to me that I felt held and empowered to unfold hidden dimensions of my inner experience? What was the source of such a transformative empathy?

## Spiritual Empathy

A key element in Roberto's ability to so intimately enter my world was that he was for the most part not operating from an agenda of any sort. I had little feeling he was trying to fix, teach, save, cure, or enlighten. Rather, he seemed absorbed in the task of being available to who I was and where I wanted to go. This included being with me in my defensiveness and respecting my own pace.

This lack of agenda was part of why I could gradually let down my guard, let him in, and be open to the movements of my soul.

Roberto was simply there, interested and compassionate, operating largely from a place beyond all roles and agendas. His attitude seemed to be what Ann Gila and I have since called *spiritual empathy* (Firman and Gila 2010, 47–58), arising from a place beyond goals and objectives, ambitions and aims; he seemed to be functioning from a ground of being that was distinct but not separate from any and all contents of experience. Here is a "self-lessness" or "ego-lessness," that in a manner of speaking could be called "noself" because there is not a particular identification imposing itself on the situation. This would account for my experience that in a way there was not an "other" present to whom I must relate. In a manner of speaking, Roberto was present by his absence.

In turn this ability to disidentify, to be non-attached, depends upon an ability to be self-empathic; one must be continuously aware of any inner feelings, thoughts, or motivations that might lead to acting from a role or an agenda and so interrupt the empathic connection. Roberto clearly had this ability, apparently born of long practice and a willingness to work through inner reactions that might tend to disrupt an empathic field. Working through such reactions to empathic intimacy can involve an uncovering and healing of childhood wounding, and I could sense that Roberto was no stranger to this deeper psychological level in himself or others.

Moreover, his profound disidentification seemed a result of his dedication to his own call or vocation in life, his own path of Self-realization. With this deeply committed relationship to Self, Roberto could come from a spiritual, disidentified, yet completely engaged place that could evoke that same spiritual, disidentified, yet completely engaged place in me. Since he was in intimate relationship with Self, I was supported in my own intimate relationship with Self, and could hear and respond to my own path of Self-realization no matter where it led me. In other words, I was allowed to recognize my own journey and travel this.

> *Moreover, each and all are included in*
> *and part of the spiritual super-individual Reality.*
> —Roberto Assagioli

For all his unconditional acceptance, however, Roberto was in no way passive. He invited me to use a variety of active techniques, including spontaneous drawing, meditation, journal writing, inner dialogue, study, dream analysis, and the production of several autobiographies focused on different personal issues. He also taught conceptual material, suggested readings, and freely asked questions and made comments about my experience. Spiritual empathy is not passive receptivity to the client; it is an active engagement with the client's unique personhood through a non-attachment to one's own experience.

## Roberto Is Human

There were those inevitable times too when Roberto missed the mark with me—he was, after all, a human being. One specific instance of this, I realized in retrospect, was that his occasional philosophical and metaphysical discussions at times seemed to supersede addressing my personal issues.

In fairness to Roberto, my sessions with him were not strictly therapy but what he had called "didactic psychosynthesis" (Assagioli 1965, 9), a furtherance of my psychosynthesis training, so some amount of conceptual work was to be expected. Furthermore, I believe these discussions were meant to help me disidentify from my problems by taking a larger view of them, to understand them in the context of a wider and more universal point of view. Ironically, rather than leading to a disidentification from my issues, these discussions tended to encourage my youthful ascetic habit of discounting my personal needs and concerns in the daily struggles of human existence.

As illustrated by the vast majority of my work with Roberto, spiritual empathy does in fact lead naturally to a sense of disidentification, of being distinct though not separate from the content of ongoing experience; it allows a non-attachment to any particular experience and therefore an openness to all experience as it arises.

This is the emergence of the human spirit, of "I" in psychosynthesis terms, within the empathic relationship. Such an openness does in effect constitute a broader perspective, an ability to see the "forest" as well as the "trees" of experience.

But in this particular instance, part of me used our discussions to confirm a belief that the forest is more real than the trees. Again, I never addressed this with Roberto, because I only became aware of this dynamic later. Was he unaware of this? Was he aware of it and chose not to address it? We can never know. I do know he would have fully supported my exploration of this issue if I had raised it. In any case, I feel the potential for my using the discussions in this way was not addressed fully enough in our work—an empathic misattunement with me.

As we have seen however, none of Roberto's misattunements could block the very rich and important work that occurred. His compassionate, spiritual empathy carried us through all limitations of technique and situation, all incompatibilities in personal style, all differences of age, culture, and belief. His "good-enough" ability to stand present with me at an essential level most of the time, without pushing and pulling, did allow me to attain a vastly expanded engagement with my inner and outer worlds, and moreover, to better hear the still, quiet whispers of Self within these worlds.

In concluding this discussion of Roberto's spiritual empathy, I can see that each of the two books he wrote in his lifetime sprung from his empathic concern for humanity. He sought not to criticize, reform, or convert, but simply to reflect back the human condition as he saw it so that we might find our way more consciously.

# Glossary

**Abraxas.** After the Gnostic teacher Basilides and C. G. Jung, a conception of God or Self as composed of both good and evil. It is basically the deification of the totality of the universe, the **uroboros**. Although perhaps derived from a valid vision of **cosmic consciousness**, the Abraxas concept can have nihilistic consequences, because there is no final basis for choosing between good or evil—both supposedly are created by the Source of the universe.

**Apophatic**, as distinguished from **cataphatic**, is any conceptual or experiential approach to Deeper Reality which disallows the use of content, process, or form. One seeks silent communion with the Divine beyond imagery, symbols, or words. Employed in the *via negativa*.

**Cataphatic**, as distinguished from **apophatic**, refers to the use of content, process, and form to approach the Divine. Examples would be active prayer, guided imagery, art, music, scripture study, and liturgy. Employed in the *via positiva*.

The **Core Personality** comprises those elements of the psyche-soma which are most central to one's sense of identity. This includes unconscious contents which were at one time closely identified with "I," but which now form the unconscious infrastructure of the adult sense of identity (e.g., core experiences and traits from childhood, the "inner child," and so forth). To be differentiated from smaller systems or complexes within the psyche-soma (e.g., **subpersonalities**), which are generally more conscious or preconscious, more immediately susceptible to transformation, and which may or may not be central to a sense of identity.

**Cosmic consciousness.** (Bucke 1967; Jung 1963; Maslow 1971; Assagioli 1973). A superconscious experience in which one apparently perceives the entire cosmos as a unity, and feels oneself an integral part of it. Can be confused with communion with Self. (See **Abraxas, Uroboros**)

**Dependent-Independent Paradox** describes the experiential dynamic by which one's recognition and acceptance of ontological dependence upon Self leads to an increased experience of independence and I-amness. The concept of **transcendence-immanence** and disidentification can help distinguish this independence of "I" from the pseudo-independence based on an idealization of "I."

**Dualism** is applied to any system which posits a fundamental, ontological separation between its two major aspects. Theories which split mind and body, self and psyche, or spirit and matter, would be examples of dualism. Dualism may view the two members of the system as parts of a greater whole, as in notions such as "mind-body harmony" or a "synthesis of spirit and matter." However, such wholeness ultimately can only be an unstable composite, given no common ontological foundation for the parts.

**Dualistic denial** begins with the view that spiritual realities are more real or more important than the mundane experiences of daily life. Spiritual experiences, practices, and beliefs are then used to distance oneself from aspects of the human condition which one does not wish to engage.

**Gnosticism** involves the belief that human salvation lies in a spiritual experience or higher state of consciousness (*gnosis*) which frees one from the "bondage" of matter. Often this salvation is couched in terms of a progression up through various levels of consciousness towards the most enlightened level at the top. Based on a **dualism** between spirit and matter. Not to be confused with "gnosticism" when this is understood as seeking direct experience of the Divine, a spiritual approach more commonly called "mysticism" or "contemplation." (See note 1.)

**Holistic Gnosticism** is the belief that although human beings are essentially spiritual and separate from the material world, the task of spirit is to penetrate matter and facilitate its evolution towards a final cosmic synthesis of spirit and matter. (See **Dualism**, **Monism**, **Gnosticism**)

**"I,"** or "personal self," is Assagioli's term for essential human being. "I" can be thought of as distinct but not separate from the content and processes of psyche-soma, i.e., as **transcendent-immanent**. "I" is a reflection or projection of a deeper transcendent-immanent source, **Self**.

**Individuality and Universality**, an ambiguous term in psychosynthesis which is applied either to: (a) a peak or mystical experience in which one apparently views the entire cosmos with no loss of personal self-consciousness (**cosmic consciousness**); or (b) the actual nature of **Self** as universally transcendent-immanent and singular. Herein we have elected the latter meaning (see appendix 4).

**Induction** indicates the energetic impact of higher human potential in the person. Induction often energizes psychological obstacles to the contact and expression of the new growing potential. For example, a burgeoning potential for love may energize latent unresolved resentments.

**Monism** is present whenever parts of a system are fused into a unity in which important characteristics of the parts are lost. An example would be the view that the human being is merely a physical organism, thus reducing psyche and self to soma.

**The Narcissistic Mistake** occurs whenever the image is taken for the subject imaged. In psychological theory, this amounts to the inability to understand "I" as essentially the subject of experience, and not a content or object of experience. If "I" is so objectified, "I" becomes something one may possess, and as with Narcissus, a "thing" with which one may become obsessed. What is missed in this mistake is the pure subjectness of "I" and thus the impossibility of making "I" into an object of experience. Such attempts at objectification will always be left with the question of who is the subjective "I" who experiences the supposed objective "I"?

**Personal Psychosynthesis** comprises those processes by which the person develops and stabilizes an independent sense of self in the world. Includes the establishment of healthy object relations, development of personal will, and the actualization of **"I."** Involves integrating contents of the lower and middle unconscious, as contrasted to **spiritual psychosynthesis** which involves the integration of higher unconscious contents. Personal and spiritual psychosynthesis together form two parameters of the larger process of Self-realization.

***Privatio Boni*** is the principle by which evil is not seen as a primary principle in and of itself, but as a privation of good. **Self** is therefore not a synthesis of good and evil, nor does Self choose evil. Rather, evil derives from willfully ignoring the fundamental reality of one's ontological connection to Self. Such misdeeds, while causing very real suffering, are nevertheless based on a lie, a privation, a non-thing—that is, on the illusion of personal self-sufficient isolation from Self.

**Self** is the deeper ontological reality of which **"I"** is a reflection. Self can be viewed as universally transcendent-immanent, and therefore as intimately present in the inner and outer life of every human being as well as throughout the entire cosmos. Such an understanding of Self seeks to accurately map reported human experience throughout history, and may or may not refer to an actual existent Self which can be established physically.

**Self-realization**. The dynamic and ongoing relationship of "I" and Self, taking place throughout all the various stages and experiences of life. Thus, it is a function of the interplay between the will of "I" and the will of Self, what can be called "morality."

**Spiritual-Moral Context**. Any system which provides ongoing spiritual and moral support for living a life in solidarity with

Self. As used in the phrase, "a larger spiritual-moral context," this refers to such a supportive system which is beyond psychosynthesis or any other psychology. Clinically, this points to the need for many clients who are experiencing a spiritual opening to have a broader context of community and tradition in which to live a life based on their spiritual values.

**Spiritual or Transpersonal Psychosynthesis** involves "the proper assimilation of the inflowing superconscious energies" into the personality (Assagioli 1965, 55). As distinguished from **personal psychosynthesis** which does not work with overt higher unconscious experience, but focuses more on the middle and lower unconscious (Assagioli 1973, 121). Also to be distinguished from **Self-realization**, which may occur in either personal or spiritual psychosynthesis.

**Subpersonality.** An aspect of the psyche-soma which functions in a semi-autonomous manner, akin to the Transactional Analysis concept of "ego states." They are socially-conditioned expressions of basic human needs which have not become harmonized into a coherent sense of identity.

**Totality-Self**. See **Abraxas**.

**Transcendence-Immanence**. By transcendence is meant, "distinct from all notions of mass, energy, space, and time, whether material, biological, or spiritual." Transcendence will be at the same time immanent, that is, present throughout, and actively engaged in, content and process. Applied to "I," the term implies the ability to experience being distinct but not separate from, in by not of, psychosomatic process.

The **Uroboros** (also "ouroboros"), the serpent endlessly eating its growing tail, is a symbol of the totality of mass, energy, space, and time of the universe. It is an unchanging cycle of endless change; it has no end in time and space, because it is a closed system which itself includes all time and space. This quality of endlessness in time and space can be confused with "eternal" (the transcendence of time) and "infinite" (the transcendence of space). Thus, the uroboric totality can be mistaken for transcendent-immanent Self. That is, the awareness of the totality of the universe; the synthesis of opposites; the Androgyne; and unending time and space, can be mistaken for communion with Self. (See **Abraxas, cosmic consciousness.**)

*Via Negativa*, or "way of negation," is the approach wherein one recognizes that Ultimate Reality is beyond any conception of mass, energy, space or time. Therefore the way to describe Reality is by describing what it is not. Applied in **apophatic** practices such as contemplation and insight meditation.

*Via Positiva*, or "positive way," is the approach wherein one uses mass, energy, space, and time as avenues towards the experience of Ultimate Reality. Applied in **cataphatic** practices such as active prayer, imagery, art, and liturgy.

# Notes

1.  When we use the term "gnosticism," we are speaking of dualistic systems such as those elaborated in Bentley Layton's *The Gnostic Scriptures* (1987) or Hans Jonas' *The Gnostic Religion* (1963). We include in the term dualisms, systems which split: soul and body; God and humanity; God and world; humanity and nature; and heaven and earth (of course such gnostic dualisms can be found in mainstream religions as well, including Christianity).

But we recognize another possible definition of the term gnosticism which is quite different from dualistic belief systems. Gnosis ("knowledge," in Greek) has also been used simply to indicate the direct experience or immediate knowing of spiritual realities, as opposed to simply formulating concepts about these realities.

See for example, Victor White's (1982, 196–97) distinction between the "Gnostic," the person who knows through direct experience or gnosis; and what he calls the "Gnosticist," the one who formulates dualistic beliefs about the experience. Following this usage, White considers gnosis as the raison d'être for the Christian Church, pointing out that the Church has never rejected gnosis, but only the dualistic "Gnosticist" systems.

But in our present work, we are using the term gnosticism in the traditional sense, to denote dualistic systems of thought, especially at the level of human personality. As a way of avoiding confusion, we reserve the usual terms "mystic" or "contemplative," rather than "Gnostic," for those who seek direct experiential communion with the Divine.

2.  Here is more Rosemary Ruether, from *Sexism and God-Talk* (1983):

> Both Gnostic and orthodox Christian thought in the
> Patristic period equate becoming virgin with becom-

ing male. Maleness expresses the spiritual nature and femaleness the carnal nature. (248)

While Gnosticism does hold generally that the feminine Sophia was the cause of The Fall, and tended to equate the feminine with "inferior" matter, they did consider women equal to men. This equality was however based on the dualistic spirituality which rejected "feminine matter" and the natural world.

> Thus a paradox arises: Gnostic Christianity affirmed women's equality, but against the goodness of nature and bodily existence. Orthodox Christianity, which affirmed doctrinally (if not in its actual spirituality) the goodness of body and creation, nevertheless used its doctrine of Creation to subordinate women. Neither orthodox nor heretical Christianity brings together the wholeness of vision that feminist theology seeks. Only by correcting the defects of each with the other do we begin to glimpse another alternative Christianity. (36–37)

**3.** Dualistic denial is a true defensive structure based on a dualistic spirituality. This is not to be confused with a healthy focused involvement with the spiritual dimension in which the depths of human suffering are *not* denied. This latter orientation can be seen for example in the person living out a genuine "call" to a life of monasticism and prayer—a vocation Assagioli himself considered well within normal healthy bounds (private conversation with author, Italy, 1973).

**4.** One important missing area in psychosynthesis theory here is the notion of the "core personality," a larger and deeper personality configuration than implied by the concept of subpersonalities. This term was first coined by Steven Kull (Psychosynthesis Institute, Palo Alto, circa 1974) to refer to those aspects of the personality integrated into one's ongoing sense of identity.

This broader concept has been extended by Ann Russell and myself as an approach to the deeper and more pervasive difficulties found in the core sense of identity. Further development of this concept in the light of the emerging work in object relations, self-psychology, family systems, childhood abuse, and multiple personality disorder, seems to promise a much-needed further development of psychosynthesis personality theory. See "Core Personality" in the Glossary.

**5.** Ann Russell (private conversation, 1989) has pointed out this problem with diagrams such as figure 3.5 which seek to represent disidentification. The problem is that this type of diagram shows "I" stepping back or moving away from the former identification, as if "I" travels from one location in space to another location in space. But this type of thinking can easily lead to dissociation—it implies a distancing from the identification, when in fact one may become *more* aware of an identification during a disidentification experience.

It is more true to the disidentification experience to say that "I" does not "move" anywhere, but rather merely becomes more "intense," to use James Vargiu's (1979) term. In becoming more intense, "I" becomes increasingly unlimited by specific psychic contents, and thus is able to experience an expanded range of content. In terms to be discussed later, disidentification is not a movement through space, but a deeper realization that "I" is transcendent-immanent.

**6.** The rejection of the "substantial self" notion in Western philosophy may be a result of a failure in maintaining clarity about the pure transcendent subjectivity of self. In *The New Dictionary of Theology,* W. Norris Clarke maintains that the rejection of substantial self is based on misunderstandings which grew up over time around the idea of substance. Clarke traces these misunderstandings as they progress through the thought of Descartes, Locke, Hume, and Kant. He says what was lost was,

> ... an older classical notion of substance as dynamic, really related to other substances by its actions, and inseparable from its accidents (and vice versa), though not reducible to any of them. (Clarke 1987, 989)

It would seem that such a notion of substantial self may be akin to our conception here of "I" as transcendent-immanent. "I" is immanent in that it is "inseparable" from changing space-time experiences ("accidents"), and transcendent in that it is not "reducible to any of them." The classical substantial self may too, then, not be as different from the Buddhist noself approach as it might at first appear.

However, today the radically different meaning of the term "substantial" is clear even in popular usage. The word now suggests a palpable mass of static content existing through changing processes—definitely not what is meant by either substantial self or transcendent-immanent "I."

7. It is interesting that the Buddhist *anatta* considers both objects of consciousness and consciousness itself as "automatic processes." We would say this points to the notion in our conception that "I" is transcendent of even consciousness itself.

One thinks too of the psalmist who says of God, "in your light we see light" (Psalm 36:10)—here seems to be some transcendence distinct from light/consciousness which can therefore reflect not simply upon illuminated objects, but upon the illuminating medium itself.

8. St. Thomas Aquinas makes this very distinction between relative and transcendent infinity. He points out that relative infinities are so like finite objects that they can even have different magnitudes:

> ...for the species of even numbers are infinite, and likewise the species of odd numbers are infinite; yet there are more even and odd numbers than even. (Aquinas 1947, Pt. III, Q. 10, Art. 3)

So here we have one infinity greater than another! Even though each infinity has no finish, yet they can be differentiated by magnitude. These infinities are therefore somewhat like measurable finite objects, for all their supposed immeasurability. And for St. Thomas, there is quite a difference between such relative infinities—the uroboric-type of infinity—and the Absolute Infinity of God who is transcendent.

St. Thomas' insight into infinity can be seen as well in the work of the famous mathematician, Georg Cantor. Cantor (1932, 378) called these different relative infinities "transfinite numbers" and distinguished these from what he called the "Absolute Infinite" beyond them all.

**9.** We would hypothesize that "I" is distinct, though not separate, from even the extreme dissociations found in dissociative identity disorder (DID). Much more research is needed into DID of course, but our formulation here would predict that "I" is the "who" who ultimately has the multiple personalities, or alters. That is, "I" is the human being who lives, suffers, and who, during the course of successful treatment, emerges from the fragmentation of this disorder into the realization of unique— that is, singular—I-amness.

We would speculate that the severe multiplicity observed in DID is an extreme instance of the multiplicity we all may recognize within ourselves (with the one tremendous difference that DID seems to be invariably connected to severe childhood abuse, often ritualistic in nature). If we undertake careful self-observation, we will find that there are many subsystems active within the personality, subsystems which have been called subpersonalities by Assagioli (1965, 74–77). It is quite common in psychosynthesis work to experience disidentification from several subpersonalities at once, allowing the realization of a singular "I" who can observe them all.

See Vargiu (1974); Carter-Haar (1975); and Rowan (1990) for elaborations of subpersonality theory; and Dummer & Greene (1988) for a beginning psychosynthesis approach to multiple personality disorder (now dissociative identity disorder). Dummer & Greene understand a dormant "core personality" within the alters which emerges during the course of successful treatment (which, we suspect, should still be considered distinct from "I").

**10.** This transcendence of—not a union of—polarities is also a characteristic of the (unsullied) Judeo-Christian notion of God. Here is Anglican deacon Mary Hayter:

> ... the objective of Old Testament writers was not to acclaim the conquest of male Yahweh over a female Asherah but to avoid, as far as possible, any projection of human sexuality on to their God. *They believed Yahweh to be neither male nor female but suprasexual.*
> (Hayter 1987, 18)

And according to feminist theologian Phyllis Trible (1978), "God is neither male nor female, nor a combination of the two" (21).

Here God is not the masculine pole in a supposed God-Goddess duality, nor the androgynous synthesis of the two, but rather is transcendent-immanent. The true Judeo-Christian conception seems then to see God as distinct from both masculine and feminine, and thus as One who can express through either or both.

**11.** I am not here speaking about the actual clinical application of psychosynthesis, but am referring only to the development of psychosynthesis theory per se (see the Introduction).

When I say "fully developed psychosynthesis theories" I mean extended theories which are integrated into the larger body of psychosynthesis thought, for example, a theory of addiction which includes the I-Self axis, the crisis of duality, the existential crisis, and the dynamics of surrender; or a precise exploration of the effect of what happens to "I" when childhood trauma breaks and falsifies one's experience of deepest identity; or a refined theory of psychosis which discerns the higher and lower unconscious dynamics here, as well as the I-Self relationship within such experience.

**12.** This view that early infancy is characterized by an undifferentiated self-other fusion can be seen in the work of Margaret Mahler (1975), and has been taken into transpersonal psychology by the work of Ken Wilber (1980). However, as we pointed out in "More Conscious Than Thou" in chapter 3, this view is challenged by the work of Daniel Stern (1985), who claims we have a sense of "emergent self" even in the first few months of life.

Stern, citing the latest studies in infant research, does not see a movement from an undifferentiated wholeness up through hierarchical stages of individuation. Rather, he describes an ongoing relationship between self and other at all stages of life, and claims that these forms of relationship are not outgrown, but continue to exist within the healthy adult experience of self and other. This is of course precisely what we would expect if human identity were transcendent-immanent, in but not of any particular phase of growth. See Stern's excellent book, *The Interpersonal World of the Infant*.

**13.** Within psychosynthesis the concept of synthesis takes on its most grand proportions in Assagioli's cosmological idea of a "Supreme Synthesis" (Assagioli 1965, 31; Assagioli 1973, 31–34). Here is envisioned a coming together of the entire cosmos, the goal of inexorable universal evolution. As Assagioli himself says, this idea is much akin to Teilhard de Chardin's concept of the "Omega Point" (Assagioli 1973, 34).

From our point of view however, we can speculate that there may be a universally transcendent-immanent Self (see appendix 4) who is not so much interested in bringing all things into a harmonious whole, as in developing an intimate relationship with every aspect of creation—whether those aspects are fragmented or whole, alone or unified, conflicted or harmonious. In short, a supreme harmonious synthesis of all things may or may not be relevant to the plans of such a Universal Self.

Also, the idea of a supreme synthesis has been found to be highly questionable not only on scientific grounds, but on philosophical and theological grounds as well. For example, here is Dr. Raymond Nogar, a Catholic priest and philosopher of science, who was known for his work in evolutionary theory (cf. his book *The Wisdom of Evolution*):

> The God of the strange world of Father Teilhard is not
> the one I have come to believe in. His is the God of the
> neat; mine is the God of the messy. His God governs

with unerring efficiency; mine provides with inexcus-
able waste. His God is impeccably regular; mine is
irresponsible. His God is the Lord of order; my God is
the Lord of the Absurd. (Nogar 1966, 126)

Such a "Lord of the Absurd" might be so transcendent-
immanent that we live and move and have our being in divine
presence *now*—not simply at the culmination of cosmic evolution.
Thus, our relationship with Self may be completely independent
of our fragmentation or wholeness.

One might then for example imagine a deep spirituality in
someone very early in human evolution (distant from a cosmic or
supreme synthesis); or in a child; or within the chaos of schizophrenia or dissociative identity disorder. With such a transcendent-
immanent deity, it is possible to imagine humanity becoming fully
Self-realized, even while nothing in the universe ever progresses a
step towards a harmonious whole.

See also Olivier Rabut (1961) for a careful and respectful
critique of the notion of a cosmic unity vis-à-vis Teilhard de
Chardin.

**14.** This brand of Gnosticism is an interesting mixture of monism
and dualism. At the cosmic level, "All is One" because all is of
the same substance as the Godhead. However, at the level of the
individual human being, we still find the dualistic flight of spirit
up through the lower levels to the Godhead at the top. We have
then a relative dualism existing within an absolute monism. We
might call this, "monistic gnosticism." But monistic gnosticism
does not in the last analysis resolve the dualism-monism problem
any more than does "holistic gnosticism" (cf. chapter 1).

**15.** While we will here take the instance of self-criticism for our
example, our argument holds too if we interpret Freud's words
above as indicating Sterba's "therapeutic dissociation" of the
ego (1934). Sterba was pointing to something much more akin to
disidentification, but nevertheless made no fundamental distinction between that "part" of the ego who observes, and that "part"
who is observed. Here still, the ego seems a pliable mass, and "I,"

as subject, is missed. The same can be said for the more recent term, "therapeutic split," which implies the patient disidentifying from negative transference in order to maintain the therapeutic alliance with the therapist.

**16.** This use of theory from modern physics to examine human personality from an energy point of view was called "psychoenergetics" by Assagioli, and is as yet an under-utilized approach within psychosynthesis (although some apparently apply the term to techniques for manipulating psychospiritual energies).

For example, in a quite similar way to Globus (1980), the usefulness of the concept of a "singularity" was recognized in psychosynthesis theory by James Vargiu (1979), who applied this concept to an understanding of important aspects of Assagioli's notion of Self. Vargiu's work represents one brief beginning of psychoenergetic thinking in psychosynthesis, and can be clearly seen in his article "Creativity" (1977). There he uses an energy-field model to elucidate the process of human creativity, drawing out implications for mystical experience; the enhancement of personal creativity; personality transformation; the formation of groups; and Self-realization.

# References

Assagioli, Roberto. 1965. *Psychosynthesis: A Manual of Principles and Techniques*. New York: Viking Press.

———. 1973. *The Act of Will*. New York: Penguin Books.

———. 1977. "Self-realization and Psychological Disturbances." *Synthesis* 3/4: 148–71.

Barrington, Jacob [pseud.]. 1988. "Twelve Steps to Freedom." *Yoga Journal* 83 (November/December): 44–47, 101–103.

Beattie, Melodie. 1987. *Codependent No More*. New York: Harper & Row.

Berger, Gaston. 1941. *Le Cogito dans la philosophie de Husserl*. Paris: Aubier/Editions Montaigne. Quoted in Roberto Assagioli, *The Act of Will* (New York: Penguin Books, 1974), 262.

Berne, Eric. 1961. *Transactional Analysis in Psychotherapy*. New York: Grove.

*Bhagavad Gita*. 1964. Translated and interpreted by Franklin Edgerton. New York: Harper & Row.

Blake, William. 1972. *Auguries of Innocence*. In *The Pickering Manuscript*. New York: Pierpont Morgan Library.

Bohm, David. 1980. *Wholeness and the Implicate Order*. London: Routledge & Kegan.

Bradshaw, John. 1988. *Bradshaw On: The Family*. Deerfield Beach, Florida: Health Communications.

Brother Lawrence. 1985. *The Practice of the Presence of God*, rev. ed. Translated by Robert J. Edmonson. Brewster, Mass.: Paraclete.

Brown, Molly Y. 1983. *The Unfolding Self*. Los Angeles: Psychosynthesis Press.

Buber, Martin. 1970. *I and Thou*. Translated by Walter Kaufmann. New York: Charles Scribner's Sons.

Bucke, Richard M. 1967. *Cosmic Consciousness*, New York: E.P. Dutton and Company.

Bugental, James. 1981. *The Search for Authenticity*. New York: Irvington Publishers.

Cantor, Georg. 1932. *Gesammelte Abhandlungen*, eds. A. Fraenkel and E. Zermelo, 378. Berlin: Springer-Verlag. Quoted in Rudy Rucker, *Infinity and the Mind* (Boston: Birkhäuser, 1982), 9.

Carter-Haar, Betsie. 1975. "Identity and Personal Freedom." *Synthesis* 2: 56–91.

Clarke, W. Norris, S.J. 1987. "Substance and Accident." Pp. 986–90 in *The New Dictionary of Theology*, eds. J. A. Komonchak, M. Collins, and D. A. Lane. Wilmington, Del.: Michael Glazier.

*Cloud of Unknowing, The, and The Book of Privy Counseling*. 1973. Edited by William Johnston. Garden City, N.Y.: Image Books.

Cooper, J. C. 1978. *An Illustrated Encyclopaedia of Traditional Symbols*. London: Thames and Hudson.

Crampton, Martha. 1981. "Psychosynthesis." In *Handbook of Innovative Psychotherapies*, ed. R. J. Corsini. New York: John Wiley and Sons.

Deikman, Arthur J. 1977. "Comments on the GAP Report on Mysticism." *Journal of Nervous and Mental Disease* 165, no. 3: 213–17.

———. 1980. "Deautomatization and the Mystic Experience." Pp. 240–69 in *Understanding Mysticism*, ed. R. Woods. Garden City, N.Y: Image Books.

———. 1982. *The Observing Self*. Boston: Beacon Press.

Detrick, Douglas W. 1986. "Alterego Phenomena and the Alterego Transferences: Some Further Considerations." Pp. 299–304 in *Progress in Self-Psychology, Volume 2*, ed. A. Goldberg. New York: Guildford Press.

Dorje, Loppon Lodro, David Steindl-Rast, Joseph Goldstein, and George Timko. 1987. Discussion: "Experiences of Self," in *Speaking of Silence*, edited by Susan Walker. Mahwah, N.J.: Paulist Press.

Dummer, Vincent, and Mary Greene. 1988. "The Core Personality: Treatment Strategies for Multiple Personality Disorder." Pp. 75–81 in *Readings in Psychosynthesis: Theory, Process, & Practice, Vol. 2*, eds. J. Weiser and T. Yeomans. Toronto: The Department of Applied Psychology/The Ontario Institute for Studies in Education.

Eckhart, Meister. 1941. *Meister Eckhart: A Modern Translation*. Translated by Raymond Bernard Blakney. New York: Harper & Row.

———. 1981. *Meister Eckhart: The Essential Sermons, Commentaries, Treatises, and Defense*. Translated by Edmund Colledge, and Bernard McGinn. New York: Paulist Press.

Eliade, Mircea. 1976. *Myths, Rites, Symbols*. New York: Harper & Row.

Eliot, T. S. 1943. *Burnt Norton*. In *Four Quartets*. New York: Harcourt, Brace & World.

Engler, Jack. 1986. Chap. 1 in *Transformations of Consciousness*, by Ken Wilber, Jack Engler, and Daniel P. Brown. Boston: New Science Library.

Fairbairn, W. Ronald D. 1990. Reprint. *Psychoanalytic Studies of the Personality*. London: Routledge. Original edition, London: Tavistock Publications Limited, 1952.

Ferrucci, Piero. 1982. *What We May Be*. Los Angeles: Jeremy P. Tarcher.

Finley, James. 1984. *The Awakening Call*, Notre Dame, Ind.: Ave Maria Press.

_____. 1988. Class Notes. Archdiocese of Los Angeles, April 15, 1988.

Firman, John, and Ann Gila. 1997. *The Primal Wound: A Transpersonal View of Trauma, Addiction, and Growth*. Albany, N.Y.: State University Of New York Press.

———. 2002. *Psychosynthesis: A Psychology of the Spirit*. Albany, N.Y.: State University of New York Press.

———. 2006. "On Religious Fanaticism: A Look at Transpersonal Identity Disorder." Palo Alto, Calif.: Psychosynthesis Palo Alto.

———. 2010. *A Psychotherapy of Love: Psychosynthesis in Practice*. Albany, N.Y.: State University of New York Press.

Firman, John, and James Vargiu. 1980. "Personal and Transpersonal Growth: The Perspective of Psychosynthesis." In *Transpersonal Psychotherapy*, edited by Seymour Boorstein, 92–115. Palo Alto, Calif.: Science and Behavior Books.

Frankl, Viktor E. 1985. *Man's Search for Meaning*. New York: Pocket Books.

———. 1988. *The Will to Meaning: Foundations and Applications of Logotherapy*. New York: Plume.

Freedman, Alfred M., and Harold I. Kaplan, eds. 1967. *Comprehensive Textbook of Psychiatry*. Baltimore: The Williams & Wilkins Company.

Freud, Anna. 1992. *The Ego and the Mechanisms of Defence*. London: Routledge.

Freud, Sigmund. 1960. *The Ego and the Id*. New York: W. W. Norton.

———. 1961. *Civilization and Its Discontents*. Translated and edited by James Strachey. New York: W. W. Norton.

———. 1965. *New Introductory Lectures on Psychoanalysis*. New York: W. W. Norton.

———. 1978. *The Question of Lay Analysis*. New York: W. W. Norton.

Friedman, Will. 1984. "Psychosynthesis, Psychoanalysis, and the Emerging Developmental Perspective in Psychotherapy." Pp. 31–46 in *Psychosynthesis in the Helping Professions: Now and for the Future*, eds. J. Weiser and T. Yeomans. Toronto: The Department of Applied Psychology/The Ontario Institute for Studies in Education.

————. 1988. "Transference and Counter-Transference in Psychosynthesis Psychotherapy." Pp. 46–54 in *Readings in Psychosynthesis: Theory, Process, & Practice, Vol. 2*, eds. J Weiser and T. Yeomans. Toronto: The Department of Applied Psychology/The Ontario Institute for Studies in Education.

Globus, Gordon G. 1980. "On 'I': The Conceptual Foundations of Responsibility." *American Journal of Psychiatry* 137, no.4: 417–22.

Goldstein, Joseph. 1988. "Self or Selflessness: A Contradiction?" *Inquiring Mind* 5, no. 1: 31.

Gordon, Richard. 1991. *The Path to the Self.* Seattle: Richard Gordon.

Govinda, Lama Anagarika. *The Way of the White Clouds* (Berkeley: Shambhala, 1970): 124–25. Quoted in Roberto Assagioli, *The Act of Will* (New York: Penguin Books, 1973), 128.

Green, Elmer and Alyce. 1977. *Beyond Biofeedback.* San Francisco: Delacorte Press/Seymour Lawrence.

Groeschel, Benedict. 1988. *Spiritual Passages.* New York: Crossroad.

Hammarskjöld, Dag. 1968. *Markings.* New York: Alfred A. Knopf.

Hardy, Jean. 1987. *A Psychology with a Soul: Psychosynthesis in Evolutionary Context.* New York: Routledge & Kegan Paul.

Hardy, Jean, and Diana Whitmore. 1989. "Psychosynthesis." In *Innovative Therapy in Britain*, ed. J. Rowan and W. Dryden. Milton Keynes, U.K.: Open University Press.

Haronian, Frank. 1972. *The Repression of the Sublime.* New York: Psychosynthesis Research Foundation.

————. 1975. "A Psychosynthetic Model of Personality and Its Implications for Psychotherapy." *Journal of Humanistic Psychology* 15, no.4: 25-53.

————. 1976. "Psychosynthesis: A Psychotherapist's Personal Overview." *Pastoral Psychology* 25, no.1: 16-33.

————. 1983. "Interview with Frank Haronian." *Psychosynthesis Digest* 2, no.1: 17-31.

Hayter, Mary. 1987. *The New Eve in Christ: The Use and Abuse of the Bible in the Debate about Women in the Church.* Grand Rapids, Mich.: Wm. B. Eerdmans.

Hoeller, Stephan. 1989. *Jung and the Lost Gospels.* Wheaton, Ill.: Theosophical Publishing House.

Hui-Neng. "Hui-Neng's Fundamental Insights." Quoted in John C. H. Wu, *The Golden Age of Zen* (Taipei, Taiwan: United Publishing Center, 1975), 89.

Huxley, Aldous. 1952. *The Devils of Loudun.* New York: Carroll & Graf.

James, William. 1918. *The Principles of Psychology*, Vol. 1. New York: Dover.

John of the Cross, Saint. 1979. *The Collected Works of St. John of the Cross.* Translated by Kieran Kavanaugh and Otilio Rodriguez. Washington, D. C.: Institute of Carmelite Studies.

Jonas, Hans. 1963. *The Gnostic Religion.* Boston: Beacon Press.

Jung, C. G. 1963. *Memories, Dreams, Reflections.* New York: Vintage Books.

————. 1966. *Two Essays on Analytical Psychology*, 2d ed. Translated by R. F. C. Hull. Vol. 7 of *The Collected Works of C. G. Jung.* Princeton: Princeton University Press.

————. 1968. *The Archetypes and the Collective Unconscious*, 2d ed. Translated by R. F. C. Hull. Vol. 9, Part 1, of *The Collected Works of C. G. Jung.* Princeton: Princeton University Press.

————. 1969a. *Psychology and Religion: West and East*, 2d ed. Translated by R. F. C. Hull. Vol. 11 of *The Collected Works of C. G. Jung.* Princeton: Princeton University Press.

————. 1969b. *Answer to Job.* Princeton: Princeton University Press.

———. 1979. *Aion*. 2d ed. Translated by R. F. C. Hull. Princeton: Princeton University Press. Pbk. reprint of Vol. 9, part ii of *The Collected Works of C. G. Jung*. Princeton: Princeton University Press, 1968.

Keen, Sam. 1974. "The Golden Mean of Roberto Assagioli." *Psychology Today* (December).

King, Vivian. 1989. "Psychosynthesis: A Spiritual Bridge: Interview with Vivian King." *Meditation* (Fall): 38–51.

Koestler, Arthur. 1967. *The Ghost in the Machine*. London: Hutchinson.

Kohut, Heinz. 1977. *The Restoration of the Self*. Madison, Conn.: International Universities Press.

Kramer, Sheldon Z. 1988. "Psychosynthesis and Integrative Marital and Family Therapy." Pp. 98–110 in *Readings in Psychosynthesis: Theory, Process, and Practice, Volume 2*, eds. J. Weiser and T. Yeomans. Toronto: The Department of Applied Psychology/The Ontario Institute for Studies in Education.

Kunkel, Fritz. 1987. Quoted in John A. Sanford, *The Strange Trial Of Mr. Hyde: A New Look at the Nature of Human Evil* (San Francisco: Harper & Row), 138–39.

Lao Tzu. 1968. *Tao Te Ching*. Translated by D. C. Lau. Baltimore: Penguin Books.

Layton, Bentley. 1987. *The Gnostic Scriptures*. Garden City, N. Y.: Doubleday.

Lewis, Hywel D. 1982. *The Elusive Self*. Philadelphia: Westminster Press.

Louth, Andrew. 1989. *Denys the Areopagite*. Wilton, Conn.: Morehouse-Barlow.

Maddi, Salvatore R. Quoted in James C. Coleman, *Abnormal Psychology and Modern Life, 5th ed.* (Glenview, Ill.: Scott Foresman, 1976), 527.

Mahler, Margaret, Fred Pine, and Anni Bergman. 1975. *The Psychological Birth of the Human Infant*. New York: Basic Books.

*Manhunter*. Directed by Michael Mann. 1986. Wilmington, N. C.: De Laurentiis Entertainment Group.

Marvell, Andrew. 2004. "To His Coy Mistress" in *Marvell: Poems*. Compiled by Peter Washington. New York: Alfred A. Knopf.

Maslow, Abraham. 1961. "Peak Experiences as Acute Identity Experiences." *American Journal of Psychoanalysis* 21, no. 1: 254–62.

———. 1970. *Religions, Values, and Peak-Experiences*. New York: Viking Press.

———. 1971. *The Farther Reaches of Human Nature*. New York: Viking Press.

Masson, Jeffrey. 1984. *The Assault on Truth*. New York: Farrar, Straus and Giroux.

May, Rollo. 1958. "Contributions of Existential Psychotherapy." Pp. 37–91 in *Existence: A New Dimension in Psychiatry and Psychology*, eds. R. May, E. Angel, and H. F.. Ellenberger. New York: Basic Books.

———. 1983. *The Discovery of Being*: *Writings in Existential Psychology*, 157–58. New York: W. W. Norton. Quoting Ludwig Binswanger. Originally quoted in Ulrich Sonnemann, *Existence and Therapy*. 1954. New York: Grune and Stratton: 255.

Meagher, Paul Kevin, Thomas C. O'Brien, and Consuelo Maria Aherne, eds. 1979. *Encyclopedic Dictionary of Religion*. Washington, D.C.: Corpus Publications.

Merton, Thomas. 1961. *New Seeds of Contemplation*. New York: New Directions.

———. 1964. "Introducing a Book: Introduction to Japanese edition of *Seven Storey Mountain*." *Queens Work*, LVI (1964): 9. Quoted in James Finley, *Merton's Palace of Nowhere* (Notre Dame, Ind.: Ave Maria Press, 1978), 146.

———. 1965. *The Way of Chuang Tzu*. New York: New Directions.

Miller, Alice. 1981. *The Drama of the Gifted Child*. New York: Basic Books.

Moustakas, Clark E. 1956. "Summary: Explorations in Essential Being and Personal Growth." In *The Self: Explorations in Personal Growth*, ed. C. E. Moustakas. New York: Harper and Row.

Needleman, Jacob. 1980. *Lost Christianity: A Journey of Rediscovery to the Centre of Christian Experience*. New York: Doubleday.

Nogar, Raymond J., O.P. 1966. *The Lord of the Absurd*. New York: Herder and Herder.

Nyanaponika, Thera. 1973. *The Heart of Buddhist Meditation*: 30. Quoted in Ken Wilber, Jack Engler, and Daniel P. Brown, *Transformations of Consciousness* (Boston: New Science Library, 1986), 20.

O'Regan, Miceal. 1984. "Reflections on the Art of Disidentification." Pp. 44–49 in *The Institute of Psychosynthesis Year Book, Vol. IV*, ed. J. Evans. London: Institute of Psychosynthesis.

Perls, Frederick S. 1992. *Gestalt Therapy Verbatim*. Gouldsboro, Maine: Gestalt Journal Press.

Plato. 1945. *The Republic of Plato*. Translated by Francis MacDonald Cornford. New York & London: Oxford University Press.

Pseudo-Dionysius. 1987. "The Mystical Theology" in *Pseudo-Dionysius, The Complete Works*. Translated by Colm Luibheid. New York: Paulist Press.

Rabut, Olivier. 1961. *Teilhard de Chardin, A Critical Study*. New York: Sheed and Ward.

Ramana Maharshi. 1978. *The Teachings of Bhagavan Sri Ramana Maharshi*. 1st Amer. ed. Edited by Arthur Osborne. New York: Samuel Weiser.

Raymond of Capua. 1980. *The Life of Catherine of Siena*. Translated by Conleth Kearns. Wilmington, Del.: Michael Glazier.

Reid, Thomas. 1973. "Of the Nature and Origin of Our Notion of Personal Identity," Pp. 194–200 in *A Modern Introduction to Philosophy, 3rd Edition*, eds. P. Edwards and A. Pap. New York: The Free Press.

Richardson, Alan, ed. 1976. *A Dictionary of Christian Theology.* Philadelphia: Westminster Press.

Robinson, Edward. 1983. *The Original Vision: A Study of the Religious Experience of Childhood.* New York: Seabury Press.

Rowan, John. 1990. *Subpersonalities: The People Inside Us.* London: Routledge.

Rucker, Rudy. 1982. *Infinity and the Mind.* Boston: Birkhäuser.

Rudolph, Kurt. 1987. *Gnosis: The Nature and History of Gnosticism.* Translation edited by Robert McLachlan Wilson. San Francisco: Harper & Row.

Ruether, Rosemary R. 1983. *Sexism and God-Talk: Toward a Feminist Theology.* Boston; Beacon Press.

Russell, Ann. 1988–90. Private conversations and material presented in professional training courses in psychosynthesis.

————. 1990. "Healing as Self Acceptance: Living Authentically and Fully Through Our Woundedness." Keynote address presented at the *Moving Beyond Survival* conference for women survivors of childhood abuse, Palo Alto, Calif.

Russell, Douglas. 1982. "Seven Basic Constructs of Psychosynthesis." *Psychosynthesis Digest* 1, no. 2: 51–79.

Ryle, Gilbert. 1949. *The Concept of Mind.* Chicago: University of Chicago Press.

Sanford, John. 1987. *The Strange Trial of Mr. Hyde: A New Look at the Nature of Human Evil.* San Francisco: Harper & Row.

Schaef, Anne Wilson. 1986. *Co-Dependence.* Minneapolis: Winston.

Schuhmacher, Stephan, and Gert Woerner, eds. 1989. *The Encyclopedia of Eastern Philosophy and Religion,* Boston: Shambhala.

Schumacher, E. F. 1977. *A Guide for the Perplexed.* New York: Harper & Row.

Sheldrake, Rupert. 1981. *A New Science of Life: The Hypothesis of Formative Causation.* Los Angeles: J. P. Tarcher.

Smith, Cyprian. 1987. *The Way of Paradox: Spiritual Life as Taught by Meister Eckhart*. London,: Darton, Longman and Todd.

Smuts, Jan Christiaan. 1986. *Holism and Evolution*. Gouldsboro, Maine: Gestalt Journal Press.

Spiegelberg, Herbert. 1964. "On the 'I-Am-Me' Experience in Childhood and Adolescence." *Review of Existential Psychology and Psychiatry* 4, no. 1: 3–21.

Sterba, Richard. 1934. "The Fate of the Ego in Analytic Therapy." *International Journal of Psycho-Analysis* 15: 117–26.

Stern, Daniel. 1985. *The Interpersonal World of the Infant*. New York: Basic Books.

Suger. 1973. Quoted in *Dictionary of the History of Ideas*, Vol. II, edited by Philip P. Wiener. (New York: Charles Scribner's Sons), 527.

Tackett, Victoria. 1988. "Treating Mental and Emotional Abuse." Pp. 15–29 in *Readings in Psychosynthesis: Theory, Process, and Practice, Volume 2*, eds. J. Weiser and T. Yeomans. Toronto: The Department of Applied Psychology/The Ontario Institute for Studies in Education.

Teilhard de Chardin, Pierre. 1975. *The Phenomenon of Man*. New York: Harper & Row.

Terr, Lenore. 1990. *Too Scared to Cry*. New York: Harper & Row.

Thomas Aquinas, Saint. 1947. *Summa Theologica*. New York,: Benziger Brothers.

Trible, Phyllis. 1978. *God and the Rhetoric of Sexuality*. Minneapolis: Fortress Press.

Trungpa, Chogyam. 1987. *Cutting Through Spiritual Materialism*. Boston: Shambhala.

*Twelve Steps and Twelve Traditions*. 1953. New York: Alcoholics Anonymous World Services.

Vaughan, Henry. 1917. "The World" in *The Oxford Book of English Verse*. Compiled by D.H.S. Nicholson and A.H.E. Lee. Oxford: Clarendon Press.

Vargiu, James. 1973. "The Superconscious and the Self." Draft. Redwood City, Calif.,: Psychosynthesis Institute. [This paper has been incorrectly attributed to Assagioli in Hardy, 1987, p. 229.]

———. 1974. "Subpersonalities." *Synthesis* 1: 52–90.

———. 1977. "Creativity." *Synthesis* 3/4: 17–53.

———. 1979. Courses taught at the Synthesis Graduate School, San Francisco.

Verny, Thomas, M. D., with John Kelly. 1981. *The Secret Life of the Unborn Child.* New York: Dell.

Walsh, Roger. 1978. "Initial Meditative Experiences: Part II." *Journal of Transpersonal Psychology* 10, no. 1: 1–28.

Weiser, John, and Thomas Yeomans, eds. 1984. *Psychosynthesis in the Helping Professions: Now and for the Future.* Toronto: The Department of Applied Psychology/The Ontario Institute for Studies in Education.

———, eds. 1985. *Readings in Psychosynthesis: Theory, Process, & Practice*, Vol. I. Toronto: The Department of Applied Psychology/The Ontario Institute for Studies in Education.

———, eds. 1988. *Readings in Psychosynthesis: Theory, Process, & Practice*, Vol. II; Toronto: The Department of Applied Psychology/The Ontario Institute for Studies in Education.

White, Victor. 1982. *God and the Unconscious.* Dallas: Spring Publications.

Whitehead, Alfred N. 1985. *Process and Reality.* New York: Free Press.

Whitfield, Charles. 1987. *Healing the Child Within.* Deerfield Beach, Fla.: Health Communications.

Whitmore, Diana. 1986. *Psychosynthesis in Education* Wellingborough, Northamptonshire: Turnstone Press.

Wilber, Ken. 1977. *The Spectrum of Consciousness.* Wheaton, Ill.: Theosophical Publishing House.

———. 1980. "The Pre/Trans Fallacy." *ReVision* 3, no. 2.

Wilber, Ken, Jack Engler, and Daniel P. Brown. 1986. *Transformations of Consciousness*. Boston: New Science Library.

Winnicott, D. W. 1987. *The Maturational Processes and the Facilitating Environment*. London: Hogarth Press.

———. 1988. *Playing and Reality*. London: Penguin Books.

Wittgenstein, Ludwig. 1974. *Tractatus Logico-Philosophicus*: 147. Translated by D. F. Pears and B. F. McGuinness. Quoted in John Hick, *Death and Eternal Life* (San Francisco: Harper & Row, 1976), 104.

Yankelovich, Daniel, and William Barrett. 1970. *Ego and Instinct: The Psychoanalytic View of Human Nature*. New York: Random House.

Zaehner, R. C. 1981. *The City Within the Heart*. New York: Crossroad.

# Index

Abraxas: and cosmic consciousness, 208–12; and god as good-evil unity, 204–10; idolatry of, 214; and Jung, 204–8

*The Act of Will* (Assagioli), 67

Analytical singularity (Globus), 193–95

*Anatta*, 75, 76, 250n. 7. *See also* noself

*Answer to Job* (Jung), 205

Apophatic, as description of *via negativa* practices, 172, 174

Assagioli, Roberto, 33, 140, 141; *The Act of Will*, 67; and birth of psychosynthesis, 1; on consciousness of Self, 104; on dependence of "I" on Self, 65; on disidentification, 98; on distinction between personal self and Self, 220, 227; dualism of, 6, 19, 43; Exercise in Disidentification, 19–23, 47, 55–56; on expansion of personal consciousness to Self, 107; on experience of universality, 222; and external unifying center, 39; on freedom in disidentification, 61; and goodness as aspect of will, 213; "human," as therapist, 239–40; on "I," 47–51; and the "I *am not*" formulation, 15–17, 19–23; on "I" and Being of existential psychotherapy, 92; and "I" as center of consciousness and will, 66–68; on "I" as center of pure self-consciousness, 48; on "I" as distinct from body, 48; on "I" as first step to Self, 103; on "I" as reflection of Self, 94, 129; on "I" as true experience, 50; and induction, 201; on Inner Christ, 108; on "links of love," 215–16; on lower unconscious, 35, 106; and nature of

"I," 6–7; not a monist, 45; on not two selves, 220; personal account of therapy with, 235–40; Self not good and evil, 213; on Self as individual and universal, 221, 222–23; on Self and superconscious, 106; on self-consciousness of inner self, 67; spiritual empathy of, 237–39; and synthesis, 41–42; and Theosophy, 17–18; on transcendence, 74–75; and transpersonal will, 115; on union of "I" and Self, 219–20, 228; on Universal Self, 225; on Universal Will, 225–26; and will, concept of, 61–63

Attachment to disidentification, 99–103

*Auguries of Innocence* (Blake), 121

Bailey, Alice, 17

Barrington, Jacob (pseudonym), on denial in meditation, 102

Beattie, Melodie, on forgiveness, 143–44

Being-doing polarity, 66–67, 161; "I" distinct from, 88; Self distinct from, 134

Berger, Gaston, 187–88

Berne, Eric, 31, 188

*Bhagavad Gita*, and via *negativa*, 173

Binswanger, Ludwig, on communication from existence to existence, 157

Blake, William, unitive experience in *Auguries of Innocence*, 121

Bohn, David, 89

Bradshaw, John, 154, 193

Brother Lawrence, *The Practice of the Presence of God*, 116

Buber, Martin, 157

Bucke, Richard M., 121

Bugental, James, on "I" as essential being, 89, 188
*Burnt Norton* (T. S. Eliot), 93

Call, 115, 135, 228–29, 248n. 3; alignment of personal and transpersonal wills, 141–142; Assagioli on, 228
Cantor, Georg, 251n.8
Carter-Haar, Betsie, 6, 57, 59, 63, 251n. 9; on freedom in disidentification, 60; on "I" transcends personality, 55
Cataphatic, as description of *via positiva* practices, 177–79
Choice. *See* will
Christian Process Theology, 75
Chuang Tzu, 170, 180
Clarke, W. Norris, and substantial self, 249n. 6
*The Cloud of Unknowing* (Anonymous), 170
Codependence, 165
*Comprehensive Textbook of Psychiatry*, on cosmic consciousness, 147, 149
Consciousness: ladder of, and elitism, 68–70; not to be split from will, 66–68
Contemplative prayer, 21, 189
Core personality, 248–49n. 4
Cosmic consciousness, 121, 227, 229; and Abraxas, 208–12; as dissociative reaction, 147; mistaken for Self-realization, 224. *See also* peak experiences
Countertransferenc: idealogical, 145; in therapy, 162–66
Crampton, Martha, on heights and depths, 108
Crisis of duality, 122
Crisis of meaning, 122

Deikman, Arthur, 77, 189; on disidentification, 62; and observing self, 195–98
Dependent-independent paradox, 133–35. *See also* I-Self union
Detrick, Douglas, on idealogical countertransference, 145
DID. *See* dissociative identity disorder

Disidentification, 249n. 5; anxiety in, 98–99, 105; attachment to, 99–103; description of, 55; vs. dissociation, 60–61, 62, 103; distinct from identification, 56–59; freedom of, 60–61; and "I *am not*" formulation, 97; idealization of, 97–102; vs. mental analysis, 56–59; and transcendence-immanence, 58–59; and *via negativa*, 170–74
Disidentification exercise, dualism in, 19–23. *See also* Exercise in Disidentification
Dissociation: vs. disidentification, 60–61, 62, 103; and peak experiences, 147–49; result of identification, 60–61, 64
Dissociative identity disorder, 251n. 9
Dorje, Loppon Lodro, 76, 81, 182
Dualism, 9–10; of Assagioli, 6, 19, 43; definition of, 19; in disidentification exercise, 19–23; and holistic Gnosticism, 42; and psyche-soma as "vehicle," 93; in therapy, 161, 162–64; transcendence without immanence, 43, 45; obstacle to acceptance of wounding, 144; world-wide, 27–28. *See also* dualistic denial
Dualisms, list of, 27–29
Dualistic denial, 33, 35, 248n. 3; as defense, 102; description of, 29–30; and human suffering, 37–40; and psychosynthesis, 31–32; and Self-realization, 107; in therapy, 143–45. *See also* dualism
Dummer, Vincent, 251n. 9

Eckhart, Meister, 170, 176, 180, 181; on detachment, 171; and *via negativa*, 172
Egg diagram. *See* oval-shaped diagram
Ego splitting (Freud), 184–89
Ego states (Berne), 31, 188
Eliade, Mircea, on Gnosticism, 24
Eliot, T. S.: *Burn Norton*, 93; and "still point," 87
Emanation, 129, 130, 131; theory of, 127

Emergent self (Stern), 193
Engler, Jack, 76, 81, 175, 189; on
 insight meditation, 101
Eternity, distinct from time, 84–85
Evil, 212–16; function of will, 212–14;
 not a content of personality, 213–14
Exercise in Dis-identification (Assagi-
 oli), 55–56; and dualism of, 19–23.
 See also disidentification exercise
Existential crisis, 10

Fairbairn, W. Ronald, central ego of, 49
False self, 28, 29, 78, 105, 159, 162,
 163, 193
Ferrucci, Piero: on Self, 104; and Self-
 idealization, 112
Field of consciousness, 51 fig. 3.1; 52;
 53 fig. 3.3; 56 fig. 3.4; 58 fig. 3.5;
 63 fig. 3.6; 106 fig. 5.1
Finley, James, 174; on contemplative
 attitude, 101
Firman, John, 9, 10, 11, 12, 104, 105,
 111, 122, 238
Frankl, Viktor, and abyss experiences,
 8, 10
Free association, 189
Freedman, Alfred M., 147
Freud, Anna, 36; and "true morality,"
 153
Freud, Sigmund, 18, 48, 113, 231; and
 child abuse as fantasy, 34; on ego
 as object, 185; and ego splitting,
 184–89; on ego as subject, 184; and
 Helmholtz School, 188–89; and
 narcissistic mistake, 187–89
Friedman, Will, 31, 107, 164; on transference in therapy, 162–63

"Ghost in the machine," 9, 19, 22, 75,
 80
Gila (Russell), Ann, 9, 11, 12, 13, 238,
 248n. 4, 249n. 5; and Heaven-Is-
 Just-Around-The-Corner Syndrome,
 29–30; on no "I," 75
Globus, Gordon, 115, 189, 193–195,
 255n. 16; on "I," 52; and "I" as
 singularity, 71–72; on transcendence-immanence of "I," 92

Gnostic elitism, and levels of
 consciousness, 128
Gnosticism, 18, 41–42, 247n. 1; and
 dualism, 24; pneumatics in, 40. See
 also holistic Gnosticism
Goldstein, Joseph, on mindfulness, 100
Good-enough therapy, description of,
 157
Good will (Assagioli), 213
Govinda, Lama, 224
Green, Elmer and Alyce, 193
Greene, Mary, 251n. 9
Groeschel, Benedict, 154
Guilt, healthy, 154

Hammarskjöld, Dag, 204
Hardy, Jean, 18
Haronian, Frank, 108, 160; on infatua-
 tion with the sublime, 31
Hayter, Mary, 252n. 10
Heaven-Is-Just-Around-The-Corner
 Syndrome, 29–30
Helmholtz School, and Freud, 188–89
Helplessness, acceptance of, 63–65, 99.
 See also strength to be helpless
Higher Self: Assagioli on will of, 238;
 no need for, 227–29. See also Self;
 Transpersonal Self
Higher unconscious, 25, 33, 107, 109;
 and avoidance of suffering, 144–45;
 forms a whole with lower uncon-
 scious, 36, 37; and peak experi-
 ences, 120; Self present in, 40–41;
 tendency toward, 36; and transper-
 sonal identification, 9; and uncover-
 ing of lower unconscious, 138–39.
 See also superconscious
Hoeller, Stephan 129; on emanation vs.
 creation, 127, 129
Holistic Gnosticism, 17, 41–43
Hui-Neng, on attachment to void, 101
Human development, not a ladder of
 consciousness, 68–70
Human suffering: and dualistic denial,
 37–40; and presence of Self in, 105
Huxley, Aldous, on induction, 201

"I," 5–7, 47–70, 103, 105, 107; as "analytical singularity" (Globus), 193–95; and being-doing polarity, 66–68; center of consciousness and will, 66–68; and confusion with feeling centered, 40; coupled to an address (Globus), 194-95; discovery of, through inner observation, 51, 55; distinct from awareness, 52; distinct from content, 71, 74; distinct from levels of consciousness, 124–26; distinct from multiplicity, 87–89, 124; distinct from psyche-soma, 15–16, 92–93; distinct from self-consciousness, 53–55; distinct from space, 81–82; distinct from states of consciousness, 225; distinct from time, 83, 84, 86–87; distinct from wholeness, 89; and dualistic denial 30; vs. Freudian ego, 48; immanence of, in *via positiva*, 169, 181; and individuality and universality, 223; is one, 89, 123–25; objectification of, 80; and observing self (Deikman), 195–98; paradoxical synthesis of permanence and change, 46; as reflection of Self, 94, 128, 129, 130–31, 133, 134; as reflection of Universal, 94; in religious traditions, 169–82; and shift between states of consciousness 123–25; source of transcendence-immanence of, 93–94; transcendence of, in *via negativa*, 169, 181; transcendence-immanence of, 65, 71–93, 122–25, 156–62; in union with Self, 131–35. *See also* personal self.
"I *am not*" formulation, 6, 15–17, 42–43, 47, 97, 101
"I" to "I," in therapy, 156–61
I-Self relationship, 129–31; and good and evil, 199–211; in therapy, 140–43
I-Self union, 131–35
"I-Thou" (Buber), 157

Idealization: of disidentification, 97–102; of Self, 103–14, 223; and timelessness, 115–17
Identification: with disidentification, 99–103; and dissociation, 60–61, 64; as distinct from disidentification, 56–59
Identity states (Tart), 188
*Imago Dei*, 93–94, 131, 232
Immanence, 90–93; description of, 46, 71; fundamental to "I," 91; implies transcendence, 41, 91–92; and split from transcendence, 122; and *via positiva*, 176–79; and "we are our psycho-soma," 92–93; without transcendence, 231. *See also* transcendence-immanence
Immanence and transcendence, not a polarity, 72
Individuality and universality, 219–27
Individuation (Jung), 189
Induction, 139, 200–208, 213; and Abraxas, 203–8; description of, 201; examples of, 201-3
Infancy: and self-other fusion, 252–53n. 12; sense of self in, 68–69
Infinity, and transcendence, 83
Insight meditation, 21, 101, 189. *See also* vipassana meditation

James, William, 176; *Auguries of Innocence*, 121
Jonas, Hans, 247n.1; on dualism, 28; on dualism and monism, 44–45
Jung, C. G., 17–18, 88, 113, 121, 208, 231; and Abraxas, 204–8; and archetype, 89; on danger of ego identifying with self, 220, 227; and definition of self, 205; on God as fact, 226; shadow, concept of, 212; on timelessness of unconscious, 85; and transcendent function, 73, 189–91

Kaplan, Harold I., 147
Keen, Sam 67, 167
King, Vivian, 104
Koestler, Arthur , 89

Kohut, Heinz, 193; nuclear self of, vs. "I," 49

Kramer, Sheldon, and pseudo-individuation, 31

Kull, Steven, 248n. 4

Kunkel, Fritz, 212

Lao Tzu, 100, 170, 172, 173–74

Layton, Bentley, on Gnosticism, 18, 24

Levels of consciousness: distinct from path of Self-realization, 141–42; and gnostic elitism, 128; "I," distinct from, 124–26; Self, distinct from, 125–26; and Self-realization, 135; as spectrums of identification, 126, 129. *See also* states of consciousness

Lewis, Hywel D., on self as constant, 49

Louth, Andrew, 129

Lower unconscious, 2, 25, 35, 43, 106, 107, 109, 110, 111, 140, 141, 149, 237; avoidance of, in dualism, 144–45; dissociation from, 31; exploration of, 138–39, 146; with higher unconscious, forms a whole, 36, 37; Self present in, 40–41; turning away from, 33, 36

Maddi, Salvatore R., 10

Mahler, Margaret, 69, 252n. 12

*Manhunter* (film), 209

Marvell, Andrew, *To His Coy Mistress*, 84

Maslow, Abraham, 121, 122–23, 124, 154, 177, 200, 201; on "core-religious experience," 210; on cosmic consciousness, 222; peak experience of, 120; and peak experiences, 1; on states of consciousness as traps, 128; on transcendence, 73; and transcendence-immanence, 191; on evil, 208-9

Masson, Jeffrey, *The Assault on Truth*, 34

May, Rollo, 92, 158, 192; on transcendence, 73

Meagher, Paul Kevin, 172

Merton, Thomas, 76, 180; on action of non-action, 66; on true self, 78; on *via negativa,* 171

Miller, Alice, 193; on mirroring, 158

Mirroring, 158–61

Monism, 9–10; immanence without transcendence, 43–45

Morality: distinct from states of consciousness, 150–54; and Self-realization, 150–54; and will, 213–14

Moustakas, Clark, and transcendence-immanence, 191–92

Multiplicity: "I," transcendent of, 89, 124; Self, transcendent of, 126

Narcissistic mistake, 77; of Freud, 187–89

Needleman, Jacob, 147–48

Nogar, Raymond, 253–54n. 13

Non-being, 99, 108

Noself, 21, 75–81, 238, 250n. 6. See also *anatta*

Nuclear self (Kohut), 193

Nyanaponika, 175

Observing self, 196–97

*The Observing Self* (Deikman), 195

O'Regan, Miceal, 16

Oval-shaped diagram, 106 fig. 5.1; 109, 110; and "I" ascending to Self, 107; and idealization of Self, 106

Peak experiences, 120–23, 147–51; description of, 1; psychological reactions to integration of, 137–39. *See also* cosmic consciousness

Perls, Fritz, 186, 198

Personal psychosynthesis, 36, 141; description of, 146; and Self-realization, 142

Personal self, 2, 4, 5, 6, 13, 125, 220, 225. *See also* "I"

Personality integration and spiritual development, healing split between, 138–39

Plato, on time, 85; ideal form of, 89

Prepersonal/transpersonal fallacy (Wilber), 149

*Privatio boni*, absence of relationship to Self, 214–16

Pseudo-Dionysius, 129, 178, 182; on knowing nothing, 79–80; and *via negativa*, 170

Psyche-soma, and immanence, 92–93

Psychoanalysis, 33, 34; and lower unconscious, 36, 37

Psychological obstacles, as response to new potential, 200-203

*Psychosynthesis* (Assagioli), 35

Psychosynthesis: heights over depths, tendency to favor, 32–36; as ongoing relationship with Self, 114

Psychosynthesis theory: dualistic denial in, 31–32; dualistic strain in, 25; lack of development of, 2–4; lacking in developmental models, 32–36, 166–67

Psychotherapist, task of, 149

Purgation, 207, 213

Rabut, Olivier, 254n. 13

Ramana Maharshi: on "I," 50; on real "I" and false "I," 78

Raymond of Capua, 76

Reid, Thomas, on I, 49

Robinson, Edward, 69

Rowan, John, 251n. 9

Rudolph, Kurt, on Gnosticism, 24

Ruether, Rosemary, on devaluation of feminine, 28, 247–48n. 2

Russell,, Ann. *See* Gila, Ann

Russell, Douglas, 104

Ryle, Gilbert, and "dogma of the Ghost in the Machine," 9, 19, 22

Sanford, John, 212

Scale of being, 127–29

Schaef, Anne Wilson, on therapist as untreated codependent, 165

Schumacher, E. F., on "I," 74

Self, 7–9; Assagioli on individuality-universality of, 221, 222–23; distinct from being-doing polarity, 134; distinct from states of consciousness, 105, 223; distinct from totality of psyche, 130; distinct from wholeness, 111–14; has no unconscious, 109; idealization of, 103–114, 223; idealization of, and oval-shaped diagram, 106; idealization of, as timelessness, 115–17; is one, not plural, 229–30; not to be confused with feeling blissful, 40; not above human suffering, 105; not synthesis of good and evil, 216; not totality of good and evil, 204–208; not totality of psychosomatic content, 110; not union of opposites, 113; present throughout lower and higher unconscious, 40–41; and *privatio boni*, 214–16; reflecting source of "I," 128, 129, 130–31, 133; transcendence-immanence of, 107–114, 223; transcendent of any polarity, 216; transcendent of multiplicity, 126; in union with "I," 131–35. *See also* Self-realization; Transpersonal Self; Universal Self

Self-consciousness: "I" as a center of, in disidentification exercise, 15, 19, 20, 48, 53, 66–67; "I" distinct from, 53–54

Selflessness, of *via negativa* and *via positiva*, 180–81

Self-realization, 107, 110–17; and acceptance of all we are, 40–41; alignment of personal and transpersonal wills, 141; Assagioli on, 219; and choosing for or against Self, 135; dependence in, 65; distinct from levels of consciousness, 152–53; distinct from states of consciousness 141–42, 149; and higher and lower unconscious, 138–39; and morality, 150–54; not combination of personal and spiritual psychosynthesis, 146; not equated with spiritual psychosynthesis, 142–43; not linear process, 110; not state of consciousness, 110; path of, in therapy, 140–43; as response to will of Self, 146; and will of Self,

150. *See also* I-Self relationship;
I-Self union; Self
Shadow (Jung), 212
Shame, healthy, 154
Sheldrake, Rupert, 89
*Shikantaza* meditation, 170, 175
Shuhmacher, Stephan, 175; on a buddha
not ruled by sensations 171, 173
Smith, Cyprian, 175
Smuts, Jan Christian, 89
Spacetime: Eckhart on transcendence
of, 171
Spiegelberg, Herbert, and "I," 192
Spiritual awakening, and need for spiri-
tual-moral context, 155–56
Spiritual development and personal-
ity integration, on healing split
between, 138–39
Spiritual empathy of Assagioli 237–39
Spiritual materialism, 128
Spiritual-moral context, 146, 212; need
for, in interpreting unitive experi-
ences, 210–12; need for, in spiritual
awakening, 155–56
Spiritual psychosynthesis, 36, 140;
description of, 146; and Self-realization, 142
States of consciousness: distinct from
morality, 150–54; Self transcendent
of, 105; and shifts of "I" between,
123–25; as traps, 128. *See also*
levels of consciousness
St. Augustine, on time, 85
St. Catherine of Siena, 76
Sterba, Richard, 254n. 15
Stern, Daniel, 152, 193, 253n. 12; and
emergent self, 54, 69
St. John of the Cross, 170, 173, 180;
and Self-realization, 112
Stream of consciousness (James),
175–76
Strength to be helpless, 63–65, 91, 163
St. Thomas Aquinas: on infinity,
250–51n. 8; on time, 85; on undivided being, 89
Subpersonalities, 31–32, 57, 188,
251n. 9

Subpersonality theory, inappropriate
approach to core trauma, 31–32
Substantial self, 75, 249–50n. 6, 81
Suger (Abbot), 178–79
Superconscious, Assagioli on Self and,
106. *See also* higher unconscious
Synthesis, concept of, 253–54n. 13

Tackett, Victoria, 163; on minimizing
childhood trauma, 31
Taoism, 170
Tart, Charles, 188
Teilhard de Chardin, Pierre, 253n. 13;
on knowing that one knows, 54
Theosophy, and Roberto Assagioi,
17–18
Therapist, and need for ongoing self-
exploration, 165–66
Therapy: dualism in, 161, 162–64; and
"I" to "I" encounter, 157–61; and
objectification of client, 156–57;
path of Self-realization in, 140–43;
and referral to spiritual-moral
context, 155–56; transference in,
162–66
Theravada Buddhism, 170
Time, transcendence of, 84–87
Timelessness, and idealization of Self,
115–17
*To His Coy Mistress* (Marvell), 84
Totality-Self, description of, 130
Transcendence, 72–89; and deeper
immanence, 90–91; definition
of, 71, 73–74; description of, 46;
distinct from union of opposites, 88;
as eternity, 84–87; without immanence, 231; and immanence, not a
polarity, 72; implies immanence,
91–92; as infinity, 83; not isolated
from immanence, 41; of space,
81–82; split from immanence, 122;
and *via negativa*, 169–76
Transcendence-immanence, 9–10;
distinct from wholeness, 111; of
"I," 71–93, 122–25; implications
for therapy, 136–68; as response to
dualism and monism, 46; of Self,

107–17; source of, 93–94. *See also*
immanence; transcendence
Transcendent function (Jung), 73,
189–91
Transcendent-immanent Self. *See* Self
Transference, in therapy, 162–66
Transpersonal identification, 9
Transpersonal psychosynthesis, 145,
146. *See also* spiritual psychosyn-
thesis
Transpersonal Self, 1,4, 5, 8, 106, 220,
227. *See also* Higher Self; Self
Transpersonal will, 115. *See also* will,
of Self
Trible, Phyllis, 252n. 10
True self, 49, 79, 159, 163, 193, 224;
Merton on, 78; not to be identi-
fied with either peak or mundane,
137–38
Trungpa, Chogyam, and spiritual mate-
rialism, 128
Twelve Steps of Alcoholics Anony-
mous, 64–65
*Twelve Steps and Twelve Traditions*, 134

Unity, and idealization of Self, 111–14
Universality and individuality, 219–27
Universal Self, 225–28; Assagioli on
will of, 228; as singular, 226–27
Universal Will, 225–26
Uroboros, 83, 85, 88, 113, 205, 208

Vargiu, James, 10, 122, 188, 201,
251n. 9, 255n. 16; on paradoxical nature of Self, 79; on Self,
104–105; and Self-idealization,
111; and universal creative field,
89; on *via negativa*, 170
Vaughan, Henry, *The World*, 85
Verny, Thomas, on unborn child, 68–69
*Via negativa*, 170–75; description of,
172; and experience of Supreme
Reality, 170–71; not separate from

*via positiva*, 176, 181; spiritual practices of, 174-75; and transcendence
of "I," 169
*Via positiva*, 176–79; and experience of
Reality, 177; and immanence of "I,"
169; spiritual practices of, 178–79;
and transpersonal psychology, 177
Vipassana meditation, 21, 76, 170, 175
Vocation. *See* call

Walsh, Roger, on "not self," 76
Way of negation. See *via negativa*
White, Victor, 247n. 1
Whitehead, Alfred N., 75
Whitfield, Charles, 193
Whitmore, Diana, 16
Wilber, Ken, 125, 150, 252n. 12; and
prepersonal/transpersonal fallacy,
149
Will, 61–63, 66–68; and acceptance
of helplessness, 63–65, 99; and
evil, 212; of "I," 141–42; and inner
freedom, 62; and morality, 213–14;
not to be split from conscious-
ness, 66–68; of Self, 141–42, 150;
Universal, 225–26; use of, and
morality, 150–54
Winnicott, D. W., 193; false self of, 28,
159; on mirroring, 159–60; true self
of, different from "I," 49; true self
of, 159
Wittgenstein, Ludwig, on eternity, 86
Woerner, Gert, 175; on a buddha not
ruled by sensations, 171, 173
*The World* (Vaughan), 85
Wounding. *See* lower unconscious

Yankelovich, Daniel, 37, 188, 189

Zaehner, R. C., on evil seen as an aspect
of good, 209
Zazen, 21
Zen Buddhism, 170

# About the Author

**John Firman**, until his death in 2008, was a licensed psychotherapist who had a private practice in Palo Alto, California. He began his career in mental health as a licensed psychiatric technician at the Neuropsychiatric Institute at the University of California, Los Angeles, in the late 1960s, and later worked in the California state hospital system as well as in a county rehabilitation program for alcoholism.

He completed advanced training in psychosynthesis at the Psychosynthesis Institute in Palo Alto and soon afterwards studied for two-and-a-half months with Roberto Assagioli in Italy. John was a director of the Psychosynthesis Institute until its closure in 1980, and during this time he led groups and conducted workshops in psychosynthesis, trained professionals in the United States and in Europe, and wrote for the journal *Synthesis*.

For three years in the late 1980s, John was a psychotherapist and spiritual director on the staff of St. Dominic's Church in Los Angeles. Beginning in 1990, in addition to his private practice and writing, he and his wife Ann Gila (formerly Ann Russell) led public and professional psychosynthesis programs both in the United States and in Europe, and were adjunct faculty members at the Institute of Transpersonal Psychology.

With Ann, he is the co-author of three books published by SUNY Press: *The Primal Wound: A Transpersonal View of Trauma, Addiction, and Growth* (1997); *Psychosynthesis: A Psychology of the Spirit* (2002); and *A Psychotherapy of Love: Psychosynthesis in Practice* (2010).

Printed in Great Britain
by Amazon

48086716R00172